SELF *and* IDENTITY

RUTGERS SERIES ON SELF AND SOCIAL IDENTITY

SELF *and* IDENTITY

Fundamental Issues

Edited by

Richard D. Ashmore

Lee Jussim

New York   Oxford
Oxford University Press
1997

Oxford University Press

Oxford   New York
Athens   Auckland   Bangkok   Bogota   Bombay   Buenos Aires
Calcutta   Cape Town   Dar es Salaam   Delhi   Florence   Hong Kong
Istanbul   Karachi   Kuala Lumpur   Madras   Madrid   Melbourne
Mexico City   Nairobi   Paris   Singapore   Taipei   Tokyo   Toronto

and associated companies in
Berlin   Ibadan

Library of Congress Cataloging-in-Publication Data
Self and identity : fundamental issues / edited by Richard D. Ashmore,
Lee Jussim.
    p.   cm.—(Rutgers series on self and social identity ; v. 1)
Papers originally presented at the First Rutgers Symposium on Self and Social Identity held at
Rutgers University in April 1995.
Includes bibliographical references and index.
ISBN 0-19-509826-9; ISBN 0-19-509827-7 (pbk.)
1. Self—Congresses.   2. Identity (Psychology)—Congresses.
I. Ashmore, Richard D.   II. Jussim, Lee J.   III. Rutgers Symposium on Self and Social Identity
(1st : 1995 : Rutgers University)
IV. Series.
BF697.S422   1997
155.2—dc20   96-8402

9 8 7 6 5 4 3 2 1

Printed in the United States of America
on acid-free paper

Series Preface

For us this is the start of a wonderful and important adventure—the Rutgers Series on Self and Social Identity, a biennial symposium-plus-book series devoted exclusively to self and social identity.

Although the notions of self and identity have long been important parts of psychology and other social sciences, it was not until the past 20 years that research and theory have begun to fulfill the promise of William James's (1890) view of self as both central to understanding human thought, feeling, and behavior and as extremely complex. These social scientific advances are apparent in the large number of references to self and identity appearing in *Psychological Abstracts* and other academic abstracting services. Also, recent years have seen the appearance of many innovative models of and methods for studying self and identity.

Given the quantity and quality of research in this field, there is a need for a continuing forum dedicated to it. The Rutgers Series on Self and Social Identity fills this need for a regular, public, and archival series on self and social identity. The Rutgers Series comprises both a symposium and book component for each topic addressed. The symposium is a public face-to-face forum where selected speakers and discussants present their ideas, and these are discussed and debated with audience members both in formal sessions and in informal settings surrounding the formal program. This interchange, plus feedback from a reviewer and the volume editors, is then used by each speaker to create a final draft chapter for the related book. This book, then, is not simply the proceedings of a symposium, as the symposium and the book are two different and complementary ways of communicating scientifically, and our experience thus far reinforces our hunch that both serve useful purposes.

A self and identity symposium will be held every other year. This makes the symposium a regular event and the book series a continuing publication forum. At the same time, not having the symposium every year allows for careful advance planning of each program and then detailed editorial supervision as the conference presentations are converted to polished chapters for the published volume. This process has certainly worked with this initial symposium and book. The symposium was exciting and informative, and we are very pleased with all the contributions to this volume. We are confident that the reader will learn much from each chapter and from the book as a whole.

Piscataway, New Jersey   Richard D. Ashmore
November 1996   Lee Jussim

Preface to Volume I

This initial volume of the Rutgers Series begins at the beginning, exploring fundamental issues in the scientific study of self and social identity. The chapters are organized around two themes: contrasting perspectives on the nature of self and identity; and contexts that are critical for understanding self and identity. The chapters address two contrasts: self as multiplicity versus unity of identity; and personal versus social nature of self and identity. They also address three critical contexts: history, culture, and modern American society at the end of the twentieth century.

One of the most exciting and provocative modern developments in this field is the notion that personal identity is both phenomenologically and behaviorally a confederacy of multiple selves. Although researchers have made great strides in identifying and understanding the organization of these multiple facets of personal definition, the idea that the self-concept is a unified and integrated whole has a long history and is crucial to many theoretical perspectives. Chapters by Seymour Rosenberg (advocating multiplicity) and Dan McAdams (advocating unity) tackle this contrast head-on.

A second major contrast in social-science work on identity is between the roles of the self as both personal (residing within the individual) and social (residing within social relationships and society). Although these views are not necessarily mutually exclusive, some perspectives place greater emphasis on the social nature of the self; others on the more personal aspects of identity. In this volume, Susan Harter reviews her own and others' research that emphasizes identity as a personal phenomenon exposed to social influences. Peggy Thoits and Lauren Virshup, by contrast, present an overview and critique of theories emphasizing the social aspects of the self.

In addition, three chapters address important contexts for understanding self and identity. Kurt Danziger describes how the phenomena of self and identity have changed over the last several centuries in the Western world. Dorothy Holland presents a historical review of the theoretical perspectives adopted by anthropologists in their quest to understand the multiple interconnections between culture and self. Both Danziger and Holland argue not only that historical and cultural contexts influence self and identity, but that attempts to understand these concepts are so bound up in historical and cultural contexts that it is nearly impossible to study them with scientific objectivity. Roy Baumeister presents a sweeping analysis of the influence on the self of one particular context: the United States at the end of the twentieth century. Baumeister shows how broad currents of U.S. history and culture have helped shape how people think about everything from personal achievement to social mores.

This book emerged from the First Rutgers Symposium on Self and Social Identity, held in April 1995. The symposium brought together for two days hundreds of researchers from many social-scientific disciplines and practitioners and students from diverse backgrounds. It provided an exciting forum that deepened and broadened participants' understanding of, and interest in, issues of self and identity. Our hope is that this volume will communicate some of that depth, breadth, and excitement to a broader audience.

Piscataway, New Jersey   R. D. A.
November 1996   L. J.

Acknowledgments

We express our gratitude to the people and organizations who have supported the overall project and this specific volume. Giving such thanks is not an easy task because we have been aided by a large number of individuals and groups. (If we miss someone, we apologize for the inadvertent omission.)

We begin by thanking our publisher and our editor for this series, Joan Bossert. She received our initial proposal with considerable enthusiasm and has been supportive throughout.

Next, we wish to acknowledge and tip our hats to the members of our editorial board. They have been actively involved in planning the series, developing and conducting the initial symposium, and helping pick future topics and speakers.

We also express our gratitude to our symposium speakers/chapter authors. At every step of the way, they kept on schedule and did so with just a tiny (and appropriate) amount of grumbling. They were tolerant of our need for structure and our desire to provide "constructive feedback" on their initial draft chapters. And, most important, we thank them for exceeding our initial high expectations for them. We picked the presenters/authors because each had established a solid track record of research and scholarship. The talks given at the symposium and the final chapters appearing in this book are just what we wanted. We could not anticipate the exact content of each contribution, but we did expect the very highest quality and that is exactly what each author has achieved. Thank you each very much.

From the outset, we have been supported by the faculty, staff, students, and administrators of Rutgers—The State University of New Jersey. We thank the people of the university.

We offer the following specific thank-yous to people in the Rutgers community: Vice-President Christine M. Haska and Harvey Trabb of the Rutgers News Service; Steven Lione, Thelma Collins, and the staff of the Rutgers Continuing Education Conference Center; Joanne Aguglia and Rolene Klinghofer of the Douglass College Center; Rosemary Manero and her colleagues in the Rutgers Dining Service; Rhonda Krauss of Rutgers Parking Services; Dan Hart, Greta Pennell, and Candace Clark for their help in picking speakers; Rae Frank, Bonita Holt-Griffin, and Anne Sokolowski for help with a thousand and one crucial details, and fretting with, and for, us; Donna Mignano and Addie Tallau for assisting with the library research reported in chapter 1.

We conclude with three special thank-yous. First, we acknowledge our huge debt to Charles Flaherty, chairman of the Department of Psychology, who has supported the Rutgers Series since its inception and also allowed us to draw considerably on the department's staff. Second, we are very grateful for the support of the students and faculty of the Social Psychology Area. Some served as hosts for speakers, others helped at the symposium registration or the social hours, still others helped contact registrants; there were many other tasks that needed to get done, and did get done with the help of Social Area members. Third, for generous financial support we thank the Rutgers University Board of Trustees, Richard F. Foley (dean, Faculty of Arts and Sciences), Joseph A. Potenza (provost and graduate dean), Charles F. Flaherty (chairman, Department of Psychology), and the Rutgers Research Council.

Contents

Contributors

Richard D. Ashmore, Department of Psychology, Rutgers University, New Brunswick, NJ 08903. E-mail: ashmore@rci.rutgers.edu.

Roy F. Baumeister, Department of Psychology, Case Western Reserve University, Cleveland, OH 44106. E-mail: rfb@po.cwru.edu.

Kurt Danziger, 32 Greengate Road, North York, Ontario Canada M3B 1E8. E-mail: kdanzig@yorku.ca.

Susan Harter, Department of Psychology, University of Denver, 2155 S. Race St., Denver, CO 80208. E-mail: sharter@pstar.psy.du.edu.

Dorothy Holland, Department of Anthropology, Campus Box 3115, University of North Carolina at Chapel Hill, Chapel Hill, NC 27514. E-mail: dholland@unc.edu.

Lee Jussim, Department of Psychology, Rutgers University, New Brunswick, NJ 08903. E-mail: jussim@rci.rutgers.edu.

Dan P. McAdams, School of Education and Social Policy, Northwestern University, 2115 N. Campus Drive, Evanston, IL 60208-2610. E-mail: dmca@nwu.edu.

Seymour Rosenberg, Department of Psychology, Rutgers University, New Brunswick, NJ 08903. E-mail: srpsych@rci.rutgers.edu.

Peggy A. Thoits, Department of Sociology, Box 1811, Station B, Vanderbilt University, Nashville, TN 37235. E-mail: thoitspa@ctrvax.vanderbilt.edu.

Lauren K. Virshup, Department of Sociology, Vanderbilt University, Nashville, TN 37235. E-mail: virshulk@ctrvax.vanderbilt.edu.

SELF *and* IDENTITY

Richard D. Ashmore
Lee Jussim

I

Introduction

Toward a Second Century of the Scientific
Analysis of Self and Identity

Among the many gems of William James's *The Principles of Psychology*
(1890), is chapter 10, "The Consciousness of Self." Although it is risky
to give a single person or publication primacy with regard to any important idea, it is fair to say that this chapter marks the introduction of self
as both a major determinant of human thought, feeling, and behavior
and as susceptible to understanding by empirical research procedures.
In 1900, Mary Whiton Calkins, a student of James, published a paper
entitled, "Psychology as Science of Selves." It is possible, therefore, to
identify the 1890s as the beginning of the scientific analysis of self and
identity.

As the end of the 1990s approaches, we are about to enter the second
century of social scientists' attempts to understand the complex set of
phenomena that we summarize as "self and identity." The overall goal
of this book is to help us move productively from the first to the second
century of the study of self. To achieve this goal, we asked a group of
talented individuals to address a set of fundamental issues in conceiving
and studying self and identity. We asked them to take stock of where we
have been and to be prescriptive about where we might go. We also
asked them to address two critical contrasts (multiplicity vs. unity,
personal vs. social) and three crucial contexts (history, culture, and
society) for understanding self and identity. Beyond these two very
general aspects, we did not specify how they should go about their task.
As a consequence, the chapters take diverse paths toward a shared
objective.

3

In setting the stage for the chapters to follow, we address the following set of questions: What is all the fuss? What exactly are we talking about? What are the highlights of the first century? What is the organizational scheme for the volume? What specific topics do the forthcoming chapters address?

What Is All the Fuss?

Are self and identity important enough to warrant this particular book and future volumes in the Rutgers Series on Self and Social Identity? There are many bits of evidence suggesting that the answer is yes. Identity issues feature prominently in popular culture of both the lowbrow and highbrow varieties. For instance, television talk shows include frequent discussions of self and identity issues, and fiction and nonfiction analyses of selfhood figure regularly in the books reviewed by *The New York Times* and other gatekeepers of high culture.

These concepts have also moved to the forefront in the social sciences. This is evident in the appearance of major publications. These include *Annual Review* articles (in sociology: Gecas, 1982; Porter & Washington, 1993; in psychology: Banaji & Prentice, 1994; Markus & Herzog, 1991; Markus & Wurf, 1987), handbook chapters (Epstein, 1990; Lewis, 1990; Markus & Cross, 1990; Stryker & Statham, 1985; Harter, 1983; Robbins, 1973), and conference proceedings (in anthropology, see Whittaker, 1993, pp. 201–202).

The upswing in social-science work on self and identity is also clear in the volume of work published on these interconnected topics. We illustrate the larger concern by focusing on self and identity in psychology.[1] Our examination of PsychLIT, the computerized version of *Psychological Abstracts*, revealed that over the past several decades the abstracting service has had to differentiate considerably just to make sense of and organize the published literature. In the 1960s, there were only four subject headings (self-concept, self-evaluation, self-perception, self-stimulation) used to encompass the publications having to do with self. In the 1970s, 14 new headings were added (e.g., self-esteem, self-reinforcement); in the 1980s, 16 more were included (e.g., self-report, self-destructive behavior), and to date in the 1990s, six new subject headings pertinent to self have been added (e.g., self-analysis, self-employment). In addition to the large number of index words, the topics identified by these index terms concern a variety of diverse phenomena, some of more interest to social and personality psychologists (e.g., self-confidence), others of primary concern to clinical psychologists (e.g., self-help techniques), still others of interest to developmental researchers and biologically oriented psychologists (e.g., child self-care).

What about the volume of publications? We counted the number of abstracts listed under each self heading and the number of publications for the six PsychLIT headings concerning identity. The total number of self- and identity-related abstracts (not counting duplicated listings) were 9,752 for 1974 to 1983 and 21,798 for 1984 to 1993. Thus, there has been a steep increase in the number of publications by psychologists on self and identity over the past two decades. The grand total of psychology publications on self and identity for 1974 to 1993 is 31,550. To put this number in some perspective, Kraus (1995) found 34,000 studies in PsychLIT published since 1974 that concerned "attitude," which is arguably the most central concept in social psychology, at least as practiced by those in psychology departments in the United States.

A more fine-grained analysis of the PsychLIT data reveals that "self-concept" and "self-perception" are the subject headings with the largest number of abstracts (7,739 and 4,897, respectively, for the period from 1974 to 1993). These are the facets of self and identity that are of primary concern in this volume.

What Exactly Are We Talking About?

Self and identity are not simple concepts. They are, instead, words that have been around for a long time in both popular and scientific discourse. They have also been used in a bewildering diversity of ways and have fostered a large number of compound concepts (e.g., objective self-awareness, identity salience). To make matters worse, the same word or phrase is sometimes used in very different ways, and different terms are sometimes used to refer to what appears to be the same phenomenon.

In this book, we have not imposed specific meanings on the terms *self* and *identity*. These words point to large, amorphous, and changing phenomena that defy hard and fast definitions,[2] though individual researchers and practitioners of particular disciplines do operate according to widely accepted conceptual and operational definitions. Stated somewhat differently, there is not a single self or identity construct/variable. Instead, there are a wide variety of self- and identity-related phenomena and terms to label these. In Table 1.1, we provide a scheme to organize these phenomena and terms. This scheme is based on a small number of big-cut distinctions.

The first big cut we make is based on the level of analysis and distinguishes self/identity as individual-level phenomena from self/identity as societal-level phenomena. At the individual level, it is possible to differentiate self as subject (or agent or process) from self as object (or content or structure). This is the "I" and "Me" differentiated by James (1890) and also referred to as *self as knower* and *self as known*, respectively.

TABLE 1.1. Distinguishing self- and identity-related terms as used by social scientists: Individual and societal (cultural) levels of analysis

Self- and Identity-Related Terms, by Level of Analysis	Reflected in Present Volume
Individual Level	
Self as knower/subject/process	
Self-states	
Self-motives	McAdams: "Selfing"
	Baumeister: Self-regulation
	McAdams: Self-consistency and life story
	Thoits & Virshup: Self-esteem maintenance and Social Identity Theory
Self as known/object/structure	
Individual self-construals	
Content-specific self definitions	Rosenberg: Multiple diverse self-construals
	Thoits & Virshup: Roles and social categories
Self-comparisons	Harter: True self
Summary self-judgments	
Evaluation: self-esteem	Harter: False self-behavior lowers self-esteem
Potency: self-efficacy	
Configurations of self-construal	
Hierarchical clustering tree	Rosenberg: Hierarchical classes analysis (HICLAS)
Self-narrative	McAdams: Life story
Self identity	Thoits & Virshup: Role-Identity and Social-Identity Models
Societal (cultural) Level	
Cultural conception of person (i.e., What is a person?)	
Cultural conception of self/identity (i.e., what is that part of a person that is labeled self?)	Danziger: Empiricist self
Cultural arrangements that constrain personhood and self of individuals (i.e., what are the bounds provided by cultural values, etc.?)	Danziger: Technologies of self; language Baumeister: Self as a moral compass in U.S. today Holland: Power arrangements in society
Selves of individuals in a particular culture (e.g., What is the modal self of people in a given culture?)	Holland: Self-in-action

Concerning self as knower, we highlight self-states and self-motives. Self-states denote acute self-processes and include objective self-awareness (Duval & Wicklund, 1972). Self-motives refer to more chronic impulses to action. Some self-motives are theorized to be universal. Roy F. Baumeister (chap. 8) argues that all humans must self-regulate in order to survive. Dan P. McAdams (chap. 3) proposes the term *selfing* to describe the individual's appropriation of her or his own experience. Other self-motives are assumed to be aroused more situationally and to show marked individual differences (Sedikides & Strube, 1995). Such self-motives can be seen as reflecting various facets of two primary self-motives: self-consistency (e.g., Lecky, 1945) and self-evaluation (e.g., Tesser's [1988] self-evaluation maintenance model). McAdams's life-story construct is predicated on a form of the self-consistency motive: the desire to integrate one's past and present with anticipated future selves. A key element of social identity theory, as described by Peggy A. Thoits and Lauren K. Virshup (chap. 5), is that people choose particular intergroup comparison dimensions in order to maintain the most positive self-esteem possible.

Within the self as known, we distinguish individual pieces of self-knowledge from organized systems, or configurations, of self-construal. With regard to the former, we highlight two types of discrete internal codings of self: (1) Content-specific self-definitions ("I am an undergraduate teacher, researcher, and jazz lover"). As Thoits and Virshup note, a particularly important source of self-definition is social-group membership, including roles ("I am a father") and demographic categories ("I am Italian-American"); (2) Self-comparisons (e.g., possible selves [Markus & Nurius, 1986], self-guides [Higgins, 1987], the long-studied ideal self and the undesired self suggested by Ogilvie [1987], as well as the true and false selves described by Susan Harter [chap. 4]). In addition, there are summary self-judgments. The most widely studied are self-esteem and self-efficacy, which capture, respectively, the evaluation and potency dimensions of connotative meaning identified by Osgood, Suci, and Tannenbaum (1957). In this volume, Harter identifies false-self behavior as a substantial input to lowered self-esteem.

In addition to discrete bits of self-knowledge, individuals organize their multiple self-definitions into systems or structures. These can be represented as spreading activation-memory networks (Fiske & Taylor, 1991), hierarchical clustering trees (Rosenberg, 1988; this book, chap. 2), and stories or narratives (Gergen & Gergen, 1988; McAdams, 1988; this book, chap. 3). Self-systems include personal-identity structures (Rosenberg, 1988; this book, chap. 2), social-identity representations (Turner et al., 1987; Thoits & Virshup, chap. 5), and self-in-action (Holland, chap. 7).

At the societal level, it is possible to identify, first, the cultural model of personhood, or "the shared conception of the person or individual" (Spiro, 1993, p. 114). Second, at a slightly less abstract level, there is "the cultural conception of some psychic entity or structure within the person, variously described as 'pure ego,' 'transcendental ego,' 'soul,' and the like" (ibid., p. 114). We add self and identity as other labels used for this "structure within the person." Third, at even a more specific and concrete level, it is possible to identify the bounds on the nature, content, and structure of individual persons and selves set by the current political, legal, economic, and informational institutions, as well as prevailing cultural values and accepted interpersonal processes. Fourth, and most specifically, one could assess the self-concepts of specific individuals and, for some purposes, determine the modal self-structure of people within a particular society. Any of these four facets of self/identity at the societal level (which are complexly intertwined and certainly not completely independent) can be compared across societies or cultures or across historical epochs within a particular society.

A crucial point for understanding diverse social-science writings on self and identity is that different "selves" tend to be studied by different types of researchers. Those interested in cross-cultural variation in self most often study a given society's (not a given person's) conception of the person (not the self; Spiro, 1993, p. 117). This tendency of cultural analysts to study a societal-level abstraction of personhood is also often true of those who do historical analyses. Thus, in this volume, the three chapters that look at context—Danziger's, Holland's, and Baumeister's—focus on somewhat different facets of self and identity from those covered by the other authors.

What Are the Highlights of the First Century?

With regard to self and identity, we can look at two types of histories. First, there is the analysis over time of cultural conceptions of selfhood and the self-concepts of individuals during different historical epochs. Baumeister (1987) has written one such history of Euro-American society, and in this volume, Danziger provides some fresh and provocative ideas on this type of analysis. The second type of history is concerned with how philosophers and social scientists have conceived of and studied self and identity through time.

There are several histories of scholarly approaches to self and identity available. We used these to construct Table 1.2 and a brief summary of the scientific analysis of self and identity over the past century.

Gleason (1983) has written a semantic history of identity in which he suggests that Freud's notion of "identification" is an important precursor to the present-day concept of identity, and that two very different routes to our concept can be identified. In psychology, Erikson (1950) proposed that ego-identity development is the crucial task of adolescence and that this task involves the individual meshing together *past* childhood identifications with *current* bodily and social changes and with *future* commitments into an *integrated* personal package. McAdams suggests that each person constructs his or her own life story to provide such identity integration. In sociology, Foote (1951) proposed that iden-

TABLE 1.2. Selected publications, eras, and trends in the first century of the social sciences' concern with self and identity and reflections in present volume

Decade(s)	Psychology	Sociology	Anthropology	Present Volume
1890s	James (1890) "Consciousness of Self"			
	Calkins (1900) "Psychology as science of selves"			
	Baldwin (1897) "socius"			Rosenberg
1900s		Cooley (1902) "looking-glass self"		
1910s–	Behaviorism: Eclipse of self			
1920s			Radin (1920): life history	
1930s–		Mead (1934): *Mind, Self and Society*		
		Linton (1936): social role		
1940s–	Self-esteem as a personality variable			Harter
		Structure: Role Theory		
		Process: Symbolic Interactionism		
1950s	Erikson (1950): ego identity			McAdams
	Foote (1951): role identification			
		Goffman (1959): *Presentation of Self* . . .		Harter
			Hallowell: universals	Baumeister
1960s	Multivariate structural analysis methods			Rosenberg
		Role-Identity Models		Thoits & Virshup
1970s–	-------------------- Cognitive Perspective ----------------------------			
	Social-Identity Theory			Thoits & Virshup
	----------------- Social-Constructivist Perspective ------------------			Danziger; Holland
1980s	Story metaphor for identity			McAdams
			self-in-action	Holland

tification is the motivation and mechanism by which the individual personally appropriates a societally prescribed role, and this insight sets the stage for the role-identity models of McCall and Simmons (1966) and Stryker (1980, 1987). Gleason (1983) suggests another sociological path to current-day conceptions of identity, which he terms symbolic interactionist, and whose originators he sees as Cooley (1902) and Mead (1934), with Goffman (1963) as the first to use "identity" in place of "self." Crucially for this volume, Gleason argues that Erikson and the psychologists who followed him viewed identity as internal to the person and persisting through time, whereas the two sociological traditions conceived of identity as social and variable.

There are also disciplinary histories of self. Scheibe (1985) described how social psychologists, in both sociology and psychology, have approached self over the past century. Gecas (1982) provided an analysis that focused more specifically on sociological traditions of investigating self. Robbins (1973) and Fogelson (1982) wrote instructive histories of self as approached by anthropologists, as did Whittaker (1993) and Holland.

Psychological and sociological analyses of self have a common parent in William James. Notwithstanding Calkins's (1900) urgings that psychology become a science of selves and the articulation of a strong and clear position for the social self by Baldwin (1897), the topic of self went underground shortly thereafter. This seemingly mysterious, elusive structure was not compatible with the behavioristic paradigm that dominated the discipline until relatively recently. Self was kept alive, however, by psychoanalytic writers, especially those who stressed the role of the ego relative to the id (Scheibe, 1985).

In the 1940s, some psychologists revived interest in the self by developing self-report measures of self-esteem—basically one's evaluation of, or attitude toward, self. From the 1940s into the 1970s, this remained the major approach in psychology to studying self. In her 1974 volume, Wylie found that three-quarters of all publications in psychology concerning self were about self-esteem. Over the past decade, interest in self-esteem has been revitalized (e.g., Baumeister, 1993), and Harter demonstrates the important role that acting according to one's "real self" has for self-evaluation.

In sociology, Cooley (1902) and Mead (1934) made major contributions to understanding self, emphasizing the central role of social factors in the development of self-conception. Following Mead, Gecas (1982) discerns two major streams of thought, one that emphasizes structure and the other, process; Scheibe (1985) identifies two related branches. The first, parallel to the structure stream according to Gecas, focuses on social roles and can be traced back to Linton (1936), through Foote (1951), and the notion of role identification. This, in turn, set the stage for the multiple-role frameworks of identity proposed by McCall and Simmons (1966) and Stryker (1980, 1987). In this volume, Thoits and Virshup provide a critical analysis of the sociological role-identity models. The second, paralleling Gecas's process stream, proceeds from Mead to Herbert Blumer's symbolic interactionism to Goffman's (1959) dramaturgy. This stream can be seen today in the work of psychologists and sociologists who study impression management (Schlenker & Weigold, 1992). Goffman's analysis of identities as publicly presented faces that individuals strategically present to different audiences, though widely applauded, was deplored by many others (Scheibe, 1985). As described by Harter, there has been a revival of interest in the authentic self and false-self behavior.

In anthropology, the history of concern with self is a bit less certain. Fogelson (1982) identifies Radin (1920) as the first ethnographer to systematically study life histories in his analysis of culture and, hence, as a pioneer figure in the analysis of self and identity. It seems, however, that this early contribution, like Calkins in psychology, has not been widely recognized. Hallowell (1955) is the major acknowledged pioneering figure in the anthropological analysis of self. Interestingly, Hallowell has apparently been misread by some of his successors, who have emphasized his argument about the individuality and distinctiveness of each culture and concluded that there are no universals. Spiro (1993) argues, however, that Hallowell suggested that there should be points on which most cultures agree and that some of these arguments should involve self and identity (see Holland). Baumeister follows Hallowell by identifying what he regards as the essential and universal features of selfhood.

Over the past two decades, a confluence of factors has brought about a resurgence of interest in self and identity in all the social sciences (Whittaker, 1993). Some of these factors, including metatheoretical ones, are internal to the social sciences. Probably the most important of these in psychology is the ascendance of the cognitive perspective (the concern with, and perceived legitimacy of, cognitive factors in accounting for human conduct). In all the social sciences, the last two decades have also witnessed the rise to prominence of the social constructivist perspective (Holland). There are also theoretical and methodological factors that have contributed to the rise of self and identity. These include a variety of new conceptual tools that have allowed us to look in new directions to discover the self, and several of these are discussed in this volume (i.e., autobiography by Rosenberg, life story by McAdams, true and false selves by Harter, role identity and social identity by Thoits and Virshup, technologies of self by Danziger, and self-in-action, also called "authoring self," by Holland). These chapters also include new methodological advances. Most important in psychology are the variety of powerful multivariate structural methods, from multidimensional scaling to the hierarchical classes (HICLAS) algorithm that Rosenberg describes. And, of course, there are broader societal and global trends that impinge from outside the disciplines. Baumeister explains how these forces impact individual selves; these forces and others have shaped how we as scientists conceive of and study self and identity.

What Is the Organizational Scheme for the Volume?

Self and identity are central to understanding the human condition. Our use of the deliberately general and vague term "human condition" is meant to highlight our contention that self and identity are important at all levels of analysis undertaken by social scientists.[3] Self and identity are crucial to making sense of the thoughts, feelings, and behaviors of individuals, and this intrapersonal level is most often the province of psychologists. The constructs self and identity are also important to explaining the formation, maintenance, and dissolution of interpersonal bonds—both personal relationships and role relationships. These are most often studied by social psychologists, in psychology and sociology, respectively. Self and identity are necessary to the study of group and intergroup processes and relations, which are of interest to all the social sciences. At the most inclusive level, self and identity figure in the production and reproduction of societies and cultures, issues most often addressed by sociologists and anthropologists.

The goal of the present book is to sharpen our understanding of self and identity at all these levels by considering a set of fundamental issues. "Fundamental issues" should not be read as "firm answers." The topics to be addressed are crucial yet irritatingly irresolvable. We do not view this irritation as bad. Rather, we liken it to the irritation caused by sand in some oysters—it can produce beautiful pearls. Thus, this book does not provide the answer for any of the issues addressed. Instead, our aim is to sharpen our analysis of these fundamental issues and point to some fruitful directions for future research and theory.

What Specific Topics Do the Forthcoming Chapters Address?

We have partitioned fundamental issues into classic contrasts and critical contexts. Classic contrasts are opposing views of the nature of self and identity, both sides of which appear to be valid. Hence, these contrasts are often regarded as paradoxes (e.g., the unity-multiplicity contrast has been labeled the "one-in-many-selves paradox" [Knowles & Sibicky, 1990]). Thus, classic contrasts are essential binary, and apparently incompatible, differences in conceiving and studying self and identity. Critical contexts are moderators of self-related phenomena; they are the spatial/temporal settings that influence how self and identity develop and play out.

Classic Contrasts

Although many important contrasts can be identified (e.g., self and identity as stable versus ephemeral and changing; Gleason, 1983), we focus on two primary issues that have vexed and prodded social scientists since James (1890): one identity versus many selves; personal self versus social identity.

One Identity versus Many Selves   Part I of this book is devoted to the unity versus multiplicity contrast, which can be traced back to James's (1890) chapter. On the one hand, James suggested that the empirical self could be divided into physical, social, and spiritual components and that each of these had multiple discrete parts. The social self, in particular, had as many selves as there were important others in the person's life. On the other hand, in his discussion of pure ego, James argued that the person experiences continuity in the stream of self-consciousness.

In chapter 2, Rosenberg makes the case for construing self as a multiplicity. He does this by using the conceptual vehicle of the "socius" offered by Baldwin (1897), in conjunction with state-of-the-art research methods adequate to capturing this complex mental structure containing an individual's organized set of multiple self-perceptions and perceptions of important others. Rosenberg adds an important time dimension by considering autobiography, including both remembered selves and others from the past and anticipated selves in the future.

In chapter 3, McAdams reviews the case for multiplicity. He admits his own ambivalence on the unity-multiplicity issue but then quickly turns to the offensive by describing the ambivalence expressed by multiplicity advocates themselves. He then steps up the attack by describing the main arguments for a unity perspective. He highlights the individual's life story as the focus of, and vehicle for, unity in identity.

Although the first two authors argue for opposing metatheoretical positions, we alert you to three areas of clear convergence: (1) Both contributors acknowledge unity and multiplicity; they take different paths to accommodating these apparent opposites. (2) Both accord importance to self over time, Rosenberg with his inclusion of autobiographical data, McAdams with his life-story construct. (3) Both argue for, and present elegant examples of, methodological approaches that integrate idiographic and nomothetic principles. That is, both study self in ways that accurately uncover identity as experienced by individuals and yet also allow for testing cross-person generalizations.

Personal Self versus Social Identity   Part II is devoted to this contrast, which has a history equal in length to that of the unity-multiplicity issue. In his "Consciousness of Self" chapter, James (1890) focused on self as a personal phenomenon but stressed that other people were intricately implicated in self-conception. The developmental psychologist Baldwin (1897) and the sociologists Cooley (1902) and Mead (1934) more fully articulated the view that identity is an inherently and thoroughly social phenomenon.

What can be said about the personal versus social contrast today? In her contribution, Harter focuses on true versus false selves. Along with self-esteem, these are quintessential personal instantiations of self and identity. True self is the *individual's* internal answer to the question, What is the core and authentic me? Harter describes recent highlights of an ambitious program of research exploring true- versus false-self perception, including the liabilities of suppressing the "real me."

Thoits and Virshup take a very different tack in analyzing the identity-as-social perspective. Instead of focusing on one construct and describing research on it, they undertake a careful analysis of two different schools of thought that emphasize identity as social. One of these is the role-identity tradition in sociology. Detailing the theories of McCall and Simmons (1966) and Stryker (1980, 1987), Thoits and Virshup describe how this approach centers on the concept of social role and the maintenance of societal-level stability. They then turn to the social-identity formulations that originated in the United Kingdom (Tajfel, 1982) and have spread across the world (e.g., Turner et al., 1987). As Thoits and Virshup note, social-identity models focus more on inter- and intragroup phenomena than on the individual's sense of identity or the maintenance of societal-level stability. Thoits and Virshup carefully weigh the strengths and weaknesses of both of the identity-as-social perspectives that they review.

As with Rosenberg and McAdams in the first two chapters, there is an area of convergence in the chapters addressing the personal versus the social self: Harter describes important social influences on self perception, and Thoits and Virshup note that the individual has an active, not passive, role in both the role-identity and social-identity formulations. Thus, self and identity are personal *and* social.

Critical Contexts

Although many critical contexts of selfhood exist (e.g., self and identity through the life course; see Harter, 1983; Markus & Herzog, 1991), Part III of the book is devoted to a consideration of three interrelated contexts that are crucial for understanding the nature and effects of self and identity: history, culture, and society.

The first two chapters in Part III offer complementary analyses of self and identity. In the first of these, Danziger takes a diachronic, or through-time, perspective and describes how the notion of self has varied over the past several centuries in Western society. Holland, in contrast, takes a synchronic look at how self and identity vary across and within cultural groups.

Danziger begins by describing why psychology must share the analysis of self with other academic disciplines and with popular and lay analysts. He then distinguishes capital P Psychology as the discipline of Psychology with its rules, procedures, and technologies for studying phenomena, including self, from lower case p psychology, by which he means the historically and culturally constructed set of understandings about selfhood. It is this complex set of understandings that provides the context within which individuals develop their own personal senses of self. A particularly important example is provided by our belief that the self can be known empirically in much the same way as other natural objects. Danziger argues that two classes of societal-level factors, which he terms "formative practices," are pivotal in constructing the framework of selfhood within which individuals must develop. The first, "technologies of self," he borrows from Foucault (1986, 1988). These are socially accepted, and often institutionally supported, procedures for action that have implicit or explicit implications for the types of selves that individuals can have. Across the past seven centuries, these technologies of self have, for example, ranged from the form of confession practiced in the twelfth-century Christian church to the many current-day psychotherapies. Next, Danziger underlines the central role that language plays in delimiting and shaping the selves that individuals can experience and enact.

Holland analyzes "selves as cultured." She begins by illustrating the great variety of self-related phenomena across different cultures. She then provides a history of anthropological approaches to self and identity. She describes the universalist versus culture-specific contrast that dominated the field up until the mid-1970s. Holland then highlights what she terms the "critical disruption," which involved critical re-evaluations of anthropological practice from multiple vantage points, including Foucauldian, feminist, and Marxist, which have resulted in greater concern with power, privilege, and perspective in both the understanding of culture and the practice of anthropology. These changes have also provoked revised theories of the relationship between culture and self. Holland concludes by describing several "new ethnographies of experience and subjectivity" that feature the notion of "self-in-action" or the "authoring self"; authoring selves are defined as public discourses and social practices that mediate between larger cultural arrangements (including power relations between men and women, or the rich and the poor) and the inner selves of specific people.

Danziger and Holland make clear that history and culture are intricately interlocking. Danziger describes how culturally conditioned practices vary through time, and Holland underlines how the current view of culture in anthropology highlights the importance of time, both for changes in the individual through the life course and for a society as conditions change through time.

In the final context analysis, Baumeister discusses "the self and society." Because society and culture are intertwined and because societies are evolving entities, Baumeister's contribution includes consideration of both historical and cross-cultural factors. After a brief examination of how the self is viewed across cultures and a detailed examination of the history of the Western self, he concludes with a consideration of the self in America today. He suggests how the current societal conception of self can pose problems for individuals attempting to live with this shared and normative view of being one's self. He highlights how the currently dominant conception of self as a moral compass can lead individuals into various activities in order to escape the self.

Conclusion

Over the last century, scientific attempts to gain insight into self and identity have been many and diverse, spanning virtually all of the social and behavioral sciences. This volume does not summarize all such existing work. Each of the following contributions, however, does present a sophisticated and detailed analysis of some of the most fundamental issues facing scholars interested in self and identity. These chapters are both descriptive, taking stock of existing work within several different disciplines, and prescriptive, as the authors suggest that certain avenues of analysis and empirical research are more likely to be productive than others. Although there is overlap in the themes among the chapters, we suspect that their diversity (in content, perspective, and tone) will stand out more than their similarities. They should, therefore, make for provocative reading for scholars as we begin this second century of the scientific analysis of self and identity.

Acknowledgments: We thank our authors for their comments on an earlier version of this chapter.

Notes

1. That the increase in attention to self and identity is not limited to the discipline of psychology is suggested by two points. First, we counted the self and identity abstracts appearing in *Sociological Abstracts* for 1974–1983 and 1984–1993 and found an increase from 1,685 to 5,647. Second, in anthropology, Whittaker (1993) documents the increased interest in self and identity by showing a large increase in the number of pertinent entries in the *Social Science Index* from 1974–1975 to 1990–1991.

2. Not only are self and identity large and amorphous concepts, but they are also related to, and overlap with, other inclusive and important concepts: in psychology, "personality" (cf. McAdams, 1988) and "memory" (cf. Fiske & Taylor, 1991); in Sociology, "role" (Thoits & Virshup, this vol.) and "language" (Mead, 1934); in anthropology, "personhood" (cf. Spiro, 1993).

3. Self and identity are not only central to basic social science, they are also important to understanding a wide variety of personal and social problems. In this book alone, we will see how self and identity figure in clinical depression, child abuse, suicide, eating disorders, and substance abuse, as well as in societal phenomena such as oppression and intergroup conflict.

References

Baldwin, J. M. (1897). *Social and ethical interpretations in mental development*. New York: Macmillan.

Banaji, M. R., & Prentice, D. A. (1994). The self in social contexts. *Annual Review of Psychology, 45,* 297–332.

Baumeister, R. F. (1987). How the self became a problem: A psychological review of historical research. *Journal of Personality and Social Psychology, 52,* 163–176.

Baumeister, R. F. (Ed.). (1993). *Self-esteem: The puzzle of low self-regard*. New York: Plenum.

Calkins, M. W. (1900). Psychology as science of selves. *Philosophical Review, 9,* 490–501.

Cooley, C. H. (1902). *Human nature and the social order*. New York: Scribner's.

Duval, S. & Wicklund, R. A. (1972). *A theory of objective self-awareness*. New York: Academic Press.

Epstein, S, (1990). Cognitive-experiential self-theory. In L. A. Pervin (Ed.), *Handbook of personality: Theory and research* (pp. 165–192). New York: Guilford.

Erikson, E. H. (1950). *Childhood and society*. New York: Norton.

Fiske, S. T., & Taylor, S. E. (1991). *Social cognition* (2nd ed.). New York: McGraw-Hill.

Fogelson, R. T. (1982). Person, self, and identity: Some anthropological retrospects, circumspects, and prospects. In B. Lee (Ed.), *Psychosocial theories of the self* (pp. 67–109). New York: Plenum.

Foote, N. N. (1951). Identification as the basis for a theory of motivation. *American Sociological Review, 16,* 14–21.

Foucault, M. (1986). *The care of the self: The history of sexuality* (Vol. 3). New York: Pantheon.

Foucault, M. (1988). *Technologies of the self*. Boston: University of Massachusetts Press.

Gecas, V. (1982). The self-concept. *Annual Review of Sociology, 8,* 1–33.

Gergen, K. J. & Gergen, M. M. (1988). Narrative and the self as relationship. In L. Berkowitz (Ed.), *Advances in experimental social psychology* (Vol. 21, pp. 17–56). New York: Academic Press.

Gleason, P. (1983). Identifying identity: A semantic history. *Journal of American History, 69,* 910–931.

Goffman, E. (1959). *The presentation of self in everyday life*. Garden City, NY: Doubleday.

Goffman, E. (1963). *Stigma: Notes on the management of spoiled identity*. Englewood Cliffs, NJ: Prentice-Hall.

Hallowell, A. I. (1955). *Culture and experience*. Philadelphia: University of Pennsylvania Press.

Harter, S. (1983). Developmental perspectives on the self-system. In P. H. Mussen (Series Ed.) & E. M. Hetherington (Vol. Ed.), *Handbook of child psychology: Vol. 4. Socialization, personality, and social development* (4th ed., pp. 275–385). New York: Wiley.

Higgins, E. T. (1987). Self-discrepancy: A theory relating self and affect. *Psychological Review, 94*, 319–340.

James, W. (1890). *Principles of psychology*. New York: Holt.

Knowles, E. S., & Sibicky, M. E. (1990). Continuity and diversity in the stream of selves: Metaphorical resolutions of William James' one-in-many-selves paradox. *Personality and Social Psychology Bulletin, 16*, 676–687.

Kraus, S. J. (1995). Attitudes and the prediction of behavior: A meta-analysis of the empirical literature. *Personality and Social Psychology Bulletin, 21*, 58–75.

Lecky, P. (1945). *Self-consistency: A theory of personality*. New York: Island.

Lewis, M. (1990). Self-knowledge and social development in early life. In L. A. Pervin (Ed.), *Handbook of personality: Theory and research* (pp. 277–300). New York: Guilford.

Linton, R. (1936). *The study of man*. New York: Appleton-Century.

Markus, H., & Cross, S. (1990). The interpersonal self. In L. A. Pervin (Ed.), *Handbook of personality: Theory and research* (pp. 576–608). New York: Guilford.

Markus, H. & Herzog, A. R. (1991). The role of the self-concept in aging. *Annual Review of Gerontology and Geriatrics, 11*, 110–143.

Markus, H., & Nurius, P. (1986). Possible selves. *American Psychologist, 41*, 954–969.

Markus, H., & Wurf, E. (1987). The dynamic self-concept: A social psychological perspective. *Annual Review of Psychology, 38*, 299–337.

McAdams, D. P. (1988). *Power, intimacy, and the life story: Personological inquiries into identity*. New York: Guilford.

McCall, G. J., & Simmons, J. L. (1966). *Identities and interactions*. New York: Free Press.

Mead, G. H. (1934). *Mind, self, and society from the standpoint of a social behaviorist*. Chicago: University of Chicago Press.

Ogilvie, D. M. (1987). The undesired self: A neglected variable in personality research. *Journal of Personality and Social Psychology, 52*, 379–385.

Osgood, C. E., Suci, G. J. & Tannenbaum, P. H. (1957). *The measurement of meaning*. Urbana, IL: University of Illinois Press.

Porter, J. R., & Washington, R. E. (1993). Minority identity and self-esteem. *Annual Review of Sociology, 19*, 139–161.

Radin, P. (1920). The autobiography of a Winnebago indian. *University of California Publications in American Archaeology and Ethnology, 16*, 381–473.

Robbins, R. H. (1973). Identity, culture, and behavior. In J. J. Honigmann (Ed.), *Handbook of social and cultural anthropology* (pp. 1199–1222). Chicago: Rand McNally.

Rosenberg, S. (1988). Self and others: Studies in social personality and autobiography. In L. Berkowitz (Ed.), *Advances in experimental social psychology* (Vol. 21, pp. 57–95). New York: Academic Press.

Scheibe, K. E. (1985). Historical perspectives on the presented self. In B. R. Schlenker (Ed.), *The self and social life* (pp. 33–64). New York: McGraw-Hill.

Schlenker, B. R., & Weigold, M. F. (1992). Interpersonal processes involving impression regulation and management. *Annual Review of Psychology, 43*, 133–168.

Sedikides, C., & Strube, M. J. (1995). The multiply motivated self. *Personality and Social Psychology Bulletin, 21*, 1330–1335.

Spiro, M. E. (1993). Is the Western conception of the self "peculiar" within the context of the world cultures? *Ethos, 21*, 107–153.

Stryker, S. (1980). *Symbolic interactionism: A social structural version.* Menlo Park, CA: Benjamin/Cummings.

Stryker, S. (1987). Identity theory: Developments and extensions. In K. Yardley & T. Honess (Eds.), *Self and identity: Psychosocial perspectives* (pp. 89–103). New York: Wiley.

Stryker, S., & Statham, A. (1985). Symbolic interaction and role theory. In G. Lindzey & E. Aronson (Eds.), *The handbook of social psychology, Vol. 1* (3rd ed., pp. 311–378). New York: Random House.

Tajfel, H. (1982). *Social identity and intergroup relations.* Cambridge: Cambridge University Press, and Paris: Editions de la Maison des Sciences del' Homme.

Tesser, A. (1988). Toward a self-evaluation maintenance model of social behavior. In L. Berkowitz (Ed.), *Advances in experimental social psychology* (Vol. 21, pp. 181–227). New York: Academic Press.

Turner, J. C., with Hogg, M. A., Oakes, P. J., Reicher, S. D., & Blackwell, M. S. (1987). *Rediscovering the social group: A self-categorization theory.* Oxford: Basil Blackwell.

Whittaker, E. (1993). The birth of the anthropological self and its career. *Ethos, 20*, 191–219.

Wylie, R. C. (1974). *The self-concept. Volume 1: A review of methodological considerations and measuring instruments.* Lincoln, NE: University of Nebraska Press.

PART I

CLASSIC CONTRASTS

Multiplicity of Self Versus Unity of Identity

Multiplicity of Selves

"Multiplicity of selves" is a rather ambiguous title. Multiplicity of selves, and its semantic relatives, subselves and subpersonalities, are used to refer to any of a variety of conceptual partitionings of self. Among the more diverse referents for these terms are complexes, archetypes, and dissociated states of consciousness, including such pathological extremes as multiple personality. This inventory, far from complete, also reflects the ubiquity of the general notion of multiplicity in psychopathology and in personality organization.

I have omitted from this inventory the conception of a multiplicity of selves that is the framework for our research on self. This framework is rooted in a social psychological tradition, first adumbrated by William James (1890) in his conception of the "empirical self" as consisting of the material self, social self, and spiritual self. A further partitioning by James of social self is reflected in his classic and often cited statement that a person "has as many social selves as there are individuals who recognize him" (James, 1890, p. 294).

Less than a decade after the publication of James's *Principles of Psychology*, Baldwin (1897/1973) proposed a more comprehensive social-psychological conception of self. For Baldwin, all aspects of the self are a social and cultural product, and there are two interrelated aspects of this social self—the "socius," as he dubbed it: ego and alter. Ego refers to the thoughts you have about yourself—how you view yourself. Alter refers to the thoughts—what is in your consciousness—you have about people that you know, that you can imagine, or that are fictional or mythical. Baldwin gave a developmental rationale for a social self that includes both ego and alter, arguing that your view of yourself and of others become inextricably linked in early development. Ego and alter constitute a dialectic, a unity, in which each shapes and is shaped by the other.

The multiple-selves framework underlying our research is that of a structure consisting of a multiplicity of ego and alter elements and their interrelationships. Associated with each element in this structure is an amalgam of features—perceived physical and psychological characteristics, feelings, values, images, and intentions—experienced by the individual. A person's "view of" or "beliefs about" a given element refer both to this amalgam and to the underlying organization of features that comprise this amalgam.

Ego elements refer to the multiple aspects of self, readily identifiable by an individual as his or her family and work roles, interests, religious and ethnic affiliations, particular interpersonal relationships, and any of these elements as the person remembers it or anticipates it. Such ego elements and the amalgam of features associated with them correspond to the "multiplicity of selves" as this phrase is typically used in the social psychological literature (Ashmore & Ogilvie, 1992; Deaux, 1991, 1992, 1993; Gergen, 1971; Kihlstrom & Cantor, 1984; Ogilvie & Ashmore, 1991; Rosenberg, 1988; Rosenberg & Gara, 1985, to name only a few). Also, in spite of the diverse inventory of referents for "multiplicity of selves," its most common use in contemporary writings (both within and outside of social psychology) is to refer to a person's views of his or her multiple aspects of self (e.g., Goulding & Schwartz, 1995; Mair, 1977; Martindale, 1980; McAdams, 1985; Rowan, 1990; Schwartz, 1987).

Alter elements refer to the "multiplicity" of persons about whom an individual has some beliefs (a view). Such persons include casual acquaintances, public figures, "types" of persons, and intimates. The content and processes associated with such beliefs is social psychology's well-established topic of person perception—the focus of a voluminous body of research.

One of the basic questions about the structure of the multiplicity of selves concerns exactly how these selves are related to one another. James (1890) ventured the notion that the empirical selves are arranged in a "hierarchical scale" in terms of the person's "self-regard." The conceptions of "identity salience" and "identity prominence" among contemporary symbolic interactionists (e.g., McCall & Simmons, 1966, 1978; Stryker & Serpe, 1982; Stryker & Statham, 1985) can be traced back (through Mead and Cooley) to James's rudimentary conception of a hierarchy. (Cooley and Mead also provided sociology with a continuity of James's and Baldwin's social-psychological conceptions of self.) Baldwin's "dialectic" suggests a structure in which there are contrastive relations between ego and alter, even within the unity of a dialectic. However, within this dialectic, Baldwin also identified certain similarities between ego and alter. He noted, for example, how early identification, particularly with parents, leads to a degree of similarity between one's view of self and of alter.

It is only recently, however, that the structural ideas of hierarchy and of similarities and contrasts among socius elements have stimulated a coherent line of empirical research in psychology. Underlying these empirical advances are two methodological ingredients for representing the organization of a multiplicity: (1) systematic data-gathering procedures, particularly those that allow a person to express his or her own categories in the descriptions of each ego and/or alter element; (2) new data-analytic methods (with feasible algorithms) for parsimoniously representing these idiographic categories and the interrelationships among ego and/or alter elements conferred by these categories. Our own data-gathering procedures were inspired initially by our research on "implicit personality theory," which focused on idiographic representations of a person's beliefs about others. It was but a short step to include aspects of ego, such as occupation, social roles and relationships, interests, and so on. We dubbed such ego elements "personal identities" (Rosenberg & Gara, 1985).

Concomitant with the inclusion of both ego and alter elements in data gathering were efforts at developing data-analytic methods particularly appropriate for a comprehensive structural representation of such a multiplicity. Standard structural models—multidimensional scaling and clustering—which we, and others, had been using to represent a person's implicit personality theory proved incomplete for such a comprehensive representation, in that such models can represent the structure of either the elements or their content, but not both (e.g., Gara & Rosenberg, 1979; Kim & Rosenberg, 1980; Rosenberg, 1977; Rosenberg, Nelson, & Vivekananthan, 1968; Rosenberg & Sedlak, 1972). Also scaling and clustering models and their associated algorithms make the simplifying assumption that for any pair of elements (or attributes) the psychological proximity is symmetrical. This precludes the representation of asymmetric relations: for example, that the description of one element subsumes that of another element, and not vice versa.

Structural models that overcome these limitations were first developed by Paul De Boeck at the University of Leuven in Belgium, who shares with me an interest in person perception and in the self. De Boeck developed both the underlying mathematical model and an associated computer algorithm for parsimoniously and comprehensively representing the rather sizable corpus of self/other descriptions obtained from each of the participants in our studies. The model and algorithm, dubbed HICLAS (HIerarchical CLASses), are based on a set-theoretical conception of hierarchy (De Boeck, 1986, 1989; De Boeck & Rosenberg, 1988; Van Mechelen, De Boeck, & Rosenberg, 1995).

The set-theoretical relations at the core of HICLAS capture quite precisely the *degree* of similarity and contrast among the elements of the socius in terms of the overlap of their descriptive content. The ego and alter elements and all the relations among them that can be represented in a HICLAS structure go considerably beyond those first explored by Baldwin (self-as-other and self-versus-other). Moreover, these set-theoretical relations imply an order—a hierarchy—among the elements, as well as among the descriptive features.

The next section is taken up with a summary of the basic features of both our data-gathering procedures and HICLAS. That is followed by three empirical applications of this methodology in which ego and alter elements are represented in the same structure. These applications, which demonstrate the feasibility of studying the socius empirically, also illustrate the relations that we have found between a person's socius and important features of their everyday life.

Also illustrated in these three empirical applications is the systematic incorporation of autobiographical memories of selected ego and alter elements into the structure of the socius. Autobiographical anticipation—a person's view of self at some time in the future—is also taken up in one of these applications. These applications clearly illustrate that a person's views of past and anticipated elements of the socius play an important role in interpersonal life. We also explore how our methods can be used in a prospective design to measure accuracy (as well as distortions) in autobiographical memory of self and other and to discover some of the determinants of accuracy. The inclusion of autobiographical memory, of autobiographical anticipation, and of a prospective design makes it possible to study the temporally dynamic socius in terms of structural shifts and the implications of these shifts in the person's life. Other applications of the HICLAS methodology are summarized elsewhere (De Boeck, Rosenberg, & Van Mechelen, 1993; Rosenberg, Van Mechelen, & De Boeck, 1996).

A final section takes up several issues raised by this research: the importance of including the alter in the multiplicity for a more comprehensive understanding of the self; how the notion of a unity of self can be incorporated into a conception of multiplicity; and the relation between structural models and the psychological reality of an organically functioning self.

Methodology

Any given study of the socius is likely to involve a rather modest subset of all the elements of ego and alter about which a person has a distinct impression. The "targets," as they are typically referred to in a particular study, are tagged for a person in a variety of ways. Here is a sampling of the kinds of ego and alter targets and an example or two (in quotes) of how a person might tag such targets.

Ego targets

Occupational and personal roles:	"psychologist," "daughter"
Particular relationships:	"me in my relationship with Nancy" (as distinct from "Nancy" as a target)
Activities and habits:	"skier," "heavy smoker"
Group membership:	"union member"
Religion, race, ethnicity:	"Illinois-American"
Hypothetical:	"how I would like to be"
Autobiographical:	"me when I was physically abused as a child"
Anticipated self:	"me as I expect to be in my relationship with Nancy"

Alter targets

Particular person:	"my mother," "Nancy"
Type of person:	"a close friend"
Hypothetical:	"how I would like for Nancy to be"
Autobiographical:	"my mother when I was a child"

Our studies of the socius make extensive use of a free-response format in order to allow each participant in the study to use their own vocabulary to describe the targets in the study. In this format, a person is asked to identify, with their own terms, the characteristics they perceive as the relatively enduring attributes of each target. These attributes may include physical traits, personality traits, attitudes, competencies, and so on. In some studies, the person is also asked to identify feelings and emotions typically experienced with each target.

In order to obtain a list of attributes for each person to use in describing their targets, a person is first asked to come up with a small sample of attributes most descriptive of each target. The person is asked to provide these attributes in the form of discrete units, but not necessarily single words. In this way, the person cumulates an attribute list from their own vocabulary. The targets are again presented, one at a time, and the person judges which of the attributes on the list are descriptive.

These judgments can be summarized in a matrix in which the rows are the targets, the columns are the attributes, and the cell entries are the person's judgments. A miniature example of such a matrix is given in Table 2.1. A cell entry of 1 in this table means that the person

TABLE 2.1. Hypothetical example of a targets by attributes matrix

	Successful	Articulate	Hardworking	Generous	Protective	Loving	Adorable
Father	1	1	1	0	0	0	0
Husband	0	0	1	1	0	0	1
Aunt	0	0	0	0	1	1	1
Sister	0	0	0	0	1	1	1
Mother	0	0	1	1	1	1	1
Me-as-Mother	0	0	1	1	1	1	1
Ideal Me	1	1	1	1	1	1	1
Baby	0	0	0	0	0	0	1

described the target in the given row with the attribute in the given column; 0, otherwise.

Table 2.1 summarizes the descriptions by a young mother of eight targets: six close relatives and two aspects of self, Me-as-Mother and Ideal-Me ("how I would like to be"). She used a vocabulary of seven attributes to describe these targets. This example was gleaned from real data; however, a real protocol usually involves considerably more targets and attributes and almost invariably contains negative as well as positive attributes. Nevertheless, this miniature example is sufficient to illustrate the basic set-theoretical relationships in HICLAS.

A set of targets having identical attributes is called a "class" of targets. In set-theoretical terminology, targets for which the attributes are identical are referred to as equivalent. Two of the target classes in Table 2.1 contain more than one member: [Aunt, Sister] and [Mother, Me-as-Mother]. That is, the table shows that both aunt and sister have the following attributes and only these attributes: protective, loving, adorable; mother and me-as-mother also have these attributes and share the following additional attributes: hardworking, generous. Thus, aunt and sister are equivalent, as are mother and me-as-mother. The remaining target classes in Table 2.1 contain only one target each.

A class of attributes is defined analogously. That is, all the attributes that apply to exactly the same targets are in the same class and are equivalent attributes. In Table 2.1, successful and articulate are equivalent, as are protective and loving. Thus, each pair constitutes an attribute class; the remaining attribute classes contain one attribute each.

Target classes can be ordered hierarchically according to the attributes that apply to them. Two target classes, A and B, are in a superset-subset relation if and only if A, the superset, as all of the attributes of B, the subset, and has other attributes that B does not have. For example, the set [Mother, Me-as-Mother] is a superset of [Aunt, Sister]; additionally, the set [Father] is a subset of [Ideal Me]. Attribute classes can also be identified as having a superset-subset relation based on the targets to which they apply. For example, [Hardworking] is a superset of

[Successful, Articulate], which means that hardworking is always attributed to a target when successful and articulate are, but not vice versa.

There may also exist pairs of target classes that are neither equivalent nor in a strict superset-subset relation because each class has attributes that the other does not. In these relations, targets may or may not share any attributes. Two examples: [Father] and [Husband] share hardworking but are otherwise nonoverlapping in the attributes they possess; [Father] and [Aunt] have no attributes in common. Analogously, there are such attribute classes. For example, [Generous] and [Protective] have partially overlapping target groups associated with them.

The target classes I have given as examples are illustrated in Figure 2.1 with Venn diagrams. These are the basic set-theoretical relations found in HICLAS and are sufficient to describe the major findings in the empirical work I summarize in the next section.

It should be noted that there are a number of other examples in Table 2.1 that I have not diagrammed in Figure 2.1. Also not diagrammed is the possibility that a class may be a superset of more than one class. An example is [Ideal Me], which is a superset of [Husband] as well as of [Father], among others. A class may also be a subset of more than one class. Moreover, there are other concatenations of the basic relations that are not diagrammed; for example, a class may be a superset of another class, which is in turn a superset of a third class. The set [Ideal Me], for example, is a superset of [Mother, Me-as-Mother], which is a superset of [Aunt, Sister]. The number of such levels is related to the dimensionality of the HICLAS structure. We refer to the dimensionality as its rank; the rank required to represent Table 2.1 completely is four.

It is possible to construct a graphic representation that summarizes all the set-theoretical relations implicit in Table 2.1 and also displays the complete hierarchy of target classes and of attribute classes and of their association to each other (cf. De Boeck & Rosenberg, 1988; De Boeck, et al., 1993; Rosenberg, 1989; Rosenberg, et al., 1996; Van Mechelen, et al., 1995).

A final note about the use of the HICLAS algorithm. The user specifies the desired rank of the HICLAS structure produced by the algorithm. Typically, a user will specify several ranks and the algorithm measures the goodness of fit for the structure that corresponds to each rank. As with other structural models—e.g., a multidimensional scaling—the rank after which there is little improvement in fit is chosen as the optimal one.

Applications

The first study is of two groups of young mothers, one group with a history of physical abuse as children, the other not. This study illustrates

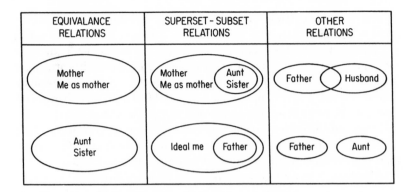

FIGURE 2.1. Example of set-theoretical relations in Table 2.1.

the value of including the memories that these mothers have about their own mothers and the value of including ego and alter targets in the same analysis. The second application, a prospective study of autobiographical memory in clinical depression, also illustrates the value of the socius framework in sorting out the memory distortions in ego and alter that occur in this group as compared with a group of nondepressed controls. The final application, that of the early development of a romantic relationship, brings in the anticipated self and demonstrates the powerful role it plays in predicting the relationship's viability.

The Socius of Mothers Physically Abused as Children

A person who was physically abused as a child is much more likely to become an abusive parent than someone who did not experience such abuse (Altemeier, O'Connor, Vietze, Sandler, & Sherrod, 1984; Fraiberg, Adelson, & Shapiro, 1975; Kaufman & Zigler, 1987; Steele & Pollock, 1968). Several years ago, Michael Gara, Elaine Herzog, and I began to raise questions about the perceptions that young mothers with a history of physical abuse have of themselves and their family members, and of the role these perceptions play in this intergenerational transmission of abuse. These questions led first to an exploratory study of five mothers, three with a history of abuse, two nonabused (Herzog, Gara, & Rosenberg, 1992). HICLAS analyses of their protocols revealed certain differences between the abused and nonabused in their view of self and significant others, including their children. This method revealed differences that related to independently obtained clinical assessments of the abused mother's care of and attachment to her infant. That is, even without any evidence that they have abused their own children, these mothers show effects from their own childhood, both in their perceptions of self and others and in the mothering of their infants. It might, then, be possible to identify high-risk mothers before abuse actually occurs.

Motivated by these findings and those from a larger subsequent study, we launched a large-scale three-year project, now in its second year; we have the complete initial protocols of the self/other descriptions of 45 mothers who were physically abused as children and 38 nonabused. The two groups of mothers are comparable in age, socioeconomic status, and ethnicity. Any mothers with psychiatric histories were screened out. For a mother to be included in the study, it was necessary that she have an infant no older than six months of age. The rationale for this criterion is that it enables us to assess the mother's perception of self and other when the likelihood of physical abuse is still small.

Each mother was seen for an individual interview, during which we obtained her free-response descriptions of a number of significant people in her life and of several aspects of herself. The significant others include her father and her mother as she views them now and, as separate targets, how she remembers viewing each of them when she was a child. The self targets are: me now, me-as-mother, me-as-child, and me-as-child-when-punished—the latter two being autobiographical memories.

The matrices created from each mother's descriptions were analyzed with HICLAS (conjunctive method, rank 4). In order to do comparisons between groups in this application, we defined a number of measures of individual differences that can be extracted from each of the idiographic HICLAS structures. These nomothetic measures are designed to reflect important facets of the socius, such as identification, contrast, and so on. Using such measures for the analyses of these mothers' initial set of descriptions yielded a number of robust findings.

One set of important findings involves the degree to which the mothers in their role as mothers implicitly identify with their own mothers as they remember her from childhood. Degree of identification was measured by coding the structural relation of the two targets: (1) me-as-mother; (2) my childhood memory of my mother. Each mother's pair of targets was classified as belonging to one of three types of set-theoretical relations:

equivalent—the two targets are in the same class; indicative of strong identification;

superset-subset—either target is a superset of the other; indicative of moderate identification;

other—the two targets each have attributes not shared by the other; indicative of minimal identification.

These three basic relations are those depicted with the hypothetical example (see Figure 2.1).

The results of this classification for the two groups are summarized in Table 2.2A. The table shows how many mothers in each group display each of the three patterns. A Fisher's exact test of this frequency table yielded a difference between the two groups that is significant beyond the .0001 level. The major source of the difference between the two groups is clear: abused mothers describe me-as-mother as less similar to my childhood memory of my mother than do mothers in the nonabused group. Moreover this difference holds up even when the father is the reported abuser (not separately tabulated). An abused mother, then, whether abused by her mother or her father, tends to disidentify with the mother she remembers during childhood, whereas a mother in the nonabused group is likely to view her mother as a model for her own mothering.

We then compared the degree to which these young mothers have the same view of their own mothers now and of their childhood memory of their mother. The consistency between these two views was judged maximal when the pair of targets fell into the same class; moderate when either target was a superset of the other; and minimal when the two targets each have attributes not shared by the other.

The results of this classification for the two groups are summarized in Table 2.2B. The table shows how many mothers in each group display each of three patterns. A Fisher's exact test here yielded a difference between the two groups that is significant beyond the .02 level. The major source of the difference between the two groups is clear: abused mothers are less consistent than nonabused mothers.

To see how different the consistency classification is from the identity classification, given that they share a common element (my childhood memory of my mother), we assigned the following similarity values to each of the set-theoretical relations: if the two targets are equivalent, similarity is two; if either target is a superset of the other, similarity is one; for other target relations, similarity is zero. A nonsignificant correlation between them ($r = .11$ in the abused group; $r = .15$ in the nonabused group) attests to the difference between consistency and identification.

Using the Bayley scales of mental and physical development (Collard, 1983), we checked whether these indices of the child's development are related to the mother's identification and consistency, particularly in the abused group. We know from the published literature that (older) maltreated children show significantly lower physical-development scores than nonmaltreated children (Lyons-Ruth, Connell, Zoll, & Stoll, 1987). While there is as yet no evidence of extensive physical abuse per se in our sample of abused mothers (although two have lost custody of their infants due to neglect), some may already be overly restrictive or hostile toward their infants. The question is whether we can detect, at this early stage, any relation between the infant's mental and/or physical development and the mother's identification and consistency.

TABLE 2.2

A. Number of mothers in each group whose structural relation between me as mother and my childhood memory of my own mother is equivalent, a superset or subset, or other

	Equivalent	Superset/Subset	Other
Abused Group	5	12	28
Control Group	21	8	9

B. Number of mothers in each group whose structural relation between my mother now and my childhood memory of my own mother is equivalent, a superset or subset, or other

	Equivalent	Superset/Subset	Other
Abused Group	22	9	14
Control Group	29	6	3

Based on the Bayley scales of 61 infants (31 from the abused group and 30 from the nonabused group), the results are largely negative at this point. That is, neither measure of the child's development correlates with the mother's identification score (0, 1, 2). There is some suggestion of a relation between the mother's consistency score and the physical subscale: the correlation is $-.26$ ($p < .10$), but it may simply be too early to gauge these relationships.

We will continue to sort out how this complex of perceptions involving mother and self-as-mother relates to the development and probability of maltreatment of the child. We will also monitor changes in the perceptions of these mothers, particularly those in the abused group who do not now identify with their own mothers. It is not at all certain that such disidentification will hold firm as the child develops.

It may be premature to draw out the implications for identifying the most at-risk mothers and for designing a treatment plan. However, it is not too early to think about altering the internalized "mothering model" of these mothers, enhancing the positive attributes in the mothering model and, if possible, providing additional models. Although more abused mothers have revised their view of their mother than mothers in the nonabused group, My Mother Now may not be a viable model for them. It is perhaps more likely that the image of the mother that these young mothers grew up with provides the model (or antimodel) for mothering.

Finally, there is another striking difference between the two groups in the general evaluative tone of the attributes they use to describe certain key targets. This difference was revealed by analyses of two different measures: one based on positive attribute classes and one on negative attribute classes. The degree of positive content was measured by counting the number of positive attribute classes associated with that target; the degree of negative content by the number of negative attribute classes. (These measures indicate target "elaboration"; cf. Robey, Cohen, & Gara, 1989, and Rosenberg & Gara, 1985). These two measures were calculated for mother now, father now, my childhood memory of my mother, my childhood memory of my father, me-as-child, me-as-child-when-punished, baby, me-now, me-as-mother.

The differences between the two groups are dramatic. The socius of a mother in the abused group is dominated by negative attribute classes. Negative attributes are focused most heavily on mother now, father now, and my childhood memory of my mother. When the measures are subjected to a discriminant analysis, the differences between the two groups on the negative measure are sufficient to accurately discriminate the two groups with but one false negative. Indeed, in our numerous studies of self and other perception in a variety of populations, we have not seen a socius that is as filled with anger, fear, and sadness as that of a physically abused mother.

Interestingly, when we look at the degree of positive elaboration of the alter, we find a significant relation between it and infant attachment, as measured by the Strange Situation test (Ainsworth, Blehar, Waters, & Wall, 1978; Ainsworth & Wittig, 1969). That is, the more elaborated the positive view of others, the more secure the attachment. This is true for both groups in our study.

Other results from this study are described in Gara, Rosenberg, & Herzog (1996). I have summarized selected findings here to illustrate the value of incorporating autobiographical memory of certain targets and the value of including both ego and alter targets (the socius framework) in the study of "multiple selves." While our framework is consistent with that of Baldwin's socius, the extensive inventory of particular socius elements allows us to explore relations far beyond those of identification and contrast envisaged by Baldwin at the turn of the century.

Autobiographical Memory of Self and Other in Depression

The analyses of retrospective memory in the study of young mothers, while novel in some ways, are also routine in the context of the voluminous literature on autobiographical memory. Indeed, much has been learned from autobiographical memory about personality and personality development and about the nature of memory itself; for example: the content of autobiography and its relation to developmental stages (e.g., Cohler, 1982), the narrative structure of memory (e.g., Spence, 1982), its content as dependent on the person's current view of self (e.g., Greenwald, 1980; Ross & Conway, 1986), the implicit beliefs contained in an autobiography about the development of self (e.g., Rosenberg, 1989), and so on. A steady stream of published collections on autobiographical knowledge provide fresh perspectives and indicate the importance of this topic in cognitive as well as social psychology (Neisser, 1993; Neisser & Fivush, 1994; Rubin, 1986; Srull & Wyer, 1993).

However, systematic studies that are prospective in design are scarce in the work on autobiographical memory. A prospective design provides the opportunity to address questions about the accuracy of autobiographical memories of self and others, as well as the role of life events in shaping and reshaping these memories. A prospective design is rather simple in principle: the data consist of self and other descriptions at time 1 and a memory test at time 2 in which the person reproduces as accurately as possible what was said at time 1. The time lapse depends on the substantive questions of the investigation and on the feasibility of conducting a longitudinal study. It is, of course, the feasibility of conducting longitudinal studies in "autobiographical time" that makes the prospective study so difficult to do.

A recently completed three-year research project on the perception of self and other in a sample of clinically depressed patients included a nine-month test-retest regimen that afforded the opportunity to use a prospective design to identify some determinants of accuracy in memories of self and other. The analysis of the autobiographical data is the subject of a doctoral dissertation (Konecky, 1996). Other findings from the project have been reported in Gara, et al. (1993), Gara, Rosenberg, and Woolfolk (1993), and Goldston, Gara, and Woolfolk (1992).

In this study one group was a sample of clinically depressed patients and the other a matched control sample of persons with no history of mental illness. We expected that the changes in life events and circumstances of the depressed patients even during a relatively brief period of nine months would lead to measurable inaccuracies in memory. We did not have the resources to identify specific life events responsible for memory inaccuracies, but we guessed that they were likely to be dramatic compared with those in the relatively stable lives of the matched controls.

Each participant completed a number of standard self-report inventories, two of which were selected as possibly related to autobiographical memory. They are the Beck Depression Inventory (BDI) (Beck, Ward, Mendelson, Mock, & Erbaugh, 1961) and the Dysfunctional Attitudes Scale (DAS) (Beck, Rush, Shaw, & Emery, 1979; Weissman, 1979). Only the DAS was found to be significantly related to memory accuracy. Thus, group membership (depressed, control) and DAS were examined for their relation to accuracy.

Of the original sample of 31 depressed patients, 23 (13 women, 10 men) remained in the study long enough for us to obtain time 2 data. Of the original control sample of 27 persons, 18 (12 women, 6 men) were available at time 2. Our comparison of participants who stayed with those who left revealed no statistically significant differences between them.

At time 1, the participants described, in a free-response format, nine persons in their lives, 10 different aspects of self, and an overall description of self ("me as I actually am"). Descriptions by the depressed patients were obtained during the first few days of treatment, before antidepressant medication and other treatments have any sizable effects.

At time 2, each participant was given the descriptive vocabulary they used at time 1 and asked to reproduce as accurately as possible the descriptions they gave at time 1 for "me as I actually am" and a significant other. For convenience of exposition, I will refer to the description of self at time 1 as actual me, and the description of this actual me from memory at time 2 as Memory Actual Me; similarly, other and Memory Other.

Time 1 descriptions and memory of time 1 descriptions obtained at time 2 were combined into one matrix and analyzed with HICLAS (rank 4). A dichotomous measure of memory accuracy was obtained from the HICLAS structure for actual me and for other. For any given participant, if actual me and Memory Actual Me occurred in the same class (that is, if they were equivalent in the set-theoretical sense), the memory was classified as accurate. A similar categorization was made for other and Memory Other.

The accuracy results are summarized in Table 2.3. The results are tabulated separately for Actual Me and Other. Within each we see the number of persons in the depressed group who accurately recalled their self-description as compared with the number in the control group, as well as the relation between high and low DAS (median split) and accuracy of recall.

A logistic regression analysis was done separately for the actual me and other counts. Within each analysis, diagnosis and DAS were the independent variables, with accuracy the dependent variable.

Both diagnosis and DAS are highly significant as predictors of accuracy of actual me: Chi-square (1) is 4.93 (p = .03) for diagnosis and Chi-square (1) is 4.68 (p = .03) for DAS. The combined effects of diagnosis and DAS are clearly revealed in Table 3. Of the eight persons who are depressed and have a low DAS, none (top left cell) are accurate; of the five persons who are not depressed and have a high DAS, only one (bottom right cell) is inaccurate. In short, depression is highly predictive of inaccurate memory of self, and so is low DAS. For accuracy in the recall of a significant other, neither independent variable is a significant predictor of accuracy: Chi-square (1) is 1.59 for diagnosis and Chi-square (1) is .16 for DAS. Thus, we cannot conclude that either depression or low DAS is necessarily associated with general memory deficits for all elements of the socius.

TABLE 2.3. Number of participants who accurately/inaccurately recalled their descriptions of actual me and of a significant other

| | Accurate in Recall of Actual Me | | | |
| | Yes | | No | |
	Low DAS	High DAS	Low DAS	High DAS
Depressed Group	0	6	8	8
Control Group	5	4	7	1
	Accurate in Recall of Other			
	Yes		No	
	Low DAS	High DAS	Low DAS	High DAS
Depressed Group	4	7	4	7
Control Group	4	2	8	3

There is the question of why a low DAS is highly predictive of decreased accuracy in memory of actual me. And why is DAS not predictive of other accuracy? The research literature (as well as the content of the questionnaire itself) is instructive (e.g., Olinger, Kuiper, & Shaw, 1987). In addition to measuring so-called "dysfunctional attitudes," the DAS is shown to be correlated with self-consciousness and self-focus. And why is the DAS not predictive of other accuracy? Essentially for the same reason: it is a measure of self-preoccupation rather than preoccupation with the nature of other people.

Anticipated Self and Commitment in a Romantic Relationship

This final application examines autobiographical anticipation in the study of multiple selves. Like the previous study of depressives, this study is prospective in design; the focus, however, is not on accuracy of memory but on how predictive an anticipated view of self in an intimate relationship is of the viability of the actual relationship.

The study is a recently completed doctoral dissertation (Reich, 1994) in our laboratory on the development of commitment in a romantic relationship. Based on a model of commitment, Reich (1994) predicted that a person will continue in the relationship and will show, on various indices, a growing involvement in the relationship if the person believes that their "real me" can be validated in the relationship. "Validation" was assessed by measuring the similarity between a person's description of anticipated self in the relationship and the person's description of the "real me."

Reich used a prospective design in which these (and other) descriptions were obtained at time 1 and again at time 2. Each participant also rated their relationship at both times on scales of commitment, satisfaction, ambivalence, attractiveness of alternatives, and active involvement in the relationship. Reich also took a *behavioral* measure of commitment to the relationship at time 2—i.e., whether the person was still seeing the partner.

Nine males and 18 females, each involved in a heterosexual relationship for less than a month, participated in this study. (Their partners did not.) Using a free-response format, each participant described a number of people in their lives and a number of ego targets. The ego targets of interest here are: "me with (name of romantic partner)"; "me with (name of romantic partner) in the near future"; "real me". For convenience, I will refer to these targets as Me with Partner, Me with Partner—Anticipated, and Real Me, respectively. At Time 2, a month later, the participants returned and repeated their free-response descriptions of all the targets, their ratings of the relationship, and a report of whether they were still seeing the partner. The attrition in this study was extraordinarily low: all but one participant (a male) returned for the second session.

Time 1 and time 2 descriptions were combined into one matrix and this matrix was analyzed with HICLAS (rank 4). Let us examine first the basic structural relations between real me at time 1 and me with partner (anticipated) for participants who were still in the relationship at time 2 with those who had broken off the relationship (Table 2.4). Also summarized are the structural relations between me with partner at time 1 and real me at time 1. At time 2, 13 participants (3 males, 10 females) reported that they were still dating their partners.

In order to do a contingency Chi-square on each of these two measures with sufficient frequencies in the cells, we grouped the equivalent, superset-subset, and subset-superset relations. The Chi-square for the resulting two-by-two table is 7.72 (p < .01) for the real me/me with partner (anticipated) relations; for the real me/me with partner at time 1, the Chi-square is 4.25 (p < .05). Obviously, both measures at time 1 are predictive of staying or leaving, with anticipated self seeming to have the edge.

In order to check on this, Reich used a more continuous measure of similarity between a person's description at time 1 of me with partner (anticipated) and real me. For comparison of relative predictive power, the same similarity measure was also calculated between a person's description of me with partner at time 1 and real me at time 1. Similarity was expressed as a proportion, obtained by dividing the number of attribute classes shared by the two selected targets by the sum of the shared and nonshared attribute classes. The higher the proportion, the more similar the descriptions of the two targets. (Reich's similarity

TABLE 2.4

A. Number of participants in each of the two groups (stay/leave) whose structural relation of me with partner—anticipated to real me is equivalent, a superset or subset, or other

	Equivalent	Superset/Subset	Subset/Superset	Other
Stay Group	1	2	6	4
Leave Group	0	0	2	11

B. Number of participants in each of the two groups (stay/leave) whose structural relation of me with partner at time 1 to real me is equivalent, a superset or subset, or other

	Equivalent	Superset/Subset	Subset/Superset	Other
Stay Group	2	2	7	2
Leave Group	0	0	6	7

measure and the categories shown in Table 2.4 are conceptually closely related.)

By far the stronger predictor at time 1 of the behavioral measure is the similarity between me with partner (anticipated) and real me. Using a log-linear regression function to predict behavior gives the results in Table 2.5. The similarity measure correctly identifies 21 of the 26 participants. The results, using the same statistical method with the other measure at time 1, showing similarity between me with partner and real me, are also in Table 2.5. The prediction does approach significance, but this measure is actually less predictive than are some of other measures available at time 1 (e.g., activity in the relationship). The similarity between me with partner (anticipated) and real me remains significant as a predictor even after controlling for these rival predictors (Reich, 1994).

These predictions about staying or leaving involve no information from the participants' partners. Since there is no reason to believe that the partner who participated in the study is the more responsible for the decision, there must have been some communication, perhaps implicit, by one member of the pair that affects the anticipated self of the other.

Observations and Conclusions

The socius is an explicit expression of a widely accepted idea that taking into account a person's views of others provides a more comprehensive understanding of the person than self-conceptions alone. In particular, there are certain categories of perception that may underlie a person's

TABLE 2.5

A. Predicted versus observed number of participants who will continue in the relationship and who will leave where the predictor is similarity between me with partner— anticipated and real me

		Predicted		
		Stay	Leave	% correct
Observed	Stay	10	3	77%
	Leave	2	11	85%
			Overall	81%

B. Predicted versus observed number of participants who will continue in the relationship and who will leave where the predictor is similarity between me with partner at time 1 and real me

		Predicted		
		Stay	Leave	% correct
Observed	Stay	10	3	77%
	Leave	6	7	54%
			Overall	65%

description of other people—categories that may or may not be accessible to, or acknowledged by, the person in the context of self-description. The relation between a self-view and the person's view of another can also be valuable in understanding the person. The measure of identification used in the study of young mothers is but one example of this principle. Another example of this research approach is the HICLAS analysis of Thomas Wolfe's fictionalized autobiography, *Look Homeward, Angel* (Rosenberg, 1988, 1989). This analysis clearly revealed Wolfe's "not me": there was no overlap between attribute classes associated with self and with members of the community. Also revealed by similar analyses are identifications and contrasts (not me) between self and family members. The contrasts in Wolfe's socius were revealed by these analyses in which the set-theoretical relations between self-targets and other targets were examined in the context of a multidimensional scaling of the attributes.

The research reported in the present paper demonstrates other ways in which views of the other can play an important role in understanding self. The finding, for example, that among depressives, memory of self is subject to distortion while memory of others do not show such distortions, tells us that a general memory deficit is not ubiquitous in clinical depression. Of course, portrayals of certain features of a person's socius may or may not require descriptions of others, just as any one study need not be exhaustive of a person's multiplicity of ego elements. The sampling of targets from the socius obviously depends on the substantive research question.

The three studies described in this paper span a considerable range in the concatenation of the two phenomena, the socius as a multiplicity and autobiography. In the study of young mothers with a history of abuse, we saw how retrospective accounts of their own mothers are playing a role in their own mothering. In the study of commitment in a developing romantic relationship, it is the account of an anticipated self that is predictive of commitment to the relationship. The study of depressives illustrates the prospective design in the study of autobiographical memory of self and others, and the potential of such a design for measuring memory accuracy and discovering its determinants.

I now turn to the issue of unity versus multiplicity of self. Depending on the way unity is defined, there may or may not be a theoretical incompatibility here. When Gara and I introduced our research on the multiplicity of personal identity a decade ago (Rosenberg & Gara, 1985), we argued for a conception of multiplicity that includes both the elements of a multiplicity and the inter-relations among them. Such a system or structure constitutes a unity in which the elements are inextricably related to one another in specifiable structural ways (and in functional ways, in that changes in the structural location of one element likely affects the location of other elements). We also argued against looking for a superordinate self in the structure as the source of unity, or at unity as the continuity of consciousness—the latter being a three-century regression to Locke's conception of identity. This is not to underestimate the psychological importance of various features of structure (e.g., a superordinate self) or of the content of consciousness. We rely on the latter for our basic data!

Another conception of unity of self is that of a person's "sense of self." However, I think it would be a mistake to use a phenomenological sense of unity as a way to define unity of self instead of the unity provided by a structural organization of the socius. Phenomenologically, for example, it may seem paradoxical that a person's view of others that he/she does not identify with is an important aspect of self; from a structural point of view, however, such views of others are part of a dichotomy that is essential to the unity of self. Even more paradoxical perhaps is the notice that the more intense the rejection of certain others as "not me," the more evident it is that the "not me" is part of "me."

Finally, I want to take up the way the set-theoretical models that we use characterizes the organization of the multiplicity of selves and others. HICLAS, in its present form, hardens the target and attribute boundaries, boundaries that are undoubtedly fuzzy in an organically functioning self. The extant model and algorithms are deterministic, and about the only way to assess the fuzziness of the structure is by the goodness-of-fit measures associated with each target and attribute. The advent of a probabilistic version of HICLAS may provide another, more explicit way to represent the fuzziness that exists within and between the elements of a multiplicity (Maris, De Boeck, & Van Mechelen, in press).

Acknowledgments: The writing of this chapter and the research described herein on mothers who were physically abused as children was supported in part by the William T. Grant Foundation (Grant 93-1442-91 to Michael Gara and Seymour Rosenberg). Support was also provided in part by NATO (Grant CRG 921321 to Iven Van Mechelen and Seymour Rosenberg). My thanks to Richard Ashmore, Nancy Cantor, Grace Cherng, Michael Gara, Lee Jussim, Iven Van Mechelen, and Warren Reich for their valuable comments on an earlier draft of this chapter.

References

Ainsworth, M. D., Blehar, M. C., Waters, E., & Wall, S. (1978). *Patterns of attachment: A psychological study of the strange situation*. Hillside, NJ: Erlbaum.

Ainsworth, M. D., & Wittig, B. A. (1969). Attachment and exploratory behavior of one-year-olds in a strange situation. In B. M. Foss (Ed.), *Determinants of infant behavior* (Vol. 4, pp. 129–173). New York: Wiley.

Altemeier, W. A., O'Connor, S., Vietze, P., Sandler, H., & Sherrod, K. (1984). Prediction of child abuse: A prospective study of feasibility. *Child Abuse and Neglect, 8*, 393–400.

Ashmore, R. D., & Ogilvie, D. M. (1992). He's such a nice boy—when he is with grandma: Gender and evaluation in self-with-other representations. In R. P. Lipka & T. M. Brinhaupt (Eds.), *The self: Definitional and methodological issues* (pp. 236–290). Albany: State University of New York Press.

Baldwin, J. M. (1897). *Social and ethical interpretations in mental development*. New York: Macmillan. (2nd ed., reprinted 1973, New York: Arno Press.)

Beck, A. T., Rush, A. J., Shaw, B. F., & Emery, G. (1979). *Cognitive therapy of depression*. New York: Guilford Press.

Beck, A. T., Ward, C. H., Mendelson, M., Mock, J., & Erbaugh, J. (1961). An inventory for measuring depression. *Archives of General Psychiatry, 4*, 561–571.

Cohler, B. J. (1982). Personal narrative and life course. In P. B. Baltes & O. G. Brim, Jr. (Eds.), *Life-span development and behavior* (Vol. 4, pp. 205–241). New York: Academic Press.

Collard, R. R. (1983). Review of the Bayley scales of infant development. In

O. Burros (Ed.), *The seventh mental measurements yearbook* (pp. 402–403). Highland Park, NJ: Gryphon Press.

Deaux, K. (1991). Social identities: Thoughts on structure and change. In R. C. Curtis (Ed.), *The relational self: Theoretical convergences in psychoanalysis and social psychology* (pp. 77–93). New York: Guilford Press.

Deaux, K. (1992). Personalizing identity and socializing self. In G. M. Breakwell (Ed.), *Social psychology of identity and the self-concept* (pp. 9–33). London: Academic Press.

Deaux, K. (1993). Reconstructing social identity. *Personality and Social Psychology Bulletin, 19,* 4–12.

De Boeck, P. (1986). *HICLAS Computer Program: Version 1.0.* Leuven, Belgium: Katholieke Universiteit Leuven, Psychology Dept.

De Boeck, P. (1989). *Brief users guide for the HICLAS program on PC version 1.1.* Unpublished manuscript, University of Leuven, Belgium.

De Boeck, P., & Rosenberg, S. (1988). Hierarchical classes: Model and data analysis. *Psychometrika, 53,* 361–381.

De Boeck, P., Rosenberg, S., & Van Mechelen, I. (1993). The hierarchical classes approach: A review. In I. Van Mechelen, J. Hampton, R. Michalski, & P. Theuns (Eds.), *Categories and concepts: Theoretical views and inductive data analysis* (pp. 265–286). London: Academic Press.

Fraiberg, S., Adelson, E., & Shapiro, V. (1975). Ghosts in the nursery: A psychoanalytic approach to the problems of impaired infant-mother relationships. *Journal of the American Academy of Child Psychiatry, 14,* 387–421.

Gara, M., & Rosenberg, S. (1979). The identification of persons as supersets and subsets in free-response personality descriptions. *Journal of Personality and Social Psychology, 37,* 2161–2170.

Gara, M. A., Rosenberg, S., & Herzog, E. P. (1996). The abused child as parent. *Child Abuse and Neglect, 20,* 797–807.

Gara, M. A., Rosenberg, S., & Woolfolk, R. L. (1993). The patient identity in major depression. *Depression, 1,* 257–262.

Gara, M. A., Woolfolk, R. L., Cohen, B. D., Goldston, R. B., Allen, L. A., & Novalany, J. (1993). The perception of self and other in major depression. *Journal of Abnormal Psychology, 102,* 93–100.

Gergen, K. J. (1971). *The concept of self.* New York: Holt.

Goldston, R. B., Gara, M., & Woolfolk, R. (1992). Emotion differentiation: A correlate of symptom severity in major depression. *Journal of Nervous and Mental Diseases, 180,* 712–718.

Goulding, R. A., & Schwartz, R. C. (1995). *The mosaic mind.* New York: Norton.

Greenwald, A. G. (1980). The totalitarian ego: Fabrication and revision of personal history. *American Psychologist, 35,* 603–618.

Herzog, E. P., Gara, M., & Rosenberg, S. (1992). The abused child as parent: Perception of self and other. *Infant Mental Health Journal, 13,* 83–98.

James, W. (1890). *Principles of psychology.* New York: Holt.

Kaufman, J., & Zigler, E. (1987). Do abused children become abusive parents? *American Journal of Orthopsychiatry, 57,* 186–192.

Kihlstrom, J. F., & Cantor, N. (1984). Mental representations of the self. In L. Berkowitz (Ed.), *Advances in experimental social psychology* (Vol. 17, pp. 1–47). New York: Academic Press.

Kim, M. P., & Rosenberg, S. (1980). Comparison of two structural models of implicit personality theory. *Journal of Personality and Social Psychology, 38*, 375–389.

Konecky, M. (1996). Autobiographical memory and clinical depression. Unpublished doctoral dissertation, Rutgers University.

Lyons-Ruth, K., Connell, D. B., Zoll, D., & Stoll, K. (1987). Infants at social risk: Relationships among infant maltreatment, maternal behavior, and infant attachment behavior. *Developmental Psychology, 23*, 223–232.

Mair, J. M. M. (1977). The community of self. In D. Bannister (Ed.), *New perspectives in personal construct theory* (pp. 125–149). London: Academic Press.

Maris, E., De Boeck, P., & Van Mechelen, I. (in press). Probability matrix decomposition models. *Psychometrika*.

Martindale, C. (1980). Subselves: The internal representation of situational and personal dispositions. In L. Wheeler (Ed.), *Review of personality and social psychology* (Vol. 1, pp. 193–218). Beverly Hills, CA: Sage.

McAdams, D. (1985). The "imago": A key narrative component of identity. In P. Shaver (Ed.), *Review of personality and social psychology* (Vol. 6, pp. 115–141). Newbury Park, CA: Sage.

McCall, G. J., & Simmons, J. L. (1966). *Identities and interactions*. New York: Free Press.

McCall, G. J., & Simmons, J. L. (1978). *Identities and interactions*. (Rev. ed.). New York: Free Press.

Neisser, U. (Ed.) (1993). *The perceived self: Ecological and interpersonal sources of self-knowledge*. New York: Cambridge University Press.

Neisser, U., & Fivush, R. (Eds.) (1994). *The remembering self: Construction and accuracy in the self-narrative*. New York: Cambridge University Press.

Ogilvie, D. M., & Ashmore, R. D. (1991). Self-with-other representation as a unit of analysis in self-concept research. In R. C. Curtis (Ed.), *The relational self: Theoretical convergences in psychoanalysis and social psychology* (pp. 282–314). New York: Guilford.

Olinger, L. J., Kuiper, N. A., & Shaw, B. F. (1987). Dysfunctional attitudes and stressful life events: An interactive model of depression. *Cognitive Therapy and Research, 11*, 25–40.

Reich, W. A. (1994). *Identities, social networks, and the development of commitment to a close relationship*. Unpublished doctoral dissertation, Rutgers University.

Robey, K. L., Cohen, B. D., & Gara, M. (1989). Self-structure in schizophrenia. *Journal of Abnormal Psychology, 98*, 436–442.

Rosenberg, S. (1977). New approaches to the analysis of personal constructs in person perception. *Nebraska Symposium on Motivation* (Vol. 24, pp. 174–242). Lincoln, NE: University of Nebraska Press.

Rosenberg, S. (1988). Self and others: Studies in social personality and autobiography. In L. Berkowitz (Ed.), *Advances in experimental social psychology* (Vol. 21, pp. 57–95). New York: Academic Press.

Rosenberg, S. (1989). A study of personality in literary autobiography: An analysis of Thomas Wolfe's "Look Homeward Angel." *Journal of Personality and Social Psychology, 56*, 416–430.

Rosenberg, S., & Gara, M. A. (1985). The multiplicity of personal identity. In

P. Shaver (Ed.), *Review of personality and social psychology* (Vol. 6, pp. 87–113). Newbury Park, CA: Sage.

Rosenberg, S., Nelson, C., & Vivekananthan, P. S. (1968). A multidimensional approach to the structure of personality impressions. *Journal of Personality and Social Psychology, 9*, 283–294.

Rosenberg, S., & Sedlak, A. (1972). Structural representations of perceived personality trait relationships. In A. K. Romney, R. N. Shepard, & S. B. Nerlove (Eds.), *Multidimensional scaling: Theory and applications in the behavioral sciences: Vol. 2 Applications* (pp. 134–162). New York: Seminar Press.

Rosenberg, S., Van Mechelen, I., & De Boeck, P. (1996). A hierarchical classes model: Theory and method with applications in psychology and psychopathology. In P. Arabie, L. Hubert, & G. De Soete (Eds.), *Clustering and classification* (pp. 123–155). Teaneck, NJ: World Scientific.

Ross, M., & Conway, M. (1986). Remembering one's own past: The construction of personal histories. In R. M. Sorrentino & E. T. Higgins (Eds.), *Handbook of motivation and cognition* (pp. 122–144). New York: Guilford Press.

Rowan, J. (1990). *Subpersonalities: The people inside us.* London: Routledge.

Rubin, D. C. (Ed.) (1986). *Autobiographical memory.* New York: Cambridge University Press.

Schwartz, R. C. (1987, March–April). Our multiple selves: Applying systems thinking to the inner family. *Networker*, 25–31, 80–83.

Spence, D. P. (1982). *Narrative truth and historical truth.* New York: Norton.

Srull, T. K., & Wyer, R. S. (Eds.) (1993). *The mental representation of trait and autobiographical knowledge about the self.* Hillsdale, NJ: Erlbaum.

Steele, B. F., & Pollock, D. (1968). A psychiatric study of parents who abuse infants and small children. In R. E. Helfer & C. H. Kempe (Eds.), *The battered child* (pp. 103–147). Chicago: University of Chicago Press.

Stryker, S., & Serpe, R. T. (1982). Commitment, identity salience, and role behavior: Theory and research example. In W. Ickes & E. Knowles (Eds.), *Personality, roles, and social behavior* (pp. 199–218). New York: Springer-Verlag.

Stryker, S., & Statham, A. (1985). Symbolic interactionism and role theory. In G. Lindzey & E. Aronson (Eds.), *Handbook of social psychology* (3rd ed., pp. 311–378). New York: Random House.

Van Mechelen, I., De Boeck, P., & Rosenberg, S. (1995). The conjunctive model of hierarchical classes. *Psychometrika, 60*, 505–521.

Weissman, A. N. (1979). The Dysfunctional Attitude Scale: A validation study. *Dissertation Abstracts International, 40*, 1389B–1390B. (University Microfilms No. 79-19, 533.)

The Case for Unity in the (Post)Modern Self

A Modest Proposal

In the opening scene of Austin Wright's (1994) novel *After Gregory*, Peter Gregory tries to kill himself by throwing his body into a freezing river on a raw November night. Peter is a high-school English teacher. He is married and has two children. But Peter's wife and children have recently left him. A sexual affair with one of his students is about to be exposed, and the girl's father has threatened to sue. And just last night Jock Hadley was killed with a hammer. Peter hated Jock, his cantankerous next-door neighbor. But did he hate him enough to kill him? Peter is confused. Perhaps he killed Jock in a drunken rage. Two years ago, so drunk he could hardly recall any of the details at the ensuing trial, Peter had driven has car the wrong way on a freeway exit ramp, past the red "Wrong Way" sign and into oncoming traffic, driving for many miles before disaster finally struck. He caused a chain-reaction collision that left a mother and her two daughters dead. Because it was his first offense, the judge suspended Peter's sentence. But the judge could do nothing to alleviate Peter's public shame and his private guilt. I haven't had a drink for two years, Peter reminds himself. Or has he? Maybe he *was* drinking last night, before Jock Hadley was hammered to death.

When Peter hits the water, he changes his mind. He finds himself swimming against the current with much greater power and effectiveness than he imagined he could summon. He sees the lights on the distant shore, and these tell him to fight, to live on. But to live on as a different person, for the old self—that is, "Peter Gregory"—seems to have died in the water. He scrambles ashore, shivering, exhausted, but now a new self. Later, he explains: "Peter Gregory wrote a suicide note and drowned himself in the river. I swam out on the other side" (pp. 41–42).

Wright's novel is a parable about the multiplicity of modern self-hood, and Peter Gregory is the first in a parade of selves to serve as protagonists in the story, each appearing in succession in the body originally inhabited by Peter. The former Peter Gregory hitchhikes to New York, changes his name a number of times, tries on a series of new roles, and makes new friends. Eventually, he meets the billionaire play-boy and philanthropist Jack Rome, who offers him thirty million dollars to finance a completely new life under the name of "Stephen Trace." In a phrase that might have come out of William James (1892), Rome provides Stephen with one of his patented "*Me* Grants"—a grant to make a new self from scratch. The only condition of the me grant is that Stephen cannot revisit the world of Peter Gregory in any way. He must sustain for the long run the clean break from Peter Gregory that he believes he has already made. If he can do this, he can construct vir-tually any kind of self or selves that thirty million dollars can buy. With some misgivings, the former-Peter-now-Stephen takes up the chal-lenge. He purchases a beautiful house on Long Island Sound. He culti-vates new interests, tastes, friendships, religion. Jack Rome even pro-vides him with a new wife.

A self-made man himself, Jack Rome is fascinated with the prospect of the making and the killing off of multiple selves. He wonders about the limits to the malleability of what James called the "social Me." Rome bets a colleague that Stephen will not be able to comply with the terms of the grant. Within two years he'll go back to being Peter Gregory, Rome wagers. His colleague bets that Stephen will make it. The self is infinitely flexible, he asserts, able to transform itself into almost any form that the situation demands. And thirty million dollars creates a rather propitious "situation."

Contemporary theorizing about the self suggests that much of the smart money is on the side of Rome's colleague. Perspectives from social psychology, personality and developmental psychology, soci-ology, contemporary psychoanalysis, and postmodern social theory tend to agree that the self is more multiple than unitary, and more so today than ever before. But Jack Rome suspects that multiplicity may have its limits. How many different selves can a person be? Is there a unity to selfhood that cuts across or undergirds (or even occasionally undermines) the apparent multiplicity of contemporary social life? There is indeed a great deal of truth in the notion that selves are multi-ple, fluid, ever changing, and constantly on the move, especially when those selves are constructed and negotiated in modern, or indeed "post-modern," societal contexts. But one should not dismiss the possibility that selves nonetheless retain a certain degree of unity and coherence. William James for one, proposed two distinct but fundamental senses of unity: one with respect to the self as "I" and a second, very different, one that pertains to the self as "me." The second sense is the unity that comes from the transformation of one's disparate and disorganized self-conception into a meaningful and vivifying life story.

Multiplicity in Selfhood Today

The Protean Self and the Postmodern World

Peter-now-Stephen may be seen as a dramatization of what Robert Jay Lifton (1993) has called the "protean self," which in the late twentieth-century West is an adaptive model for how to live amid relentless cultural and technological change and ideological ambiguity. Like the Greek god Proteus, one takes on whatever forms and qualities that a particular life situation demands. One juggles multiple roles, tries on different hats, different lives, forging selves whose unity is at best tentative and provisional, selves waiting to be dissolved into new combinations or even discarded for brand new editions when life changes and new challenges arise. The multiplicity of the protean self exists in both a temporal and a spatial sense. Over time, people change, new selves replace or improve upon the old. In a given time period, too, across social space and roles, a person assumes many different personas—"wife," "mother," "member of the church council," "tennis player," "party girl," "friend of Louise." As James foretold, there are perhaps as many potential social selves as there are significant social audiences. To think of the self as unitary in today's world, some would say, is to long for simpler times when people played fewer roles, cultural change was slow, and one grew up to be one particular thing, fitting a culturally sanctioned niche grounded in tradition.

Proteanism has moved to the center of the psychocultural stage in many modern societies over the last eighty years, argues Lifton, because of a confluence of disorienting factors such as world wars, campaigns of genocide, rapid technological and ideological change, the breakdown of moral authority, and the saturation of the mass media. Modern men and women feel few connections to the past and little faith in the future. The protean self represents, therefore, an adaptation to cultural trauma wherein modern people find it impossible to make meaningful and long-term commitments to each other, to their institutions, or to the more enduring aspects of selfhood that may reside beneath the surface of everyday role-playing (see also Lifton, 1979). Yet there is much to admire in this adaptation, Lifton (1993) suggests, for proteanism makes available "explorations and new combinations, for life-enhancing" responses (p. 24). Rather than lament the superficial multiplicity of the protean self, one may celebrate its adaptive and life-transforming power. As a metaphor for the latter, Lifton quotes Salman Rushdie in *The Satanic Verses*, describing the pieces of human lives that are left when an airplane blows up: "equally fragmented, equally absurd, there floated the debris of the soul, broken memories, sloughed-off selves, severed mother-tongues, violated privacies, untranslatable jokes, extinguished futures, lost loves, the forgotten meaning of hollow, booming words, *land, belonging, home*" (Rushdie, 1988, p. 4). But those very fragments, those sloughed-off selves eventually bring "newness into the world," new "fusions, translations, conjoinings" that have lives of their own (p. 8). One of the monumental literary works of our time, *The Satanic Verses* "celebrates hybridity, impurity, intermingling, the transformation that comes of new and unexpected combinations of human beings, cultures, ideas, politics, movies, songs. It rejoices in the mongrelisation and fears the absolutism of the Pure" (Weatherby, 1990, p. 233). Among other things, the "absolutism of the Pure" can refer to the traditional Western belief in the unity of selfhood. Like Peter-now-Stephen, the contemporary protean self is a hybrid or "mongrel," intermingling and interbreeding, transforming "itself" over time and across situations into new combinations that work in the here and now, in order to live on to meet the next here and now.

Rushdie's affirmation of mongrelization reflects a central theme in contemporary "postmodernist" approaches to conceptualizing the self. Gergen (1992), Sampson (1989a, 1989b), and other postmodern scholars view the self as an indeterminate "text" that is continually created and recreated through social discourse. Each moment of social discourse brings with it a new and particular expression of the self. Over time, expressions are collected and patched together, much like a montage or collage. Because all texts are indeterminate, no single life can really mean a single thing, no organizing pattern or identity can be validly discerned in any single human life. In *The Saturated Self*, Gergen (1992) makes this point forcefully:

> The postmodern condition more generally is marked by a plurality of voices vying for the right to reality—to be accepted as legitimate expressions of the true and the good. . . . Under postmodern conditions, persons exist in a state of continuous construction and reconstruction; it is a world where anything goes that can be negotiated. Each reality of self gives way to a reflexive questioning, irony, and ultimately the playful probing of yet another reality. The center fails to hold. (p. 71)

Gergen questions the ability of contemporary Westerners to find unity and purpose in the self amid the wild "multiphrenia" of the postmodern world. His account of "the plurality of voices" in post-modern life, furthermore, resonates with the writings of Watkins (1986) on the "internalized dialogues" that constitute contemporary selfhood and with the theory of the "dialogical self" proposed by Hermans and Kempen (1993; Hermans, Kempen, & van Loon, 1992). According to Hermans and Kempen, the dialogical self is a dynamic multiplicity of relatively autonomous "I-positions," each providing a unique voice and viewpoint. Different aspects of a person are personified as voices in dialogue, creating a multivocal self that takes the form of an internalized "polyphonic novel." In a related vein, object-relations theories in the psychoanalytic tradition tend to construe the self as an evolving conversation between personified internalizations (Fairbairn, 1952; Guntrip, 1971; Kohut, 1977). "Internalized objects" and "self-objects" are representations of significant people in one's world that interact with each other on a crowded intrapsychic stage. The stage *is* the self.

Multiple Personality

The most dramatic expressions of multiplicity in the self occur when the actors on stage and the voices in the polyphony come to take on "personalities" of their own. In multiple personality disorder (MPD), a person reports the experience of a number of distinct and autonomous executive selves who possess their own moods, memories, and behavioral repertoires. Hacking (1995) reports that a wave of multiplicity swept across France between the years 1874 and 1886, shortly after the first cases of MPD were reported in the psychiatric literature. But the disorder seemed to vanish shortly after World War I. He reports that fewer than a dozen cases of multiple personality may be found in the psychiatric literature during the 50 years before 1972. Since then, however, clinicians have reported thousands of cases, with some estimates suggesting that as many as 1 in 20 adults living in the United States today may suffer some type of "dissociative disorder," of which MPD is the most celebrated form. While clinical interest in multiple personality has mushroomed (Cardena, 1994; Klein & Doane, 1994), MPD patients have also organized their own self-help and advocacy groups, leading some observers to classify MPD as a "social movement" (Hacking, 1995; Kihlstrom, 1995). Once considered the rarest of clinical oddities, multiple personality disorder has re-emerged as an astonishing cultural phenomenon in North America during the past 25 years.

A controversial line of clinical thinking has it that MPD originates in childhood abuse, especially sexual abuse. Some theorists have argued that repeated childhood trauma may lead some children to defend themselves by splitting off these experiences into dissociated parts, forming the kernels of multiple, autonomous egos (Bliss, 1986). Many others, however, are highly skeptical of the evidence for a link between trauma and dissociation. They question the validity of the mainly retrospective data upon which trauma theorists rely; they point to the growing number of fantastical accounts of repressed memory, satanic cults, and other increasingly implausible scenarios that patients have summoned forth to explain dissociation; they further suggest that MPD probably has multiple causes and is associated with a host of other psychiatric illnesses as well (e.g., Tillman, Nash, & Lerner, 1994). Still others dismiss out of hand any psychiatric explanation for dissociation and MPD. Spanos (1994) argues that MPD, like other forms of multiplicity seen in other cultures, is socially constructed, manifesting itself as context-bound, goal-directed, social behavior geared to the expectations of significant others in the environment. Chief among those significant others are the many psychotherapists who buy into and encourage their clients to think in terms of the prevailing characterizations of MPD. Writes Spanos, "patients learn to construe themselves as possessing multiple selves, learn to present themselves in terms of this construal, and learn to recognize and elaborate on their personal biography so as to make it congruent with their understanding of what it means to be a multiple" (1994, p. 143).

However one characterizes multiple personality in contemporary American society, it is clear that a segment of the population today understands its own unhappiness and pathology in terms of the severe multiplicity manifest in dissociation. In the late 19th century, multiple personality provided a new way to be an unhappy person. After a long hibernation, this most florid example of multiplicity in the self seems to be back on the cultural stage today. As Hacking observes: "Even many supporters of the multiple personality diagnosis [as a medical category] are willing to agree that it has become, to use one popular phrasing, a culturally sanctioned way of expressing distress" (1995, p. 236).

The Many-Splendored Self

Multiplicity in selfhood need not be couched in the contexts of personal distress and cultural unrest. Indeed, the prevailing view in sociology and social psychology is that people's self-concepts are almost cheerfully multiple—the more selves the merrier. Beginning with Mead (1934) and Goffman (1959), symbolic-interactionist and dramaturgical perspectives on the self have emphasized the ways in which individuals adopt multiple roles and enact multiple performances in order to negotiate meanings, status, and position in everyday social life. Social identities are linked to the particular exigencies of external role and situational demands, and as those demands change the corresponding identities change as well. In that selves reflect the social world, therefore, as the world becomes more complex, unity and coherence in self-conceptions should become rarer and rarer. In a social world that demands flexibility in self-presentation and role-playing, the most adaptive form for selfhood may be a loose confederacy of multiple self-conceptions.

Representative of the prevailing emphasis on multiplicity, social-identity theory (Tajfel & Turner, 1979) conceives of the self-concept as a collection of self-images ranging on a continuum from the most personal ("I have three children") to the most social ("I am a member of the Catholic church"). Deaux (1992) defines identity as the personal meanings people ascribe to the multiple social categories to which they claim membership. Markus (1977; Markus & Kitayama, 1991) argues that knowledge about the self is represented in numerous self schemas, each of which encodes in memory personal attributes or social relationships within a particular life domain. Linville (1985) conceives of multiple self-aspects representing different contexts of experience (e.g., student, friend, at home, in small social gatherings). Associative network models for the self typically represent self-knowledge as a set of propositions linking a "self node" to specific self-relevant episodes or attributes (e.g., Bower & Gilligan, 1979; Kihlstrom & Cantor, 1984). Retrieval of self-knowledge occurs via spreading activation, as when the demand to judge oneself in terms of a specific attribute activates corresponding memories and characteristics associated with that self-relevant characteristic. Wyer and Srull (1989) propose a bin model in which multiple selves are represented as multiple self-bins, each with a header describing a specific domain or experience such as "self as father" or "self at parties." Much theorizing in sociology, furthermore, tends also to underscore multiple identities and multiple roles in contemporary social life (e.g., Burke, 1980; Stryker, 1980; Thoits, 1983).

Theorists have identified several basic dimensions upon which multiple selves may vary (Linville & Carlston, 1994). On the temporal dimension, theorists have proposed past, present, and future selves. With respect to the dimension of centrality, some self-conceptions reside closer to the "core" of one's individuality whereas others may be more peripheral. On the evaluative dimension, selves may be seen as positive or negative, desired or undesired. In his self-discrepancy theory, Higgins (1987) distinguishes among actual, ideal, and ought selves, each of which may be construed from the standpoint of the actor or the observer. Higgins's research suggests that discrepancies between ought and actual selves may result in anxiety whereas discrepancies between actual and ideal selves lead to depression. Working with the undesired self, Ogilvie (1987) finds that the psychological distance between one's actual and undesired self is a stronger predictor of well-being than is the distance between one's actual and ideal self. Markus and Nurius (1986) add possible selves to the mix. Finally, Ogilvie and Ashmore (1991) have conceptualized the multiplicity of self-understanding in terms of self-with-other representations. Employing a sophisticated idiographic procedure, Ogilvie and his colleagues are able to chart the complexity of an individual's self-structure in terms of multiple representations of how the person sees him- or herself when interacting with each of a large number of important people in his or her life.

People differ with respect to the multiplicity they express in their self-conceptions. Linville's (1985) self-complexity model assumes that there are individual differences in the number of domain-specific self-structures and in the degree to which these structures are interconnected. People high in self-complexity organize self-knowledge in terms of a greater number of self-aspects and maintain greater distinctions among self-aspects than those low in self-complexity. Being high in self-complexity helps insulate a person from emotional extremes. A threat to one's "self-as-father," therefore, may have little negative impact on one's "self-as-best-friend-to-Jim" if these two different self-aspects are separated from each other by a large number of other, clearly delineated self-aspects that act as buffers to the threat. Through multiplicity in self-understanding, therefore, a person can distribute his or her precious self-esteem eggs into many different self-baskets (or bins), spreading out the risk and minimizing the chances of a big break.

Mixed Messages about Multiplicity

Amid the many credible arguments made for multiplicity in the (post)modern self, one may still encounter ambivalence, uncertainty, and mixed messages. Two kinds of mixed messages are fairly common. One suggests that multiplicity is not very desirable, the other that multiplicity may not be as prevalent as one might initially suppose. Lifton (1993), for example, believes that a tenuous unity of the self *can* emerge in proteanism, as the individual struggles to maintain a "certain poise or balance" in order to "function in the world." "That poise is bound up with agility, with flexible adaptation, and is less a matter of steady and predictable direction than of maneuverability and talent for coping with widely divergent circumstances," he writes. To maintain the poise, it may be necessary to cultivate and sustain "strong tendencies toward mockery and humor for 'lubricating' experience, emotions, and communities that are 'free-floating' rather than clearly anchored, [a] preference for fragmentary ideas rather than large belief systems, and continuous improvisation in social and occupational arrangements and in expressions of conciliation and protest" (p. 93). Psychosocially speaking, this is not an easy kind of unity to achieve. Failure to maintain Lifton's desirable protean poise may result in "negative proteanism": "fluidity so lacking in moral content and sustainable inner form that it is likely to result in fragmentation (or near fragmentation) of the self, harm to others, or both" (Lifton, 1993, pp. 190–191).

Contemporary psychologists and other social scientists may like the word "multiplicity," but they generally do not find appealing the related notion of fragmentation. While Lifton worries about the dangers of fragmentation in negative proteanism, postmodern theorists express a great deal of ambivalence about multiplicity in selfhood, and they stimulate an even greater amount of ambivalence in their readers and critics (e.g., Smith, 1994). Gergen (1992) cannot decide if he should lament or celebrate the passing of both 19th-century romanticism and 20th-century modernism for the arrival of the contemporary postmodern condition. Indeed, uncertainty and ambivalence may be part and parcel of a postmodern sensibility. Thus, one can be postmodern and still long for the unity of self. The mixed messages of postmodern writings often pit unity versus fragmentation, commitment versus alienation, and meaning versus nihilism. In this regard, it is noteworthy when one scholar describes an intriguing brand of "plebeian postmodernism" in which men and women "still honor the quest for a unifying vision capable of allowing the individual to see it all and see it whole" (Inchausti, 1991, p. 129). Inchausti writes that "unlike many of their contemporaries, plebeian postmoderns do *not* celebrate the plurality of selves, or the indeterminate, modernist environment of endless change. They seek totality and organize the plurality of selves through a Self above the selves . . . expressible only through such complex forms as the novel, the drama, or religious ritual" (p. 129).

Multiplicity writ large, therefore, would appear to be undesirable, perhaps even from the standpoint of postmodernity. Reviewing a number of contemporary novels and biographies in the context of "postmodernist notions of personality," one reviewer for the *New York Times* recently wrote that the idea of multiple selves is "amusing enough in fiction, but it represents a false option in real life. To believe that one need never really commit to a set of values or beliefs is ultimately to deny accountability, just as to believe that one can continually assume new identities is to end up having no identity at all" (Kakutani, 1995, p. B4).

A second kind of mixed message suggests that there may be less there than initially meets the eye when it comes to multiplicity in the self. Mixed messages of this sort can even be found in the arena with arguably the most arresting data to display: multiple personality. Recently, the psychiatric community replaced the traditional label of MPD with the name "dissociative identity disorder" to dampen the idea that such a disorder involves the proliferation of autonomous, executive agents possessing complete alternative personalities. Hacking (1995) suggests that the name change is partly "an attempt to get away from solidified alters, agents who cope; it wants instead to emphasize disintegration, the loss of wholeness, the absence of the person, that some of these patients exhibit" (p. 266). MPD may ultimately involve, therefore, too little selfhood rather than too many selves.

A close look at the social-psychological literature on self-conceptions reveals countermessages suggesting that unity may still be found amid the multiplicity of the self. Rogers (1981) posits a unitary self-proto-type. Some hierarchical models argue for a superordinate self-structure that serves to coordinate or integrate the multiple lower-level components of the self (e.g., Rogers, Kuiper, & Kirker, 1977). Epstein (1973) argues that the self is structured as a single "theory." Furthermore, while social-psychological models typically underscore multiplicity in self structures, they tend toward a much less pluralistic conception of the self's motivational functions (Banaji & Prentice, 1994). Social psychologists have long highlighted two primary functions of the self-concept. Regardless of how many different self-schemata, self-aspects, self-exemplars, self-bins, or subselves comprise the loose confederacy of an individual's self, the various members of the confederacy all function in the common service of self-consistency (Lecky, 1945; Swann 1983) and self-enhancement (Taylor & Brown, 1988).

Finally, it is worth noting that even William James gave mixed messages on multiplicity. Social psychologists delight in quoting James's assertion that "a man has as many social selves as there are distinct groups of persons about whose opinions he cares" (1892, p. 169). But in that same chapter on self, James made an eloquent statement on potential unity under the heading of "Rivalry and Conflict of the Different Me's." He wrote:

> I am often confronted by the necessity of standing by one of my empirical selves and relinquishing the rest. Not that I would not, if I could, be both handsome and fat and well-dressed, and a great athlete, and make a million a year, be a wit, a *bon vivant*, and a lady-killer, as well as a philosopher; a philanthropist, statesman, warrior, African explorer, as well as a "tone poet" and saint. But the thing is simply impossible. The millionaire's work would run counter to the saint's; the *bon vivant* and the philanthropist would trip each other up; the philosopher and the lady-killer could not well keep house in the same tenement of clay. Such different characters may conceivably at the outset of life be alike *possible* to a man. But to make any one of them actual, the rest must more or less be suppressed. So the seeker of his truest, strongest, deepest self must review the list carefully, and pick out the one on which to stake his salvation. All other selves thereupon become unreal, but the fortunes of his self are real. Its failures are real failures, its triumphs real triumphs, carrying shame and gladness with them. This is as strong an example as there is of that selective industry of the mind on which I insisted some pages back. Our thought, incessantly deciding, among many things of a kind, which ones for it shall be realities, here chooses one of many possible selves or characters, and forthwith reckons it no shame to fail in any of those not adopted expressly as its own. (James, 1892, p. 174)

What James called "that selective industry of the mind" works to constellate the entire confederacy of selves around a unifying "character." A unifying "I" may at times seek to fashion a unified and purposeful "me."

The Unity of the I: Selfing

Following James's (1892) distinction between the subjective and objective aspects of selfhood, there are two senses in which unity may be conferred upon the self, even amid the multiplicity of (post)modern social life. With respect to the I, the self functions as a unifying process through which subjective experience is synthesized and appropriated as one's own. On the side of the me, the process of appropriating experience as one's own results in a reflexive conception of self (the me that the I constructs), and such a reflexive product may itself express unity and purpose. Identity in the me is the extent to which the me can be arranged (by the I) as a unifying and purpose-giving story. For contemporary adults, therefore, the synthesizing I-process creates unity in the me by fashioning a self-defining product that ideally assumes the form of an integrative life narrative.

The first step to discerning unity in the self is to understand that James's "I" should refer not to a noun but to a verb. The I is not a thing. Nor is it a part, a piece, a component, or even a facet of the self. The I is rather the process of being a self—a process we give the label *selfing* (McAdams, 1995, 1996). To self—or to maintain the "stance" of an I in the world (Blasi, 1988)—is to apprehend and appropriate experience as a subject, to grasp phenomenal experience as one's own, as belonging "to me." To self, furthermore, is to locate the source of subjective experience as oneself. Thus, selfing is responsible for human feelings of agency, the sense that one is potentially a causal agent in the world (Blasi, 1988). From the standpoint of the agential I, I "know" in a fundamental sense that when I voluntarily raise my hand it is I who am raising it; I control that action of raising my hand. To feel that one's hand is being raised by some other agent—say, by God or by an internalized interloper who has "taken me over," or even by a reflex action— is to experience a breakdown in the fundamental and usually taken for granted experience of agential selfhood. Selfing is responsible for the sense of otherness as well (Blasi, 1988; Hart, 1988): I am I; you are you. Rarely do people mix this up. As James (1892, pp. 188–189) observed, rarely does Peter go to bed and wake up the next morning thinking he is Paul. Whether or not Peter knows precisely who he is and where is life may be heading, he virtually never forgets *that* he is, that his experience is his and not Paul's. To do so would be to suffer a selfing problem of rather dynamic proportions.

Selfing is inherently a unifying, integrative, synthesizing process about which psychologists of widely different pedigrees have written with great conviction. Within the psychoanalytic tradition, selfing has typically been regarded as the essence of the *ego*. Freud's (1923/1961) word for the ego—*das Ich*—translates as "the I." Within Freud's id-dominated psychology, the ego negotiates compromises among the conflicting forces of instinct, superego, society, and reality. The ego psychologists, however, expanded the powers of the I, arguing that the ego promotes healthy adaptation to life through the functions of learning, memory, perception, and synthesis (Hartmann, 1939; Kris, 1952). More than Freud's beleaguered defender against anxiety, the ego is a master integrator. It organizes experience so that the organism can become an effective and competent member of society (White, 1959). Still, the ego psychologists' conceptions tended, like Freud's, to reify the ego, as if it were a thing that interacted with other things, such as the id and the outside world.

In her theory of ego development, Loevinger (1976) was one of the first to make the critical move from thing to process when she wrote that "the synthetic function is not just another thing that the ego does, *it is what the ego is*" (p. 5). For Loevinger, the I is a synthesizing process, a putting together of experience from the standpoint of a subject. Ryan (1995) shows how a number of different theories in developmental and personality psychology have traditionally invoked a general organismic function or process for integrating subjective experience, as captured in such terms as the orthogenetic principle (Werner, 1948), organization (Piaget, 1971), individuation (Jung, 1961), and actualizing tendencies (Goldstein, 1939; Maslow, 1968). While these various concepts differ from each other in important ways, they converge on the idea that human experience tends toward a fundamental sense of unity in that human beings apprehend experience through an integrative selfing process. The I puts experience together—synthesizes it, unifies it—to make it "mine." The fact that it *is* mine—that when I see the sunset, *I* am seeing it; that when you hurt my feelings, those were *my* feelings, not yours, that were hurt—provides a unity to selfhood without which human life in society as we know it would simply not exist.

It is because selfing is such a fundamental psychological process, therefore, that we find the phenomenon of multiple personality disorder so bizarre. For it is precisely the selfing process itself that seems to have gone so strangely awry when a woman claims that what would appear to be *her* subjective experience is not experienced as hers at all but belongs to another with whom she shares the same body. In MPD, selfing breaks down as experience comes to be dispersed across different subjective selves, each of which appropriates that experience as his or her own. Indeed, it would appear that MPD fundamentally involves the operation of two or more autonomous selfing processes within the same person. Woody and Bowers (1994) describe MPD as the development of "two [or more] alternative, coexisting executive control systems, each with its own memory-management processes and access to unique records" (p. 75). Other forms of selfing breakdown are seen in schizophrenia and other extreme conditions under which an individual feels that there is no self there, or that the self that is there is not theirs or that the self is empty or dead or inhabited by aliens. While these are extraordinarily debilitating conditions, they are still relatively rare; most people can only imagine these kinds of aberrations in selfing by relating them to dreams, trances, hallucinations, drug-induced states of consciousness, and so on—all of which act as temporary breakdowns of the normative selfing mode for most people in virtually all cultures.

Research in developmental psychology suggests that selfing emerges in the first year and a half of human life. Reviewing decades of infancy research, Kagan (1989) writes of the development of "the I-feeling" as "the universal emergence in the second year of an awareness that one can have an effect upon people and objects, together with a consciousness of one's feelings and competence" (p. 243). Research examining how infants relate to images of themselves in mirrors and other reflecting devices charts a series of stages that they move through on their way to the consolidation of a sense of I (Lewis & Brooks-Gunn, 1979). Concluding that such a consolidation typically occurs between 15 and 18 months of age, Harter (1983) writes:

> The infant's first task is the development of a sense of self as subject. Thus, the infant must come to appreciate that he or she exists as an active causal agent, a source and controller of actions, separate from other persons and objects in the world. Once this "existential" self . . . has been differentiated from others, the infant must learn to recognize those particular features, characteristics, and categories that define the self as object. A representation of the self that the infant can identify must be developed. (p. 279)

In other words, the existential process of selfing emerges as the infant comes to experience the world as a subject. Once consolidated, selfing (the I) works to construct a "representation of the self," which is the me.

The development of selfing in infancy and early childhood is probably strengthened and sustained through the child's place in a warm and attentive interpersonal milieu (Ainsworth & Bowlby, 1991). As attachment may develop in a wide variety of ways, ranging from the most secure to the most anxious interpersonal bonds, so too may the vicissitudes of selfing vary dramatically from one person to the next, although virtually all children in all cultures become attached in some way. Similarly, it would appear that amid the variety in selfing styles and orientations that can develop, selfing, nonetheless, "happens" for most, but not all, people in the first two years of life. Sacks (1995) describes in moving detail how for some autistic children and idiot savants the "I-feeling" never seems to emerge. Sacks tells the story of Stephen Wiltshire, an autistic prodigy who, despite his extraordinary artistic talents, never achieved I-ness: "I had the feeling that the whole visible world flowed through Stephen like a river, without making sense, without being appropriated, without becoming part of him in the least. That though he might, in a sense, retain everything he saw, it was retained as something external, unintegrated, never built on, connected, revised, never influencing or influenced by anything else" (1995, p. 56). Sacks asks himself, Can a person be an artist without having a self? Perhaps. But one cannot live normally, humanly in the world without the I-feeling, bereft of the integrative power of selfing. Sacks writes:

> A mind is not just a collection of talents [or modules]. . . . Completely modular view of the mind removes the personal center, the self, the "I." Normally there is a cohering and unifying power (Coleridge calls it an "esemplastic" power) that integrates all the separate faculties of mind, and integrates them, too, with our experiences and emotions, so that they take on a uniquely personal cast. It is this global, or integrating, power that allows us to generalize and to reflect, to develop subjectivity and a self-conscious self. (1995, p. 60)

Like MPD, autism provides a window into what can go terribly wrong in selfing. In the example Sacks describes, Wiltshire never comes to appropriate personal experience from the standpoint of a subject. He never comes to own his own experience. It is as if he does not realize that his own mind is his. One line of recent theorizing suggests that autistic children never develop a "theory of mind" (Baron-Cohen, Tager-Flusberg, & Cohen, 1993). Normal children are able to attribute mental states such as beliefs, desires, and intentions to themselves and to other people, as a way of predicting and making sense of human behavior (Meltzoff, 1995; Wellman, 1993). They develop a mentalistic folk psychology which assumes that people have (their own) minds and that minds guide (their own) behavior. The primitive theory of mind that underlies childhood (and eventually adult) experience would appear to be premised on the assumption of selfing. A person can operate from the standpoint of a subject because he or she apprehends that he or she is a mindful agent who desires, feels, thinks, and acts. One appropriates experience as one's own by virtue or experiencing oneself as "having a mind." Not only does the autistic child find it difficult to apprehend his or her own experience as his or her own, but he or she also finds it difficult to apprehend the experience of others as *theirs*. In severe autism, there are no minds, inside or outside. Without an I, there are no other I's.

The Unity of the Me: Identity as a Life Story

A second sense in which the contemporary self may exhibit unity is in the striving to construct a me—a self-conception—that is itself expressive of life unity and purpose. If the I is the process of selfing, then the me is the product of that selfing process; the me is the evolving result of the I's self-appropriating power. There is no psychological law that says that the me must be a unified or unifying thing, and in that it contains all that the I considers to be "mine," the me is a motley collection of self-attributions, as James (1892) foretold. For example, my self-conception includes my understanding of myself as a professor, as a person who tends toward introversion but enjoys public performance, as somebody who hit one home run in an otherwise undistinguished Little League career, as someone married to Rebecca Pallmeyer, as the father of two children, as a lover of Mexican food, as one who drives a Toyota Camry, one who thinks a lot about the I and the me (to the amusement of my relatives), who wants his daughter to play the oboe, who never went fishing with his father, and who hates to cook but does it anyway because it is in keeping with the socially constructed role of the progressive husband living in a dual professional family in America in the 1990s. There is nothing necessarily unified about this short list.

For many adults in contemporary modern societies, unity in the me is rather a cultural expectation that arises when one seeks to move from a self-list like mine to a more patterned and purposeful integration of the me. In modern societies, there is no need to make such a move before late adolescence or young adulthood, and according to cognitive developmental theory and research, one cannot, in fact, make this move very well before then (Breger, 1974; Elkind, 1981). For the most part, whether or not the me is patterned in a unified and unifying way is not a problem for children. If I ask my eight-year-old daughter, "Who are you, Amanda?" she will say: "I'm Amanda, silly. I live in a white house. I am a good ice skater. I am best friends with Julie. My sister, Ruth, gets me mad when she tries to be so bossy. My favorite TV show is *Full House*." "But I know all that," I tell her. "I want to know how the different items on the list relate to each other. I want to know who you are beyond the list. I want to know who you are beneath the surface. I want to know who you think you really are. I want to know how you understand *your life*." She rolls her eyes, or maybe yells for her mother. These kinds of concerns mean little to Amanda because she is not prepared to construe the me as something that conveys life unity and purpose. But in late adolescence and young adulthood identity arises as a desired quality of selfhood in a society that expects individual lives to express an individuated patterning suggestive of life unity and purpose (Erikson, 1963).

Identity and Modernity

Identity is the problem of unity and purpose in human life (McAdams, 1985). To suggest, then, that the self lacks unity in contemporary social life is to suggest that the self-conceptions that contemporary men and women fashion for themselves are too diffuse, incoherent, or multi-faceted to qualify as selves that "have identity" (e.g., Gergen, 1992). When I wonder what gives my collection of self-attributions a sense of unity and purpose, I am wondering about my identity. To say that a person "lacks" identity, then, is not to suggest that (1) the person has no I (as in the case of severe autism), (2) the person has no me (as for a person who is unable to offer much self-description), or (3) the person has no self (which could refer to either I or me). Instead, it is to say that a person's selfing process is currently experiencing difficulty in integrating self-conceptions into a pattern that suggests life unity and purpose. Multiplicity, therefore, poses a direct challenge to identity, for the difficulty we experience in forging selves that are unified and purposeful typically goes up as we face a greater number and variety of life possibilities and greater uncertainty about what an integrated me should in fact look like.

Identity is a psychosocial issue of particular salience for modern Westerners. For the past 200 years or so (Baumeister 1986), Westerners have expressed repeated doubts about the extent to which they experience themselves as (1) essentially the same person from one situation to the next and over time and (2) a unique and integrated person who is consistently different from, as well as related to, other unique persons in the environment. Beginning with the elites and spreading to the expanding professional and working classes, modernity ushered in a new quality of consciousness about the me, prescribing that selves should exhibit identity. Whether one views the current cultural scene in Western democracies as a new period of postmodernity (Gergen, 1992) or as the culmination of modernity's central themes within a period of high modernity (Giddens, 1991; Smith, 1994), many social observers suggest that the problem of unity and purpose in the me is as great today as it has ever been. Thus, Langbaum (1982) writes that identity is "the spiritual problem of our time" (p. 352).

What is it about the modern self that renders identity such a problem? There are at least five characteristics of selfhood in many modern societies that may be invoked to address this question (McAdams, 1996):

1. *In modernity, the self is viewed as a reflexive project that the individual "works on."* In the modern view, selves are not given or conferred, but rather they are made. One's very identity becomes a product or project that is fashioned and sculpted, not unlike a work of art or technological artifact (Giddens, 1991). Like the artist or the technician, modern men and women are ultimately responsible for the selves they make. In James's terms, the I reflexively creates a modern me for which the I assumes authorship and responsibility.

2. *The individual works on the self in everyday life.* Taylor (1989) sees

"the affirmation of ordinary life" as a hallmark of the modern self (p. x). One need not be a king or philosopher to possess a unique self, to be involved in a self-defining project of significant proportions. One need not have a special relationship with God or some other external authority who legitimates the self. Instead, beginning in the 19th century, legitimacy could reside in common bourgeois life, with its emphasis on moral rectitude and good works (Gay, 1984), much as modern men and women find legitimacy in the everyday social life of work and family, the main domains wherein the me is made and remade.

3. *The modern self is multilayered, possessing inner depth.* Even before Freud proclaimed the power of the unconscious, 19th-century men and women were keenly aware of the distinction between the public and the private selves and of the possibility of profound depth and layering within (Baumeister, 1986; Ellenberger, 1970; Gay, 1984, 1986). Thus, the reflexive project of the self involves a concerted examination of the modern person's rich inner life, where, it is assumed, some form of truth or meaning may be discerned (Taylor, 1989). Given the modern skepticism about external moral authority, the me becomes, for many, an inner moral source. It becomes especially important in modernity, therefore, to be "true to one's self."

4. *The self develops over time.* Modern men and women routinely adopt a developmental rhetoric in making sense of their own lives (e.g., Bellah, Madsen, Sullivan, Swidler, & Tipton, 1985; Linde, 1990). Improvements in nutrition and stupendous advances in medical science have dramatically increased life expectancy among modern adults, resulting in "the regularization of biography" (Hagestad, 1988) as modern men and women now fully expect to live well into their seventies and beyond. Anticipating that they will experience the full normative life course, modern adults think of themselves as growing, changing, moving through passages and stages as the self forms a trajectory of development from the remembered past to the anticipated future (Langbaum, 1982). Such developmental thinking provides a comfortable conceptual environment for modernist notions of progress and self-improvement, as captured in such well-worn humanist ideas as self-actualization, self-fulfillment, and self-transcendence (Jung, 1961; Maslow, 1968; Rogers, 1951). According to this pervasive view, life is like a journey with attendant opportunities and risks; one must make the most of the opportunities as they arise and minimize risks, though risks must sometimes be taken to entertain opportunities for growth and positive change (Giddens, 1991).

5. *The developing self seeks a temporal coherence.* If the me keeps changing over the long journey of life, then it may be incumbent upon the I to find or construct some form of life coherence and continuity in order for change to make sense. How are temporal lives made sensible in the modern world? It is no coincidence that the rise of the novel as a

Western art form and the growing popularity of keeping journals, diaries, and other autobiographical devices neatly parallel the rise of modernity in the West (Giddens, 1991; Rose, 1984), for making sense of the modern self as it changes over time centrally involves the construction of self-narratives. Narratives, or stories, have the capacity to integrate the individual's reconstructed past, perceived present, and anticipated future, rendering a life in time sensible in terms of beginnings, middles, and endings (McAdams, 1985; Polkinghorne, 1988). Therefore, "a person's identity is not to be found in behavior, nor—important though this is—in the reactions of others, but in the capacity *to keep a particular narrative going*" (Giddens, 1991, p. 54).

Life Narrative

The challenge of identity demands that the modern adult construct a narrative of the self that synthesizes the synchronic and diachronic elements of the me to suggest that (1) despite its many facets the me is coherent and unified and (2) despite the many changes that attend the passage of time, the me of the past led up to or set the stage for the me of the present, which in turn will lead up to or set the stage for the me of the future. What form does such a construction take? A growing number of theorists have argued recently that the predominant way in which human lives are given unity and purpose is indeed through narrative (Bruner, 1990; Charme, 1984; Cohler, 1982; Cohler & Cole, 1994; Hermans & Kempen, 1993; Howard, 1991; Kerby, 1991; Kotre, 1984; Linde, 1990; MacIntyre, 1981; McAdams, 1984, 1985, 1990, 1993; Polkinghorne, 1988; Singer, 1995; Singer & Salovey, 1993).

While the multiplicity of (post)modern life renders it unlikely, and perhaps undesirable, that a person's me can be packaged neatly into a simple narrative form, adults still seek to bestow upon the me a modicum of unity and purpose (i.e., identity) by constructing more or less coherent, followable, and vivifying stories that integrate the person into society in a productive and generative way and provide a purposeful self-history. Identity is the story that the modern I constructs and tells about the me. To the extent the modern I can indeed relate the me as a meaningful story, the I succeeds in meeting the modernist challenge to construe the self as a dynamic, multileveled project that is integrated in time and across social space. Success in this regard is, of course, never total. But nor is failure the inevitable fate, even amid the ambiguities and pluralities of (post)modern life. By binding together different elements of the me into a broader narrative frame, the selfing process can make a patterned identity out of a scattered and pluralistic me.

A life story is a psychosocial construction (McAdams, 1995, 1996). While the story that comprises a person's identity is constructed by that person, the story has its constitutive meanings within culture. Indeed, one can speak of a sense in which the life story is jointly authored by the person and his or her defining culture or cultures. Different stories make sense in different cultures. Within modernity, furthermore, different groups are given different narrative opportunities and face different narrative constraints. Especially relevant in this regard are gender, race, and class divisions. Heilbrun (1988) remarks that many women "have been deprived of the narratives, or the texts, plots, or examples, by which they might assume power over—take control of—their own lives" (p. 17). The empowerment of women's narratives is a major theme in some feminist social-science writings (e.g., Franz & Stewart, 1994; Riessman, 1992). The historical and contemporary life experiences of many African-Americans do not coalesce nicely into the life-narrative forms most valued by the white majority (Boyd-Franklin, 1989). Life stories, therefore, echo gender and class constructions in society and reflect, in one way or another, prevailing patterns of hegemony in the economic, political, and cultural contexts in which human lives are embedded (Franz & Stewart, 1994; Rosenwald & Ochberg, 1992).

People offer different stories about themselves in different contexts. The demanding characteristics of everyday life require that men and women operate in strategic ways to manage the impressions of others, seeking status and acceptance in their self-defining groups (Goffman, 1959; Hogan, 1987). That storied accounts of the self are always embedded in the discourse of everyday life, however, does *not* mean that (1) the me is hopelessly ephemeral and indeterminate because it transforms itself with every move in discourse, as some postmodernists seem to suggest (Sampson, 1989b), or (2) the me is forever stable and well-defined as the "real," inner, essential me that lives behind the public presentation of self (Jung, 1961). In that the me is a psychosocial construction of selfing, it obviously does not have the kind of material reality that, say, a chair or a garden has. New Age psychology to the contrary, there is no single essential, and deeply ingrained "real me." Yet the modern me has enough solidity as a construction that it does not typically change dramatically from day to day. Still, it is supple enough to undergo remarkable transformation over more extended periods of time. The modern me includes both those private narrative musings about "who I really am" and those public narrative maneuverings that are strongly driven by role and situational demands. In principle, neither the private musing nor the public maneuvering is any more "real" or "authentic" than the other.

Like any story, identity has certain recognizable features of structure and content, such as a setting, characters who strive for goals, conflict between characters, significant scenes, and endings that (sometimes) resolve the plot (Bruner, 1986; Mandler, 1984). Furthermore, identity comes out of a set of literary traditions. In the modern West, life stories are typically expected to have beginnings in the family, to involve growth and expansion in the early years, to locate later problems in early dynamics, to incorporate "turning point" moments or epiphanies that leave their mark on subsequent events, and to couch narrative movement in terms of progress or decline (Denzin, 1989; Gergen & Gergen, 1986). Over the past 12 years, my students and I have examined the structure, content, and function of life stories and their relations to other aspects of adult personality (e.g., Mansfield & McAdams, 1996; McAdams, 1982, 1984, 1985, 1993, 1994; McAdams, Booth, & Selvik, 1981; McAdams, de St. Aubin, & Logan, 1993; McAdams, Diamond, de St. Aubin, & Mansfield, in press; McAdams, Hoffman, Mansfield, & Day, 1996; McAdams, Ruetzel, & Foley, 1986). Analyzing over 250 full-length accounts from life-story interviews as well as hundreds of shorter accounts of key episodes and turning points in people's lives, we have learned that life stories can be understood in terms of at least seven related features, each of which may exhibit how the I makes unity in the me through narrative.

1. *Narrative Tone.* Life stories typically manifest an overall emotional tone or attitude, ranging simply from hopeless pessimism to boundless optimism. In Western literary traditions, affectively positive stories often take the forms of comedy and romance whereas negatively toned narratives may assume the forms of tragedy and irony (Frye, 1957). Any given life story may draw upon comedic, romantic, tragic, and ironic forms to effect a range of tones that the I appropriates to the me.

The case of Jessica C. (McAdams, 1985, pp. 96–98) illustrates the integrative power of a romantic narrative tone. In romance, the hero or heroine moves ahead vigorously and optimistically from one adventure to the next, growing, expanding, and often emerging victorious in the end. The dominant emotion is excitement or interest, as the protagonist learns lessons about life, love, and power on the quest. In Jessica's life story, she is the ever-moving, ever-changing heroine in quest of the new, the beautiful, and the true. From an early age, she says, Jessica was preoccupied with "where I stand in the world." She tells a story wherein this preoccupation stems directly from her ethnic lineage, half German (her mother) and half Sicilian (her father). She has traveled around the world, and on each of her sojourns she has come to a new understanding of how her rational German side and her impetuous Sicilian side play off against each other, sometimes experiencing conflict and other times rapprochement. With each new lesson, she moves closer to self-fulfillment, to "finding the balance" and "knowing where I stand." "Life goes from achievement to achievement," Jessica asserts. She adds, "You can always do better tomorrow." This narrative realization gives her hope, keeps her moving, and provides a unifying frame for the me.

2. *Imagery.*   Life stories display a characteristic quality of imagery. The imagery of a story is determined by the word pictures, the sounds, even the smells and tastes the author creates, the metaphors, similes, and so on that provide the narrative with a distinctive feel. Selfing involves the choice of the right kind of imagery to convey the unique quality of the person's experience. Therefore, an individual's favorite metaphors and symbols are reflective of what his or her identity is all about (McAdams, 1993, 1994).

As discerned in her diaries and letters of late adolescence and young adulthood, the life story of Karen Horney, the prominent psychoanalytic theorist, displays a preoccupation with the imagery of "movement" and "light" (McAdams, 1994). In love for all of two days with Ernst Schorschi—a young man with "sunny sparkle" in his eyes— she finds herself "chasing after happiness in every form." Months later, as she comes to reflect on Ernst's rejections of her, she writes that her "blood flowed sluggishly after the great loss, but it is already beginning to pulse more rapidly." A heroine "lit the sacred flame of enthusiasm for me," Karen writes. She was "the lustrous star toward which my soul directed its way," the one name that above all else "shines brightly" above me, and so on. Horney's early writings are filled with metaphors of and references to movement as a symbol of youth and vigor and to light as a signal for truth, understanding, and clarity. Across the many different domains of an extraordinarily complex and multifaceted life, Horney employed these same images to express her narrative understanding of herself and her world. The images even appear prominently in her later theorizing as she delineates the three basic neurotic positions of moving toward, moving away, and moving against the world (Horney, 1945).

3. *Theme.*   Themes are goal-directed sequences that characters pursue in narrative. Themes convey human motivation: what characters want, what they strive to get and to avoid over time (McAdams, 1985). In Western literary traditions, characters often seek some variation on power or love or more generally what Bakan (1966) termed agency and communion. Agency refers to separation of the individual from and his or her mastery of the environment, subsuming such overlapping motifs as power, autonomy, achievement, control, and isolation. Agency denotes story material in which characters assert, expand, or protect themselves as autonomous and active "agents." Communion refers to union of the individual with the environment and the surrender of individuality to a larger whole, covering such motifs as intimacy, love, reconciliation, caring, and merger. Agency and communion have also been identified as fundamental axes for social interaction more generally, as represented in circumplex models of interpersonal behavior (Leary, 1957; Wiggins & Broughton, 1985). Life stories may be com-

pared and contrasted, therefore, by the degree to which thematic lines of agency and communion dominate the text.

4. *Ideological Setting.*   MacIntyre (1981) and Taylor (1989) argue that the creation of identity through narrative typically involves the establishment of some sort of moral stance—an implicit perspective on the good—from which the individual can judge the quality of his or her own life and the lives of others. In line with this idea, most modern life stories may be viewed as suggesting an ideological setting or a particular backdrop of fundamental beliefs and values. The ideological setting, then, refers to the person's religious, political, and ethical beliefs and values as they are instantiated in the story, including the individual's accounts of how those values and beliefs came to be.

Research suggests that individuals whose selfing processes operate at a highly complex and differentiated level (individuals high in ego development) tend to construct highly personalized ideological settings that are viewed as evolving significantly over time (McAdams, 1985; McAdams, Booth, & Selvik, 1981). By contrast, individuals with less complex selfing strategies (low ego development) tend to create stories of ideological stability that follow conventional, authority-driven scripts. In these cases, deviations from the straight and narrow may be described as shameful missteps or mistakes. Their counterparts, by contrast, tell stories in which the protagonist searches for and struggles with what is right and true, even when this means violating the norms the protagonist learned as a child. The ideological setting shifts and moves over the course of time, making for more turning points in the narrative, alternating moments of sudden confusion and sudden insight. In response to a question about religious doubts, one young woman tells a story to suggest that a unifying force in her life is the tension between doubt and faith:

> I think that most of [my] serious questioning evolved out of ethical problems—friends aborting fetuses, shady practices at my place of work, etc. Right and wrong were no longer clear—if they ever had been. These single issues were maybe resolved one by one, but greater ones arose. I guess one's appreciation (in the pure sense) of evil increases proportionate to age and experience. I stood at the ovens of Dachau and asked how my Sunday-school-class God could have let it happen. The questioning has not yet been resolved, but nor has it been abandoned. I rejoice in the opportunity to rail like Job against my God. (McAdams, 1985, p. 221)

5. *Nuclear Episodes.*   Particular scenes that stand out in the life story may be called "nuclear episodes." Of most importance are high points, low points, beginning points, ending points, and turning points in the story. These reconstructed scenes typically affirm self-perceived continuity or change in the me over time (McAdams, 1985). As an affirma-

tion of continuity, a person may give high priority to a particular event that encapsules in a narrative nutshell an essential and enduring "truth" about the me. Thus, the event may be symbolic proof that "I am what I am." As a declaration of change, a person may single out a particular event as an epiphany through which the me experienced rather sudden or decided transformation, as in a "loss of innocence," a "fall from grace," a "lucky break," and so on (Denzin, 1989; McAdams, 1985). Therefore, what may be most important in a nuclear episode is not so much what actually happened but what the memory of it symbolizes in the context of overall life narrative. Research suggests, furthermore, that the extent to which the content of nuclear episodes reflects the thematic lines of agency or communion correlates with personality variables such as the needs for power and achievement and the needs for intimacy and affiliation (McAdams, 1982; McAdams, Hoffman, Mansfield, & Day, 1996).

6. *Imagoes.* All stories contain human or humanlike characters (Bruner, 1986). In a life story, the main character is the person whose life the story is about. But the main character may appear in a multitude of guises, each personifying particular aspects of the me (McAdams, 1984). Therefore, an imago is an idealized personification of the self that functions as a main character in narrative. Imagoes are often one-dimensional stock characters who act and think in highly personalized ways. The concept of the imago bears some resemblance to the idea of possible selves (Markus & Nurius, 1986) or ideal and ought selves (Higgins, 1987), and it shares conceptual space with certain psychoanalytic ideas such as internalized objects (Fairbairn, 1952), ego states (Berne, 1964), dialogical voices (Watkins, 1986), and personifications (Sullivan, 1953). Within the life story, the I may personify aspects of the me to produce such imagoes as "the good boy (or girl) who never gets into trouble," "the sophisticated and intellectual professor," "the rough-around-the-edges working-class kid from the wrong side of the tracks," "the corporate executive living out the American dream," "the worldly traveler in search of all that is new and exotic," "the athlete," "the loyal friend," "the sage," "the teacher," "the soldier," "the clown," "the peacemaker," and many more. While certain archetypal characters from myth and folklore may provide models for imago construction (Feinstein & Krippner, 1988), the main characters in modern life stories seem to reflect more clearly contemporary culture, including the implicit character models a society lays out for the good and appropriate life (Bellah et al., 1985; MacIntyre, 1981).

A main character in the life story of Tom H. is "the good soldier" (McAdams, 1993, pp. 136–137). Growing up on the south side of Chicago, Tom recalls a number of significant events in his early years associated with war, death, and authority. His earliest memories concern the air-raid sirens and a childhood fear of "imminent invasion" resulting from the regular air-raid drills organized by Chicago neighborhoods. The unexpected deaths of his grandmother and his dog, the latter killed by a speeding automobile, were two early events associated with a feeling of rage toward those who were larger, stronger, and in authority. In 1943, Tom's family moved to a farm community outside Chicago. This resulted in considerable stress for Tom. The major conflict in his new community was between the "farm kids" and the displaced "city kids." He describes his role in the conflict as that of a diplomat: "I was like Henry Kissinger doing shuttle diplomacy," negotiating fragile peace treaties between warring factions. Tom found himself assuming a similar role in family arguments.

All of Tom's childhood heroes were soldiers. He is quick to link his own life history to violent world events such as the beginning of the Korean War, the construction of the Berlin Wall, and the assassination of President Kennedy. Tom contrasts his glory years at the military academy where he attended high school with his subsequent "first big failure" at Notre Dame University. There he repeatedly battled a host of authority figures, unwittingly cultivating what he now calls the role of "the rebel." Soon after dropping out of college, Tom enlisted in the air force and began another glorious chapter. His life story since then alternates between periods of glory, when he moves forcefully and successfully in the world as the noble warrior (in the guise of a good citizen, dedicated husband, or courageous politician), and times of depravity and shame, when he falls into heavy drinking and generally irresponsible behavior. This second way of being seems to be personified in an undesirable imago that encompasses the rebel of his college years and stands in sharp opposition to the soldier.

Tom provides his self-conceptions with narrative unity through a story of warfare. There is always some battle to be fought. The soldier is victorious when he is able to channel aggressive energy into the arts of preparing for war, negotiating treaties among warring factions, and making war so as to keep the peace. In Tom's story, the imago of the good soldier is the self-controlled vanguard of domestic tranquility who promotes peace and stability through strength. When he fails to live up to an implicit warrior code—a regimen of conformity, impulse control, and Spartan austerity—the story lapses into dereliction and defeat. For Tom, the soldier imago serves to embody his goals of attaining power over others and control over himself—that is, agency. Tom perceives himself as a dominant and aggressive individual, though he knows he can be very weak. His role models include strong and disciplined men such as Henry Kissinger and his early war heroes. In keeping with the soldier imago, Tom tends to be somewhat combative and wary when engaging in new relationships. He calls his friends and acquaintances "allies." Many others, especially people in authority, are adversaries Tom must fight. Relationships provide opportunities for heroic action.

They challenge Tom to remain strong and true, to fight the good fight and win the battle in the end. The imago of the good soldier signals his central conflict between self-discipline and losing control.

It is as much through the narrative delineation of imagoes as anything else that modern men and women manage multiplicity in the me. By construing the me in a number of different guises, each of which functions as a main character, the I can explore how multiple aspects of the me interact and play off of one another. The life story provides an integrative framework within which a number of different personifications—possible selves, ought selves, ideal selves, undesired selves, selves-with-particular-others—can find a common narrative home. Modern life does not demand that the story integrate *all* divergent aspects of the self, but it does compel many men and women to work out a self-defining life story that enables different imagoes to enact different roles and express different voices. As such, the construction of multiple imagoes within a unifying life story provides what Knowles and Sibicky (1990) call a "metaphoric resolution" to "William James's one-in-many-selves paradox" (p. 676).

7. Endings: The Generativity Script. Stories are expected to have endings as well as beginnings and middles. An increasingly pressing identity task for modern adults as they move through middle age is the fashioning of an anticipated ending for the life story that ties together the beginning and middle to affirm unity, purpose, and direction in life over time. Modern adults may seek in narrative an ending that enables them to attain a kind of symbolic immortality, generating a legacy of the me that will "live on" even after they are no longer living (Becker, 1973; Kotre, 1984; McAdams, 1985). That is, the ideal ending should produce new beginnings. As a result, adults are challenged to fashion a "generativity script" (McAdams, 1985; McAdams, Ruetzel, & Foley, 1986) that concerns how the adult generates, creates, nurtures, or develops a positive legacy of the self for subsequent generations. In this sense, the generativity script provides a narrative mechanism whereby the I can create a me that may "outlive the self" (Kotre, 1984). As midlife and older adults compose their lives around their emerging understanding of an expected legacy, they may discover a new narrative focus that brings greater unity to the me, placing their lives and their stories in a sequence of generations within which they occupy a particular, self-defining position.

My students and I recently completed an intensive study of a set of life stories whose unifying power seemed to be driven by generativity scripts (McAdams, Diamond, de St. Aubin, & Mansfield, in press). Comparing the life stories of 40 highly generative schoolteachers and community volunteers to the life stories constructed by a matched group of 30 less generative adults, we discovered a particular narrative form that tended to differentiate the two groups. Highly generative adults tended to construe identity in terms of a commitment story. Overall, in the prototypical commitment story the protagonist comes to believe early on (in childhood) that he or she has a special advantage or blessing that contrasts markedly to the pain and misfortune suffered by many others. Experiencing the world as a place where people need to care for others, the protagonist commits the self at an early age to living in accord with a set of clear and enduring values and personal beliefs that guide behavior throughout the life span. Moving ahead with the confidence of early blessing and steadfast belief, the protagonist encounters a series of personal misfortunes, disappointments, and tragedies in life, but these bad events often become transformed or "redeemed" into good outcomes, sometimes because of the protagonist's own efforts and sometimes by chance or external design. Thus, while many bad things happen, they often turn into good, whereas good things rarely turn bad. Looking to the future with an expanded radius of care, the protagonist sets goals that aim to benefit others, especially those of the next generation, and to contribute to the progressive development of society as a whole and of its more worthy institutions.

This kind of commitment story is not the only kind of life story that a highly generative person can tell about the self. And whether one aspires to make a significant contribution to the next generation or not, the I can find many different ways to confer upon the me at least a modicum of unity and purpose through story. Some stories work better than others, and within a cultural context some stories are probably better stories—more vivifying, health-inducing, socially exemplary, and so on (McAdams, 1996). Some stories unify better than others do, and some people in some contexts are better able to integrate self-conceptions around narrative than others are. Yet with due acknowledgment of all of these caveats and many more, I still conclude that it is primarily through the life story that contemporary adults in (post)modern societies create unity in the me.

Peter Gregory and Stephen Trace

After Peter Gregory jumped into the river, he became Stephen Trace. Stephen's me grant subsidizes the development of a brand-new self, and for many months he seems to live more or less happily on Long Island Sound. He thinks he may even be in love with his new wife. But his irrepressible memory of the Peter Gregory self keeps Stephen from making the clean break he had hoped to make, prevents him from becoming fully protean. Aspects of his former me keep insinuating themselves into his now-self and into his thinking about the future. When Jack Rome dies in a plane crash, Stephen's grant support is withdrawn. His new wife leaves to marry the colleague who had bet that Stephen would never go back to Peter Gregory. Stephen moves west, takes on the name of Mitchel Grape, starts up a relationship with Bonnie Brown, who is a social activist. He tells her about his previous selves. She does not believe him at first. But after a while she begins to encourage him to seek out unity with the past: "Time to think about your life, she said. You had a wife, you had children. They meant something to you. People can't live divided from themselves. You need to heal yourself. Close your wounds. Bring your divided selves together. A reunion" (Wright, 1994, p. 263).

Spoken like this, in formulas, Bonnie's advice sounds a bit naive, like a New Age self-help book. Nonetheless, Mitchell does go back to the town of Peter Gregory. There he finds few traces of his former self. What should he do?

He begins to write his story—the one story of his many selves. As he reconstructs the past in order to tell it in such a way as to provide the me with unity and purpose, he comes to believe that he never really intended to kill himself when he jumped into the river that night, and that he absolutely could not have killed Jock Hadley—both actions are too inconsistent with the newly storied past and future; they do not make narrative sense now. At first, he imagines that his reader for this story will be Peter Gregory's former wife and his children. He thinks that maybe he'll run a personal advertisement in a number of newspapers across the country. It might read: "Peter Gregory your once husband and father is alive and well and has *a story* for you. Please write or call" (p. 290). He never does that, though. Eventually, he finds that the writing of this life story is intrinsically rewarding. And he comes to wonder if indeed the most important reader of the book may ultimately be himself.

Acknowledgments: I would like to thank Lee Jussim, Richard Ashmore, Dan Ogilvie, and Dan Lewis for their helpful comments on earlier drafts of this manuscript. Preparation of the manuscript was aided by a grant from The Spencer Foundation.

References

Ainsworth, M. D. S. & Bowlby, J. (1991). An ethological approach to personality development. *American Psychologist, 46*, 333–341.

Bakan, D. (1966). *The duality of human existence: Isolation and communion in Western man*. Boston: Beacon.

Banaji, M. R., & Prentice, D. A. (1994). The self in social contexts. *Annual Review of Psychology, 45*, 297–332.

Baron-Cohen, S., Tager-Flusberg, H., & Cohen, D. J. (Eds.) (1993). *Understanding other minds: Perspectives from autism*. New York: Oxford University Press.

Baumeister, R. F. (1986). *Identity: Cultural change and the struggle for self.* New York: Oxford University Press.

Becker, E. (1973). *The denial of death.* New York: Free Press.

Bellah, R. N., Madsen, R., Sullivan, W. M., Swidler, A., & Tipton, S. M. (1985). *Habits of the heart: Individualism and commitment in American life.* Berkeley and Los Angeles: University of California Press.

Berne, E. (1964). *Games people play.* New York: Grove.

Blasi, A. (1988). Identity and the development of the self. In D. K. Lapsley and F. C. Power (Eds.), *Self, ego, and identity: Integrative approaches* (pp. 226–242). New York: Springer-Verlag.

Bliss, E. L. (1986). *Multiple personality, allied disorders, and hypnosis.* New York: Oxford University Press.

Bower, G. H., & Gilligan, S. G. (1979). Remembering information related to one's self. *Journal of Research in Personality, 13,* 420–461.

Boyd-Franklin, N. (1989). *Black families in therapy: A multisystems approach.* New York: Guilford Press.

Breger, L. (1974). *From instinct to identity: The development of personality.* Englewood Cliffs, NJ: Prentice-Hall.

Bruner, J. S. (1986). *Actual minds, possible worlds.* Cambridge, MA: Harvard University Press.

Bruner, J. S. (1990). *Acts of meaning.* Cambridge, MA: Harvard University Press.

Burke, P. J. (1980). The self: Measurement requirements from an interactionist perspective. *Psychology Quarterly, 43,* 18–29.

Cardena, E. (1994). The domain of dissociation. In S. J. Lynn and J. W. Rhue (Eds.), *Dissociation: Clinical and theoretical perspectives* (pp. 15–31). New York: Guilford Press.

Charme, S. T. (1984). *Meaning and myth in the study of lives: A Sartrean perspective.* Philadelphia: University of Pennsylvania Press.

Cohler, B. J. (1982). Personal narrative and the life course. In P. B. Baltes and O. G. Brim, Jr. (Eds.), *Life-span development and behavior* (Vol. 4, pp. 205–241). New York: Academic Press.

Cohler, B. J., & Cole, T. R. (1994). *Studying older lives: Reciprocal acts of telling and listening.* Paper presented at the conference for Society for Personology, Ann Arbor, MI.

Deaux, K. (1992). Personalizing identity and socializing self. In G. Breakwell (Ed.), *Social psychology of identity and the self-concept* (pp. 9–33). London: Academic Press.

Denzin, N. K. (1989). *Interpretive biography.* Newbury Park, CA: Sage.

Elkind, D. (1981). *Children and adolescents* (3rd Ed.). New York: Oxford University Press.

Ellenberger, H. (1970). *The discovery of the unconscious.* New York: Basic Books.

Epstein, S. (1973). The self-concept revisited: Or a theory of a theory. *American Psychologist, 28,* 404–416.

Erikson, E. H. (1963). *Childhood and society* (2nd Ed.). New York: Norton.

Fairbairn, W. R. D. (1952). *Psychoanalytic studies of the personality.* London: Routledge and Kegan Paul.

Feinstein, D., & Krippner, S. (1988). *Personal mythology: The psychology of your evolving self.* Los Angeles: Jeremy P. Tarcher.

Franz, C., & Stewart, A. J. (Eds.) (1994). *Women creating lives: Identities, resilience, and resistance.* Boulder, CO: Westview Press.

Freud, S. (1923/1961). *The ego and the id.* In J. Strachey (Eds.), *The standard edition of the complete psychological works of Sigmund Freud* (Vol. 18). London: Hogarth.

Frye, N. (1957). *Anatomy of criticism.* Princeton, NJ: Princeton University Press.

Gay, P. (1984). *The bourgeois experience: Victoria to Freud: Vol. 1. The education of the senses.* New York: Oxford University Press.

Gay, P. (1986). *The bourgeois experience: Victoria to Freud: Vol. 2. The tender passion.* New York: Oxford University Press.

Gergen, K. J. (1991). *The saturated self: Dilemmas of identity in modern life.* New York: Basic Books.

Gergen, K. J., & Gergen, M. M. (1986). Narrative form and the construction of psychological science. In T. R. Sarbin (Ed.), *Narrative psychology: The storied nature of human conduct* (pp. 22–44). New York: Praeger.

Giddens, A. (1991). *Modernity and self-identity.* Stanford, CA: Stanford University Press.

Goffman, E. (1959). *The presentation of self in everyday life.* Garden City, NY: Doubleday.

Goldstein, K. (1939). *The organism.* New York: American Books.

Guntrip, H. (1971). *Psychoanalytic theory, therapy, and the self.* New York: Basic Books.

Hacking, I. (1995). *Rewriting the soul: Multiple personality and the sciences of memory.* Princeton, NJ: Princeton University Press.

Hagestad, G. O. (1988). Demographic change and the life course: Some emerging trends in the family realm. *Family Relations, 37,* 405–410.

Hart, D. (1988). The adolescent self-concept in social context. In D. K. Lapsley and F. C. Powers (Eds.), *Self, ego, and identity: Integrative approaches* (pp. 71–90). New York: Springer-Verlag.

Harter, S. (1983). Developmental perspectives on the self-system. In P. H. Mussen (Series Ed.) & E. M. Hetherington (Vol. Ed.), *Handbook of child psychology: Vol. 4. Socialization, personality, and social development* (4th ed., pp. 275–385). New York: Wiley.

Hartmann, H. (1939). *Ego psychology and the problem of adaptation.* New York: International Universities Press.

Heilbrun, C. G. (1988). *Writing a woman's life.* New York: Norton.

Hermans, H. J. M., & Kempen, H. J. G. (1993). *The dialogical self.* New York: Academic Press.

Hermans, H. J. M., Kempen, H. J. G., & van Loon, R. J. P. (1992). The dialogical self: Beyond individualism and rationalism. *American Psychologist, 47,* 23–33.

Higgins, E. T. (1987). Self-discrepancy: A theory relating self and affect. *Psychological Review, 94,* 319–340.

Hogan, R. (1987). Personality psychology: Back to basics. In J. Aronoff, A. I. Rabin, and R. A. Zucker (Eds.), *The emergence of personality* (pp. 79–104). New York: Springer.

Horney, K. (1945). *Our inner conflicts.* New York: Norton.

Howard, G. S. (1991). Culture tales: A narrative approach to thinking, cross-cultural psychology, and psychotherapy. *American Psychologist, 46,* 187–197.

Inchausti, R. (1991). *The ignorant perfection of ordinary people.* Albany, NY: State University of New York Press.

James, W. (1892/1963). *Psychology.* Greenwich, CT: Fawcett.

Jung, C. G. (1961). *Memories, dreams, reflections.* New York: Vintage.

Kagan, J. (1989). *Unstable ideas: Temperament, cognition, and self.* Cambridge, MA: Harvard University Press.

Kakutani, M. (1995, March 20). An era when fluidity has replaced maturity. *New York Times,* pp. B1, B4.

Kerby, A. P. (1991). *Narrative and the self.* Bloomington, IN: Indiana University Press.

Kihlstrom, J. F. (1995). Dissociation: It's ba-ack! [Review of R. M. Klein and B. K. Doane (Eds.), *Psychological concepts and dissociative disorders* (Hillsdale, NJ: Erlbaum)] *Contemporary Psychology, 49,* 949–950.

Kihlstrom, J. F., & Cantor, N. (1984). Mental representations of the self. In L. Berkowitz (Ed.), *Advances in experimental social psychology* (Vol. 17, pp. 1–47). New York: Academic Press.

Klein, R. M., & Doane, B. K. (Eds.) (1994). *Psychological concepts and dissociative disorders.* Hillsdale, NJ: Erlbaum.

Knowles, E. S., & Sibicky, M. E. (1990). Continuity and diversity in the stream of selves: Metaphorical resolutions of William James's one-in-many-selves paradox. *Personality and Social Psychology Bulletin, 16,* 676–687.

Kohut, H. (1977). *The restoration of the self.* New York: International Universities Press.

Kotre, J. (1984). *Outliving the self: Generativity and the interpretation of lives.* Baltimore, MD: Johns Hopkins University Press.

Kris, E. (1952). *Psychoanalytic explorations in art.* New York: International Universities Press.

Langbaum, R. (1982). *The mysteries of identity: A theme in modern literature.* Chicago: University of Chicago Press.

Leary, T. (1957). *Interpersonal diagnosis of personality.* New York: Ronald.

Lecky, P. (1945). *Self-consistency: A theory of personality.* New York: Island.

Lewis, M., & Brooks-Gunn, J. (1979). *Social cognition and the acquisition of self.* New York: Plenum.

Lifton, R. J. (1979). *The broken connection.* New York: Simon and Schuster.

Lifton, R. J. (1993). *The protean self.* New York: Basic Books.

Linde, C. (1990). *Life stories: The creation of coherence.* Palo Alto, CA: Institute for Research on Learning.

Linville, P. W. (1985). Self-complexity and affective extremity: Don't put all your eggs in one cognitive basket. *Social Cognition, 3,* 94–120.

Linville, P. W., & Carlston, D. E. (1994). Social cognition of the self. In P. G. Devine, D. L. Hamilton, and T. M. Ostrom (Eds.), *Social cognition: Impact on social psychology* (pp. 143–193). San Diego: Academic Press.

Loevinger, J. (1976). *Ego development.* San Francisco: Jossey-Bass.

MacIntyre, A. (1981). *After virtue.* Notre Dame, IN: University of Notre Dame Press.

Mandler, J. M. (1984). *Stories, scripts, and scenes.* Hillsdale, NJ: Erlbaum.

Mansfield, E., & McAdams, D. P. (1996). Generativity and themes of agency and communion in adult autobiography. *Personality and Social Psychology Bulletin, 22,* 721–731.

Markus, H. R. (1977). Self-schemata and processing information about the self. *Journal of Personality and Social Psychology, 35,* 63–78.

Markus, H. R., & Kitayama, S. (1991). Culture and the self: Implications for cognition, emotion, and motivation. *Psychological Review, 98,* 224–253.

Markus, H. R., & Nurius, P. (1986). Possible selves. *American Psychologist, 41,* 954–969.

Maslow, A. (1968). *Toward a psychology of being.* New York: D. Van Nostrand.

McAdams, D. P. (1982). Experiences of intimacy and power: Relationships between social motives and autobiographical memory. *Journal of Personality and Social Psychology, 42,* 292–302.

McAdams, D. P. (1984). Love, power, and images of the self. In C. Z. Malatesta and C. E. Izard (Eds.), *Emotion in adult development* (pp. 159–174). Beverly Hills, CA: Sage.

McAdams, D. P. (1985). *Power, intimacy, and the life story: Personological inquiries into identity.* New York: Guilford Press.

McAdams, D. P. (1990). Unity and purpose in human lives: The emergence of identity as a life story. In A. I. Rabin, R. A. Zucker, R. A. Emmons, and S. Frank (Eds.), *Studying persons and lives* (pp. 148–200). New York: Springer.

McAdams, D. P. (1993). *The stories we live by: Personal myths and the making of the self.* New York: William Morrow.

McAdams, D. P. (1994). Image, theme, and character in the life story of Karen Horney. In C. Franz and A. J. Stewart (Eds.), *Women creating lives: Identities, resilience, and resistance* (pp. 157–171). Boulder, CO: Westview Press.

McAdams, D. P. (1995). What do we know when we know a person? *Journal of Personality, 63,* 363–396.

McAdams, D. P. (1996). Personality, modernity, and the storied self: A contemporary framework for studying persons. *Psychological Inquiry, 7,* 295–321.

McAdams, D. P., Booth, L., & Selvik, R. (1981). Religious identity among students at a private college: Social motives, ego stage, and development. *Merrill-Palmer Quarterly, 27,* 219–239.

McAdams, D. P., de St. Aubin, E., & Logan, R. L. (1993). Generativity among young, midlife, and older adults. *Psychology and Aging, 8,* 221–230.

McAdams, D. P., Diamond, A., de St. Aubin, E., & Mansfield, E. (in press). Stories of commitment: The psychosocial construction of generative lives. *Journal of Personality and Social Psychology.*

McAdams, D. P., Hoffman, B. J., Mansfield, E., & Day, R. (1996). Themes of agency and communion in significant autobiographical scenes. *Journal of Personality, 64,* 339–378.

McAdams, D. P., Ruetzel, K., & Foley, J. M. (1986). Complexity and generativity at midlife: Relations among social motives, ego development, and adults' plans for the future. *Journal of Personality and Social Psychology, 50,* 800–807.

Mead, G. H. (1934). *Mind, self, and society from the standpoint of a social behaviorist.* Chicago: University of Chicago Press.

Meltzoff, A. N. (1995). Understanding the intentions of others: Re-enactment of intended acts by 18-month-old children. *Developmental Psychology, 31,* 838–850.

Ogilvie, D. M. (1987). The undesired self: A neglected variable in personality research. *Journal of Personality and Social Psychology, 52,* 379–385.

Ogilvie, D. M., & Ashmore, R. D. (1991). Self-with-other representation as a unit of analysis in self-concept research. In R. C. Curtis (Ed.), *The rational self: Theoretical convergences in psychoanalysis and social psychology* (pp. 282–314). New York: Guilford.

Piaget, J. (1971). *Biology and knowledge.* Chicago: University of Chicago Press.

Polkinghorne, D. (1988). *Narrative knowing and the human sciences.* Albany, NY: State University of New York Press.

Riessman, C. K. (1992). Making sense of marital violence: One woman's narrative. In G. C. Rosenwald and R. L. Ochberg (Eds.), *Storied lives: The cultural politics of self-understanding* (pp. 231–249). New Haven, CT: Yale University Press.

Rogers, C. R. (1951). *Client-centered therapy.* Boston: Houghton Mifflin.

Rogers, T. B. (1981). A model of the self as an aspect of human information processing system. In N. Cantor and J. F. Kihlstrom (Eds.), *Personality, cognition, and social interaction* (pp. 193–214). Hillsdale, NJ: Erlbaum.

Rogers, T. B., Kuiper, N. A., & Kirker, W. S. (1977). Self-reference and the encoding of personal information. *Journal of Personality and Social Psychology, 35,* 677–688.

Rose, P. (1984). *Parallel lives: Five Victorian marriages.* New York: Knopf.

Rosenwald, G. C., & Ochberg, R. L. (Eds.) (1992). *Storied lives: The cultural politics of self-understanding.* New Haven, CT: Yale University Press.

Rushdie, S. (1988). *The satanic verses.* New York: Viking.

Ryan, R. M. (1995). Psychological needs and the facilitation of integrative processes. *Journal of Personality, 63,* 397–427.

Sacks, O. (1995, January 9). Prodigies. *The New Yorker,* pp. 44–65.

Sampson, E. E. (1989a). The challenge of social change for psychology: Globalization and psychology's theory of the person. *American Psychologist, 44,* 914–921.

Sampson, E. E. (1989b). The deconstruction of the self. In J. Shotter and K. J. Gergen (Eds.), *Texts of identity* (pp. 1–19). Newbury Park, CA: Sage.

Singer, J. A. (1995). Seeing one's self: Locating narrative memory in a framework of personality. *Journal of Personality, 63,* 429–457.

Singer, J. A., & Salovey, P. (1993). *The remembered self.* New York: Free Press.

Smith, M. B. (1994). Selfhood at risk: Postmodern perils and the perils of postmoderism. *American Psychologist, 49,* 405–411.

Spanos, N. P. (1994). Multiple identity enactments and multiple personality disorder: A socio-cognitive perspective. *Psychological Bulletin, 116,* 143–165.

Stryker, S. (1980). *Symbolic interactionism: A social structural version.* Menlo Park, CA: Benjamin/Cummings.

Sullivan, H. S. (1953). *The interpersonal theory of psychiatry.* New York: Norton.

Swann, W. J., Jr. (1983). Self-verification. Bringing social reality into harmony with the self. In J. Suls and A. G. Greenwald (Eds.), *Psychological perspectives on the self* (Vol. 2, pp. 33–66). Hillsdale, NJ: Erlbaum.

Tajfel, H., & Turner, J. C. (1979). An integrative theory of intergroup conflict. In W. J. Austin and S. Worchel (Eds.), *The social psychology of intergroup relations* (pp. 33–48). Monterey, CA: Brooks-Cole.

Taylor, C. (1989). *Sources of the self: The making of the modern identity*. Cambridge, MA: Harvard University Press.

Taylor, S. E., & Brown, J. D. (1988). Illusion and well-being: A social psychological perspective on mental health. *Psychological Bulletin, 103*, 193–210.

Thoits, P. A. (1983). Multiple identities and psychological well-being: A reformulation and test of the social isolation hypothesis. *American Sociological Review, 48*, 174–187.

Tillman, J. G., Nash, M. R., & Lerner, P. M. (1994). Does trauma cause dissociative pathology? In S. J. Lynn and J. W. Rhue (Eds.), *Dissociation: Clinical and theoretical perspectives* (pp. 395–414). New York: Guilford Press.

Watkins, M. (1986). *Invisible guests: The development of imaginal dialogues*. Hillsdale, NJ: Analytic Press.

Weatherby, W. J. (1990). *Salman Rushdie: Sentenced to death*. New York: Carroll and Graf.

Wellman, H. M. (1993). Early understanding of mind: The normal case. In S. Baron-Cohen, H. Tager-Flusberg, and D. J. Cohen (Eds.), *Understanding other minds: Perspectives from autism* (pp. 10–39). New York: Oxford University Press.

Werner, H. (1948). *Comparative psychology of mental development*. New York: International Universities Press.

White, R. W. (1959). Motivation reconsidered: The concept of competence. *Psychological Review, 66*, 297–333.

Wiggins, J. S., & Broughton, R. (1985). The interpersonal circle: A structural model for the integration of personality research. In R. Hogan and W. H. Jones (Eds.), *Perspectives in personality* (Vol. 1. pp. 1–47). Greenwich, CT: JAI Press.

Woody, E. Z., & Bowers, K. S. (1994). A frontal assault on dissociated control. In S. J. Lynn and J. W. Rhue (Eds.), *Dissociation: Clinical and theoretical perspectives* (pp. 52–79). New York: Guilford Press.

Wright, A. (1994). *After Gregory*. Dallas, TX: Baskerville.

Wyer, R. S., Jr., & Srull, T. K. (1989). *Memory and cognition in its social context*. Hillsdale, NJ: Erlbaum.

PART II

CLASSIC CONTRASTS

Personal Self Versus Social Identity

The Personal Self in Social Context

Barriers to Authenticity

Although this chapter appears in the section entitled "Classic Contrasts: Personal Self Versus Social Identity," these constructs should not be considered in opposition to one another. Instead, the personal self is very much embedded within multiple social contexts. Three historical scholars, Cooley (1902), Mead (1934), and Baldwin (1897), set the conceptual stage on which the drama of the self in social interaction was enacted. For these symbolic interactionists, the self was primarily a social construction, crafted through linguistic exchanges with others. Thus, the personal self is crafted through the incorporation of attitudes that significant others appear to hold about one's self. There has been a resurgence of interest in their formulations emphasizing how interactive processes, initially with care givers, profoundly shape the developing self. Contemporary attachment theorists (e.g., Bretherton, 1991; Cicchetti, 1990; Sroufe, 1990) emphasize how working models of self arise from an organized care-giving matrix. Cognitive developmentalists (e.g., Case, 1991), in paying homage to Baldwin, Cooley, and Mead also observe that the first sense of self is formed in the crucible of children's interactive experiences with significant others. Those who have examined self-processes across the life span have highlighted how others continue to impact the formation of one's self-portrait (see review by Harter, in press-b).

But there are liabilities associated with the construction of a personal self so highly dependent on social interaction. One such liability is the potential for constructing a false self that does not mirror one's authentic experiences. Thus, one may incorporate opinions of others toward the self that do not correspond to events as experienced. Alternatively, the demands of significant others, coupled with the need to garner their approval, may alternatively lead to the suppression of authentic opinions or behaviors and the display of what others need to observe or want to hear. I will briefly touch upon how a concern with false self-behavior emerged historically and then surfaced within three different psychological literatures, representing clinical, social, and developmental perspectives. Recently, there has been a resurgence of interest in the causes and manifestations of lack of authenticity across the life span, as well as sociocultural treatments of how societal and economic changes pose challenges to authenticity for entire generations of individuals. Despite these trenchant analyses, there has been little empirical work thus far on the causes and consequences of false self-behavior. Thus, we have embarked upon research to study these issues during adolescence and adulthood, examining the larger implications regarding lack of authenticity.

The Historical Emergence of Interest in False Self-Behavior

An interest in the distinction between true and false self-behaviors appears to date from the 16th century (Baumeister, 1987; Trilling, 1971). Trilling describes the obsession with deception and pretense that found its way into politics, philosophy, and literature (such as in the works of Shakespeare) in England. Baumeister observes that people were particularly worried that others (not themselves) might be hiding their true selves. With the advent of Puritanism, people became concerned about whether they were deceiving *themselves* with regard to those attributes (piety, faith, and virtue) essential to acceptance into the kingdom of heaven. Emphasis on the hidden parts of the self was exacerbated by Victorian repressiveness; self-scrutiny, coupled with impossibly high moral standards, forced individuals to become self-deceptive. Freud's later revelations concerning the unconscious lead to the conclusion that certain parts of the true self may be inaccessible even to oneself.

The theme of true and false self-behavior emerged more explicitly in the clinical literature among those psychoanalytically oriented theorists who built on Freudian formulations. Horney (1950) described the person's alienation from the real self. Other theorists noted that imposter tendencies represented the need for narcissistic enhancement as a defense against core feelings of worthlessness (Deutsch, 1955; Kohut, 1984). Bleiberg (1984) and Winnicott (1965) focused more on the developmental precursors of false self-behavior. For Bleiberg, false self-behavior resulted from care givers who did not validate the child's true self, thus leading the infant to become alienated from the core self. Winnicott argued that parents who are intrusively overinvolved with their infant cause the child to develop a false self based upon compliance (see also Sullivan, 1953). These clinical formulations emphasize the more pathological avenues to the developments of a false self.

Within the sociological and social psychological literatures, lack of authenticity among adults is considered to be motivated by attempts to present the self in a manner that will impress or win the acceptance of others. Goffman (1959), in his treatment of the presentation of self in everyday life, described the manipulative motives that compete with our desire to be sincere. Various forms of "facework" communicate to others that we are competent, likable, moral, or worthy of respect, motives designed not only to protect and promote the self but to curry favor, obtain social currency or power, and preserve critical relationships. Earlier in the same decade, Riesman (1950) distinguished between inner-directed individuals who were self-determining and, by definition, more true to themselves, and outer-directed individuals whose malleability in the face of social demands marked them as less authentic. A similar distinction has been echoed by Snyder (1987) in identifying high and low self-monitors. High self-monitors are presumed to suppress features of their true self in order to gain the approval of others. Concern with the social appropriateness of their self-presentations leads necessarily to inconsistency in their self-presentations from one social situation to another. While some condemn the high self-monitor for superficiality if not deceit, Snyder suggests that high self-monitoring reflects the individual's flexibility in coping with the diversity of social roles one is expected to assume.

Finally, within the developmental adolescent literature, false self-behaviors are considered by some theorists to be a dimension of normative role experimentation (Broughton, 1981; Selman, 1980). Thus, a contemporary female adolescent may well don the mantle of Madonna in one situation, but then shift to Nancy Kerrigan in another. Elkind (1967) cites an additional motive, observing that the adolescent becomes more self-conscious as it becomes more apparent that one is the object of others' evaluations. Thus, adolescents may attempt to obscure their true selves if they feel that they do not measure up to the standards and values set by others whose opinions are critical.

Contemporary Interest in the False Self

Lerner (1993) points to the vast vocabulary we have developed to describe deception. Verb forms make reference to fabricating, withholding, concealing, distorting, falsifying, pulling the wool over someone's eyes, posturing, charading, faking, and hiding behind a facade. Adjectives include elusive, evasive, wily, phony, artificial, two-faced, manipulative, calculating, pretentious, crafty, conniving, duplicitous, deceitful, dishonest. Noun forms include hypocrite, charlatan, chameleon, impostor, fake, and fraud. Interestingly, there are common threads in the analyses of lack of authenticity across the life span.

Infancy

From a normative, developmental perspective, the emergence of language is a double-edged sword. On the positive side, the attainment of language is potent in the service of union and connectedness, since it provides a common symbol system allowing for new levels of shared meaning. In addition, verbal representation provides a powerful vehicle through which the child can begin to construct a narrative of one's life story (Stern, 1985), preserved in autobiographic memory (see Crittenden, 1994; Eisenberg, 1985; Fivush & Hudson, 1990; Hudson, 1990; Nelson, 1986, 1993; Snow, 1990). However, these theorists also alert us to the liabilities of language. Stern argues that language can drive a wedge between two simultaneous forms of interpersonal experience: as it is lived and as it is verbally represented. The very capacity for objectifying the self through language allows one to transcend, and therefore potentially distort, immediate experience.

Moreover, the narrative that is constructed initially is highly scaffolded by parents who dictate which aspects of the child's experience parents feel are important to codify in the child's autobiographical memory, leading to potential misrepresentations of the child's actual experience (Bowlby, 1980; Bretherton, 1991; Crittenden, 1994). Children may receive subtle signals that certain episodes should not be retold or are best "forgotten" (Dunn, Brown, & Beardsall, 1991). If one accepts the falsified version of experience, such distortions may well contribute to the formation of a false self. Thus, displaying behavior to meet the needs and wishes of someone else incurs the risk of alienation from those inner experiences that represent one's true self (Crittenden, 1994; Stern, 1985; Winnicott, 1965).

Childhood

Issues involving displays of true and false self-behavior during childhood have also been related to differences in the socialization experiences of children. For example, Deci and Ryan (1995) contend that a child's true self is fostered by care givers who love the child for whom he or she is, rather than for matching a socially imposed standard. In contrast, a false self will emerge to the extent that care givers make their love contingent upon the child's living up to their particular standards, since the child must adopt a socially implanted self. Such children display what Deci and Ryan label "contingent self-esteem." Consistent with their analysis are findings revealing that those experiencing support that is conditional on meeting the externally imposed standards of parents and peers display more false self-behavior (see Harter, Marold, Whitesell, & Cobbs, 1996).

Abusive treatment by care givers also places the child at serious risk for suppressing the true self and displaying various forms of false self-behavior (Harter, in press-a). Lack of attunement to the child's needs, empathic failure, lack of validation, threats of harm, coercion, and enforced compliance all cause the true self to go underground (Bleiberg, 1984; Stern, 1985; Winnicott, 1965) and lead to what Sullivan (1953) labelled "not me" experiences. Secrecy pacts around sexually abusive interactions further lead the abused child to defensively exclude such episodic memories from awareness. Thus, sexual and physical abuse at the hands of family members causes the child to split off experiences, relegating them to either a private or inaccessible part of the self. The very disavowal, repression, or dissociation of one's experiences coupled with psychogenic amnesia and numbing as defensive reactions to abuse therefore set the stage for the loss of one's true self. Herman (1992) describes a more conscious pathway in that the abused child comes to see the true self as corroded with inner badness and as therefore to be concealed at all costs. Persistent attempts to be good, in order to please the parents, lead the child to develop a socially acceptable self that is experienced as false or unauthentic.

Adolescence

These processes can and do continue into adolescence. However, other developmental features emerge, making the issue of false self-behavior even more problematic. The adolescent is confronted with the demand to create multiple selves associated with different social roles or contexts: one may display different selves with father, mother, close friends, romantic partners, peers, and don different persona in the role of student, worker, or athlete (see Erikson, 1950; Griffen, Chassin, & Young, 1981; Harter & Monsour, 1992; Kolligian, 1990; Smollnar & Youniss, 1985). This proliferation of selves naturally introduces concern over which is "the real me," particularly if attributes in different roles appear contradictory (e.g., cheerful with friends but depressed with parents). When asked to define true and false behavior, adolescents describe true self-behavior as the "real me inside," "saying what you really think," "expressing your opinion." In contrast, false self-behavior includes "being phony," "not stating your true opinion," "saying what you think others want to hear" (Harter et al., 1996).

These observations converge with what Gilligan and colleagues (Gilligan, 1982; Gilligan, Lyons, & Hammer, 1989) have referred to as "loss of voice"—namely, the suppression of thoughts and opinions. They feel this is a liability for females in particular, beginning in adolescence. Gilligan contends that prior to adolescence, girls seem to be clear about what they know and most are able to express their opinions forcefully. With the onset of adolescence, however, many cover over what they knew as children, suppressing their voices, compromising themselves, and hiding their feelings in a "cartography of lies." Gilligan argues that many adolescent females identify with the stereotype of the "good woman" in our culture, often exemplified by one's own mother, who is nice, polite, pleasing to others, and unassertive. Adolescent girls also silence their voices as they come to observe that in our society women's opinions are typically not sought, not valued, and not supported. Another motive, according to Gilligan, stems from the fear that to speak one's mind might well cause tension within relationships. She contends that connectedness to others is particularly important for females and therefore behaviors that threaten relationships are to be avoided at all costs. Gilligan's analysis is quite provocative, and her observations, including interviews and dialogues with adolescent girls, clearly reveal that many female adolescents do suppress their voices. Her efforts, however, have not resulted in any systematic empirical demonstration of the prevalence of loss of voice among females, nor has she chosen to address these issues in adolescent males. Thus, many questions remain.

Adulthood

The issue of authenticity during adulthood has been highlighted by a number of women scholars who have spoken to the potential for false self-behavior within close relationships (see Chodorow, 1978; Gilligan, 1982; Jordan, 1991; Miller, 1986). As a starting point, these theorists argue that connectedness to others is as essential as the development of autonomy. They argue that relatedness with others brings clarity, reality, and authenticity to the self. However, an overemphasis on connectedness and care giving may jeopardize authenticity and the development of one's true self. For example, women who adopt a position of subordination in relationships typically "transform" their own needs, seeing others' needs as their own. As Miller (1986) cogently argues, subordination and authenticity are totally incompatible. There is increasing convergence in the literature (Gilligan, 1982; Gilligan et al., 1989; Jordan, Kaplan, Miller, Stiver, & Stiver, 1991; Lerner, 1993; Miller, 1986; Stiver & Miller, 1988) that such women are fearful that should they act on their own needs and desires, such an expression of their true self would cause conflict and threaten the relationship. Lerner (1993) in her recent book *The Dance of Deception* contends that pretending is closely linked with femininity in our culture, providing challenges for women to live authentically. Yet truth telling, she argues, is central to intimacy, self-regard, and joy. Thus, cultural factors conspire to force many women to compromise the true self, an adaptation that takes its toll in other arenas of their lives.

Sociocultural Analyses

A more sociocultural perspective on how false self-behavior has become a contemporary societal problem has been offered by Gergen (1991). He argues that in the previous period of Modernism authenticity was a major commodity, as well as an expectation. However, marked advances in technology have vaulted us into an era of postmodernism. Gergen develops a portrait of the "saturated" or "populated" self, observing that easy access to air travel, electronic and express mail, fax machines, cellular phones, beepers, and answering machines have all dramatically accelerated our social connectedness. As a result of these technological developments, contemporary life is a dizzying swirl of relationships where the "social caravan in which we travel through life remains always full" (p. 62).

For Gergen, these changes have profound implications for the self. The demands of multiple relationships split the individual into a multiplicity of self-investments leading to a "cacophony of potential selves" across different relational contexts. Such multiple selves become increasingly crafted to conform to particular relationships and are likely to possess many voices that do not necessarily harmonize, casting doubt on one's true identity. Thus, in playing out many roles as a "social chameleon," the sense of an obdurate, core self is compromised. Gergen argues that strategically adopting multiple roles for social gain, consciously managing the impressions one wishes to create, depends for its palpability on a contrasting sense of a real self. Such a "pastiche personality" must, in turn, lead the individual to conclude that he or she is not true to one's self. For some, the guise of strategically manipulating others will lead to distress, while for others such superficiality gives way to an optimistic sense of enormous possibility, particularly if it is successful in enhancing social currency.

Lifton (1993) offers a similar analysis describing what he terms the "protean self," derived from the Greek sea god Proteus, who displayed many forms. For Lifton, the protean self emerges from the confusion of contemporary society, in which we feel buffeted by unmanageable historical, economic, political, and social uncertainties. The protean self, therefore, requires tactical flexibility that may well be experienced as lack of authenticity. However, Lifton also emphasizes the resilience of the human condition. Cultural crises may force the self to evolve in numerous directions, creating opportunities for personal expansion and growth.

Summary

Across the various literatures, addressing different age periods, there are common themes and definitions of false self-behavior. From a symbolic-interactionist perspective, one may incorporate certain attitudes that others hold about the self, attitudes that do not mirror one's own experience. At a behavioral level, an individual may engage in actions designed to please or impress others, actions that violate one's sense of a core self. A common motive for failing to express one's true self resides in the belief that this "real" self has not been, or will not be, validated or accepted by significant others. Implicit in this formulation is perceived tension between one's sense of true self and the false self that is on display; there is the perception that one is compromising who one really is. Therefore, false self-behavior is experienced as phony or artificial. Merely acting differently in different relational contexts does not necessarily constitute false self-behavior (although one may appear chameleonlike to others). False self-behavior must be accompanied by the phenomenological experience that one's actions and words lack authenticity.

Both false and true selves are very personal constructs. However, the false self is experienced as socially implanted against one's will, and as such it feels foreign. According to symbolic interactionists, the true self is also social in origin, derived from the incorporation of the perceived opinions of significant others. However, one has consciously or unconsciously internalized these messages in a form that the individual comes to own as a personal rendering of the true self. Thus, both true and false selves are primarily social in origin, although the true self is experienced as a self-defining core sense of who one really is. In the remainder of this chapter, I will present research that examines certain hypothesized causes, correlates, and potential outcomes of true and false self-behavior among adolescents and adults.

True versus False Self-Behavior among Adolescents

We first became alerted to the salience of false self-behavior during adolescence within the context of studies on the proliferation of multiple selves. In describing the seemingly contradictory attributes that define the self in different roles, certain adolescents agonize over "which is the real me." In pursuing this issue we discovered that adolescents are quite sensitive to whether they themselves, as well as others, are being true to themselves or being phony, defined as putting on an act or behaving in ways that someone else wants you to be. Although our initial interest focused on the normative, developmental concern that many adolescents express over false self-behavior, subsequent studies revealed considerable variability in adolescents' reports of the level of their own true and false self-behavior with parents and peers. Thus, we sought to examine certain antecedents of the level of false self-behavior in order to understand these marked individual differences. We looked to features of adolescents' parent and peer support systems, given our own previous research on the impact of approval on self processes and those literatures described above that implicated certain patterns of support in the display of false self-behavior.

We predicted that adolescents reporting that they were not receiving high levels of approval would be motivated to suppress their true selves, altering their behavior in hopes of garnering support from significant others. In addition, we hypothesized that the conditionality of support would affect false self-behavior. Conditional support was defined as the perception that approval will only be forthcoming if one meets very high expectations of significant others. It represents the antithesis of what Rogers (1951) termed "unconditional positive regard." Our interviews with adolescents demonstrated their awareness of conditional support from parents. As one put it, "My mom is really on my case because I'm not living up to what she wants me to be. If I get A's in school she acts like she is proud of me. But if I don't she doesn't approve of me, you could say how she treats me is conditional on how I do. There is no way I can ever please her, it's pretty hopeless." What such verbal descriptions make clear is that conditional "support" is not perceived as supportive, since typically it does not validate one's core self. Rather, it represents contingencies, it specifies the psychological hoops through which one must jump to try to please the parents by meeting their standards. In earlier work (Harter, Marold, & Whitesell, 1991) we demonstrated that those who report high parental conditionality also report low levels of parental approval. We subsequently extended the conditionality construct to the peer domain, where acting, dressing, and adopting attitudes touted by peers whose opinions were important represent the pathway to peer acceptance. With both parents and peers, attempts to meet the conditions set by others should result in more false self-behavior.

Since a number of our interviewees spontaneously added that they felt somewhat hopeless about being able to please parents or peers, we also hypothesized that hopelessness may well be implicated in false self-behavior. Employing path-analytic techniques, the best-fitting model revealed that the effect of level and conditionality of support on false self-behavior is mediated by hopelessness about obtaining support (Harter et al., in press). Thus, the highest levels of false self-behavior are reported by those adolescents who are receiving relatively low levels of support that they feel is conditional, leading them to feel hopeless about pleasing others, which in turn causes them to suppress their true selves. It was our interpretation that they did so as a means of garnering the desired support. But are adolescents themselves aware of such motives?

We found that adolescents can readily report on their reasons for engaging in false self-behavior. Interestingly, these reasons parallel the three motive categories identified in the different literatures described at the outset. Some cite reasons paralleling the motives identified in the clinical literature, namely devaluation of the self (e.g., parents or peers do not like them or they do not like themselves). Motives more consonant with the social psychological literature include wanting to please, impress, or gain the acceptance of others. Finally, some adolescents suggest the normative developmental motive of experimenting with different selves, trying different ways of acting around other people to see what it feels like.

There are powerful correlates to these three motive choices. Those citing motives emphasizing devaluation of the self report the worst outcomes in that they (1) engage in the highest levels of false self-behavior, (2) are more likely not to know who their true self really is, and (3) report the lowest self-esteem coupled with depressed affect. Those endorsing role experimentation report the most positive outcomes (least false self-behavior, most knowledge of true self, highest self-esteem and cheerful affect), with the approval seekers concerned with impression management falling in between. It is possible that those who expressed the devaluation motives identified in the clinical literature may have experienced the most negative history of disapproval. If care givers failed to validate the child's expressions of authentic self, compliance to the parents' wishes and expectations may have established a pattern of false self-behavior. Such a pattern may be exacerbated at adolescence when these issues become more salient, leading to the most negative consequences for this group.

Lack of Voice Among Adolescents

Although Gilligan has claimed that many adolescent girls lose their voices, there is no systematic empirical evidence on whether voice declines developmentally for adolescent females or on whether there are gender differences in level of voice. In our work, we became alerted to lack of voice since not stating one's opinions, suppressing what one really thinks, was a common theme in adolescents' descriptions of false self-behavior. Thus, Patricia Waters and I, in collaboration with Nancy Whitesell, Eric Johnson, and Ramona Gonzales, embarked upon a program of research to examine predictors and correlates of level of voice among adolescent males and females. Between the ages of 12 and 18, what happens to the level of voice among girls as well as boys? Does voice vary as a function of the particular relationship? Are there individual differences in level of voice within each gender? If so, might they be predicted by gender orientation (rather than gender per se) as well as by perceived support for voice in each relational context?

We first developed questionnaire items that tapped adolescents' ability to "share what they are thinking," "say what's on their mind," "express their opinions," "let others know what is important to them," and "express their point of view." A sample item: "Some teenagers usually don't say what's on their mind to (particular persons) BUT Other teenagers *do* say what's on their mind to (particular persons)." Subjects first select the kind of teenagers they are most like and then indicate whether that choice is "Really True for Me" or "Sort of True for Me." Items are scored on a four-point scale where 1 equals the lowest level of voice and 4 the highest. (Internal consistencies range from .82 to .89.) The particular persons have varied across studies and have included parents, teachers, classmates (males versus females in one study), close friends, and boys in social situations. To date, we have collected data in both a coeducational middle school (6th through 8th grades) and high school (9th through 12th grades) and in an all-girls, parochial, high school.

Although Gilligan has not presented prevalence data on level of voice in different relationships, she does observe that one arena in which adolescent girls are able to maintain their voices is with close friends. We were interested in whether there were meaningful differences across relational contexts. The pattern reveals that voice is highest with close friends, followed by classmates of the same gender. However, voice is consistently lower with classmates of the opposite gender, as well as with parents and teachers. In the all-girls high school, voice was lowest with males in social situations. Thus, clearly, the social context is important in that adolescents are more comfortable expressing their opinions in some contexts than in others.

Of particular relevance to Gilligan's thesis is whether there are age and gender differences across 6th through 12th grades. With regard to developmental differences, our cross-sectional data reveal no significant mean differences associated with grade level for either gender, nor are there even any trends, in either the coeducational or all-girls school. Thus, as we have assessed it, level of voice does not decline for adolescent females. One possibility is that by sixth grade (age 12 to 13) the processes cited by Gilligan may have already taken place. However, the mean levels we obtain (average scores of around 3.0 on a four-point scale) reveal that levels of voice are relatively high among young female adolescents, arguing against such an interpretation.

We have also found no evidence for gender differences favoring males. In the middle school, scores were quite comparable for males and females. At the high-school level, girls actually reported significantly higher levels of voice with close friends, female classmates, parents, and teachers, and comparable scores in the context of male class-mates. Thus, these findings caution against making generalizations about the developmental trajectory of voice for most or all adolescent females. Rather, the most impressive discoveries in our data have been the marked individual differences in level of voice among both male and female adolescents, differences we have examined as a function of gender orientation and social support for voice.

Gender Orientation

To assess gender orientation, we have drawn from instruments including the Personality Attributes Questionnaire (Spence, Helmreich, & Stapp, 1975), the Sex Role Inventory developed by Bem (1985), and Boldizar's (1991) adaptation for children and adolescents. Masculine items tap dimensions such as competitiveness, ability to make decisions, independence, risk-taking, confidence, athleticism, mechanical aptitude, individualism, leadership, and enjoyment of math and science. Feminine items tap themes that include sensitivity, warmth, empathy, expressions of affection, enjoyment of babies and children, gentleness, and concern for others who are in distress. We were particularly interested in the hypothesis that among adolescent girls those displaying a predominantly feminine orientation (endorsing feminine but not masculine items) would report lower levels of voice, compared to those displaying an androgynous orientation (endorsing both feminine and masculine items). (We did not have a sufficient number of masculine females to make meaningful comparisons.)

The findings revealed that femininity does represent a liability for girls in certain, but not all, relational contexts. Interestingly, feminine girls report significantly lower levels of voice than do androgynous girls in more public social contexts—namely, with teachers, classmates (where the effect is stronger with male classmates), and, among those in the all-girls high school, with boys in social situations. However, in more private, interpersonal relationships—namely, with close friends and parents—these differences were not obtained, suggesting that femininity is not a liability in these contexts. Dimensions of femininity such as empathy and concern for others may well facilitate expression of voice. It is in the more public social contexts that one might expect those highly feminine adolescent females to display behaviors consistent with the "good woman" societal stereotype (Gilligan et al., 1989), leading to their suppression of voice. Our findings, therefore, caution against making generalizations based on gender alone since they reveal that it is not gender per se but gender orientation that predicts level of voice among females.

Among males, we were able to identity both masculine and androgynous subgroups. No differences in level of voice were observed with teachers, parents, and female classmates. However, masculine boys did report higher levels of voice with male classmates than did androgynous counterparts, suggesting that androgyny is a liability for males in this context. However, with close friends, androgynous boys reported higher levels of voice than did masculine boys, suggesting that the possession of certain feminine characteristics allows one to more comfortably express oneself within a more intimate relationship.

Support for Voice

In our initial studies, low levels of approval coupled with conditional support were predictive of general displays of false self-behavior. We then reasoned that support for voice, specifically, should be associated with the level of voice expressed. We created items in which support-for-voice items tapped others' interest in what one had to say, respect for one's ideas even if there is disagreement, ability to listen to one's opinions and take them seriously, and attempts to understand one's point of view. We have obtained marked effects for both genders that occurred across all relationships, where correlations between support for voice and level of voice range from .46 to .70. To take but one relational context (high-school girls with teachers) to convey differences in the absolute levels of voice as a function of level of support, those perceiving low levels of support from teachers reported voice scores of 2.3. Those with moderate levels of support reported voice scores of 2.8, and those with high levels of support had voice scores of 3.5.

Differences in voice as a function of the responsiveness of significant others highlight the importance of how the personal self is affected by social interactions. The ability to be one's true self, to express one's inner thoughts and opinions, is profoundly influenced by the extent to which others listen to, attempt to understand, and respect what the adolescent has to say, even if they do not always agree. Such an analysis implies that support in this form promotes the adolescent's expression of voice. However, it is also likely that if adolescents voice their opinions, this may generate supportive interest in others, suggesting a causal link in the other direction as well.

The pattern of findings also reveals the additive effects of support and gender orientation, particularly in more public relational contexts. In the all-girls high school we had enough subjects to cross support with gender orientations. Figure 4.1 presents the findings for one such context, with female classmates. The same pattern was observed for voice with teachers, parents, and with males in social situations (where we consistently obtained two highly significant main effects and no interaction). The differences associated with the combination of support for voice and gender orientation are dramatic. Those most at risk for lack of voice are feminine girls who also report low levels of support. Those

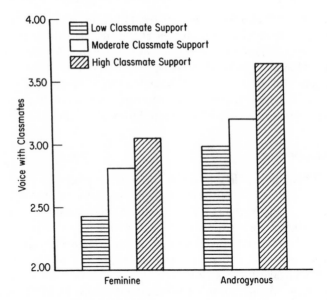

FIGURE 4.1. Level of voice with female classmates as a function of gender orientation and support for voice.

most able to express their voices are those androgynous girls who also report high levels of support.

Is Lack of Voice Perceived as False Self-Behavior?

Our analysis has assumed that lack of voice represents false self-behavior, in large part because adolescents cite the inability to express their opinions as one manifestation of the false self. There could, however, be other motives for lack of voice that do not imply lack of authenticity. For example, (1) one may be shy, temperamentally, (2) one may feel that it is not socially appropriate to express one's opinions in certain contexts, or (3) one may choose not to share certain opinions that are considered private. In our coed sample, therefore, we created items to determine whether adolescents perceive lack of voice as false or true self-behavior. For example: "When I don't say what I am thinking around (particular persons) I feel like I am *not* being the 'real me'" versus "When I don't say what I am thinking around (particular persons), it feels like I *am* being the 'real me.'" A second set of items addressed the extent to which adolescents were bothered or upset by not expressing their opinions in each relationship.

Approximately 75% of adolescents of both genders indicated that failure to express their opinions did constitute false self-behavior. By way of converging evidence, 75% also reported that they were bothered when they did not say what they really think. The percentages were quite similar across the different relationship contexts, bolstering our assumption that, for the large majority of adolescents, lack of voice *is* perceived as suppression of the true self. Moreover, when we inquired into the reasons why one would not express one's opinions among those with low levels of voice, both males and females reported that saying what one really thought would threaten a relationship with parents and classmates, although not with teachers. With classmates, they also reported that the expression of one's views could lead to embarrassment and social censure if, for example, what one said was "stupid."

The Liabilities of Lack of Voice as a Form of False Self-Behavior

A basic claim of theorists concerned with false self-behavior is that lack of authenticity has negative outcomes or correlates. In our earlier studies those highest in false self-behavior, motivated by devaluation of the self, reported the lowest level of global self-esteem and were the most likely to report depressive affect. In our high-school coed subsample of those who acknowledged that suppression of one's opinion was indeed a manifestation of false self-behavior, we were also interested in a new construct that we have labeled "relational self esteem." We anticipated that just as approval, support for voice, and level of voice may vary across relationships, so might self-esteem, in that one may feel more worthwhile as a person in some relationships than in others. Evidence for the validity of the relational self-esteem construct came from a very clean factor structure, as well as from the discrepancies between individual's self-esteem scores across relationships. At the extreme, one student reported her self-esteem to be 1.0 with parents and 4.0 with female friends, the maximum difference possible.

We divided subjects with those with low and with high levels of voice for each relationship and then examined their corresponding relational self-esteem. The findings were strikingly comparable for males and females (combined below) across each context: low-voice subjects had significantly lower self-esteem than did high-voice subjects with parents (2.5 vs. 3.4), teachers (2.8 vs. 3.3), male classmates (2.6 vs. 3.2), and female classmates (2.7 vs. 3.2). However, is it that lack of voice in a given relationship leads one to devalue the self in that context, or that if one doesn't like the kind of person one is in a given relationship one then stifles one's opinions or feels that one doesn't have anything worthwhile to say? It is likely that both dynamics contribute to this link. In addition to the findings for relationship self-esteem, similar patterns were obtained for global self-esteem as well as affect (cheerful to depressed). Thus, lack of voice among those who view it as false self-behavior is clearly associated with liabilities that in turn may well interfere with the adaptive functioning among adolescents. Converging evidence comes from Kolligian (1990) who reports that perceived fraudulence in adults is accompanied by self-criticism and depressive tendencies.

Double Jeopardy for Females Who Are to Be Seen and Not Heard

Feminist scholars have viewed the suppression of voice as distressing for females, particularly given societal messages to the effect that, in comparison to men, women's voices as not as valued and their opinions are not taken as seriously. Moreover, such messages are coupled with communications about how a woman's looks are potentially her greatest commodity. Popular culture and the media perpetuate the stereotype of the desirable woman who should be seen and not heard. Movies, television, magazines, rock videos, and advertising all tout the importance of physical attractiveness, glamorizing the popular role models people should emulate. Standards regarding desirable bodily characteristics such as thinness have become increasingly unrealistic and demanding for women within the past two decades (see Heatherton and Baumeister, 1991; Garner, Garfinkel, Schwartz, & Thompson, 1980).

The difficulty for females in meeting the cultural stereotypes for appearance seems to be brought home over the course of development, the closer one comes to adopting the role of a woman in this society. Our own data (Harter, 1993) reveal that, for females, perceptions of physical attractiveness systematically decline with grade level, whereas there is no such drop for males. In middle childhood, girls and boys feel equally good about their appearance; however, by the end of high school, females' scores are dramatically lower than males'. We find similar gender differences in perceived appearance among college populations as well as among adults in the world of work and family, particularly for women who are full-time homemakers.

In addition to assaulting adolescent and adult females with exhortations that they become thinner and more attractive, there is the implicit message that looks are more critical than intelligence and the expression of one's opinion. Observe for example, the number of headless women in ads for clothing, perfume, and other women's products. If women are depicted with heads, they are often deprived of a cortex. Images of these headless and decorticated females unconsciously communicate the message that women are mindless, brainless, and therefore perhaps should be voiceless. A recent ad depicting a woman applying perfume put it quite explicitly. The caption read: "Make a statement without saying a word."

Not all adolescent girls and women fall victim to this mentality by buying into these media messages. But what are the consequences for those who do adopt these cultural expectations? We addressed this issue by dividing female high-school students into four groups based on their levels of voice (high vs. low) crossed with their ratings of the importance of appearance (high vs. low). We examined four correlates: perceptions of appearance, global self-esteem, relational self-esteem, and affect. Across every relationship, those most likely to endorse the view that females should be seen and not heard—namely, those low in voice who rated appearance as highly important—reported the worst outcomes. In contrast, those high in voice who reported appearance as unimportant reported the best outcomes, with the other two groups falling in between (manifest in two significant main effects with no interaction). To give one example (with male classmates), those with low voice who also touted the importance of appearance, compared to those with high voice who reviewed appearance as unimportant, reported appearance scores of 2.3 (vs. 2.9), global self-esteem scores of 2.9 (vs. 3.4), relational self-esteem scores of 2.65 (vs. 3.25), and affect scores of 2.9 (vs. 3.45). The differences were equally dramatic and significant in other relationships (with parents, teachers, and female classmates). Thus, not only does lack of voice bring with it liabilities, but when coupled with an emphasis on the importance of appearance it places females in double jeopardy, leading to negative evaluations of both one's outer and inner selves.

In summary, our studies of voice reveal no evidence that adolescent girls, in general, lose their voices between ages 12 and 18, nor do they report lower levels of voice than males at any of these ages. These findings caution against generalizations based upon age and gender. What did emerge were dramatic individual differences in level of voice. In both genders, support for voice was a powerful predictor. For females, gender orientation was also a determinant in that feminine girls reported lower levels of voice in more public, relational contexts. For both genders, lack of voice is associated with liabilities such as low self-esteem and depressed affect. Low-voice females who also tout the importance of appearance are at the greatest risk.

Barriers to Authenticity in Adulthood

Dichotomies that pit the constructs of a personal self against a more socially oriented self misrepresent the embeddedness of the self in social contexts. One such dichotomy can be observed in treatments of the adult self, where two orientations, self-focused versus other-focused have been sharply contrasted (see Gilligan, 1982; Jordan, 1991; Markus & Kitayama, 1991). The self-focused individual has been characterized as overly autonomous, independent, and dominating, with sharply defined boundaries between the self and others. Such an individual experiences uncomfortableness with intimacy and acknowledges greater clarity about one's own needs and feelings than about a partner's. In contrast, the other-focused individual is oriented toward caring and concern for others, as well as toward compliance, typically subordinating one's own needs to those of a partner. As a result, there is often greater attentiveness to, and therefore clarity about, the partner's feelings than about one's own (Miller, 1986).

These styles have been dichotomized too sharply (see also Holland, this volume). Moreover, they have been too readily generalized to characterize the styles of men as self-focused versus women as other-focused. Views of development that have focused solely on growth toward self-focused autonomy or the primacy of other-focused connection have each contributed to distortions about what constitutes healthy development. Our perspective is more in keeping with the recent emphasis on healthy adaptation as an integration of autonomy or individuality and connectedness. Within the infancy literature (Emde, 1988; Stern, 1985) as well as the adolescent literature (Allen, Hauser, Bell, & O'Connor, in press; Cooper, Grotevant, & Condon, 1983; Hill & Holmbeck, 1986), certain theorists and investigators are now arguing that a major developmental task involves movement toward autonomy that is best achieved in the context of meaningful relationships with significant others (see also Guisinger & Blatt, 1993; Powers, Hauser, & Kilner, 1989; Ryan & Lynch, 1989).

Recently (Harter, Waters, Pettitt, Whitesell, Kofkin, & Jordan, in press), we have extended this framework to adulthood, suggesting that the integration of appropriate forms of autonomy and connectedness within the context of one's relationship with a spouse or intimate partner will result in the most positive outcomes. This has resulted in a trichotomy of relationship styles rather than the typical dichotomy. The three styles we have identified are (1) self-focused autonomy, (2) other-focused connection, and a third new style, (3) mutuality— namely, a balanced integration of autonomy and connection. Those displaying the mutual style attempt to balance their needs with those of their partner; they try to be clear about, and empathize with, their partner's feelings while also trying to be clear about their own. They also value closeness and the relationship but balance this with an appropriate differentiation from their partner as well as with interests outside the relationship.

Our data were obtained from a newspaper survey in which 3,800 adults reported on their own style as well as that of their partner. In examining partner combinations, the most common pairings were women and men both displaying the mutual relationship style. As expected, other-focused women subjects were most likely to report that their partners were self-focused men. Similarly, the majority of self-focused men subjects reported that their partners were other-focused women. We anticipated this combination given the initial complementary fit between such styles—i.e., a submissive female paired with a dominant male.

We were particularly interested in two correlates of these partner pairings: perceived validation by the partner and the ability to be one's authentic self within the relationship. Consistent with our adolescent studies, we hypothesized that the ability to be one's authentic self within the relationship would be directly related to the extent to which one felt supported or validated by the partner. Thus, if a person feels validated in that his or her partner listens, takes what they say seriously, and values them as a person, then he or she is able to be authentic within the relationship. Conversely, if a person is not validated in the sense that one is not listened to or taken seriously, he or she will suppress the "real me."

We found support for the prediction that other-focused women paired with self-focused men would feel least validated of any group and would therefore also report the lowest levels of authentic self-behavior within the relationship. Not only do the self-focused partner's attributes contribute to lack of validation by definition, but the other-focused women adopt a submissive stance that may well not invite validation. The other-focused woman's subordinate stance precludes authenticity; transforming one's own needs in the service of pleasing one's partner necessarily involves the suppression of one's authentic self within the relationship (Miller, 1986). The much smaller group of other-focused men paired with self-focused women displayed a similar pattern. Thus, it would appear that the dynamics of the relationship are primarily responsible for these outcomes, rather than gender per se. Strong support was also obtained for the prediction that partners who both identify with the mutuality style would report the highest levels of perceived validation and authentic self-behavior. Men and women reporting this style have, as one relationship goal, mutual understanding, which in turn would appear to allow them to be their authentic selves within the relationship.

Somewhat unanticipated was the finding that self-focused men with other-focused women partners reported less validation and authentic self-behavior than couples displaying mutuality, since self-focused men feel entitled to have their needs met and have partners who are presumably attentive to their needs and feelings. Self-focused individuals' feelings of entitlement may lead to expectations that cannot be realistically fulfilled, causing the self-focused people to feel insufficiently validated. Alternatively, the self-focused male may primarily desire validation for instrumental accomplishments outside of the relationship, whereas his other-focused female partner may seek to provide validation for intimacy and the expression of emotions by her partner, resulting in a mismatch of goals.

In summary, the findings reveal liabilities associated with the two extreme relationship styles. Within both genders, individuals reporting these styles acknowledge that they feel less validated and are less able to be their true selves than individuals reporting mutuality. Moreover, through path-analytic techniques, we examined a more general process model in the entire sample that revealed that not only does the level of validation by a partner predict one's ability to be one's authentic self in the relationship but that authentic self-behavior, in turn, appears to mediate self-esteem and affect. Those individuals who feel lack of validation, leading to an inability to be one's true self, also report low self-esteem and depressed affect. Thus, this package of findings provides further evidence for links between the reactions of significant others and dimensions of the personal self.

Conclusions

The emergence of the personal self is deeply embedded in the crucible of interpersonal relationships, particularly with regard to the impact of significant others on the ability to display one's authentic self. Across numerous analyses of the development and display of false self-behavior, a central theme emerges. If significant others ignore, reject, devalue, or actively denigrate one's authentic self, individuals—whether children, adolescents, or adults, female or male—will be driven to suppress the true self and to display manifestations of false self-behavior. Such behaviors are motivated by attempts to obtain approval, to avoid rejection, and to maintain some form of connection. Paradoxically, however, efforts to sustain a relationship and please others that require *distortion* of the self not only lead to disconnection from one's true self but disconnection from significant others, since they also prevent an authentic relationship (Jordan, 1991; Miller, 1986).

A central focus of our research program has been to address individual differences in the display of false self-behavior. Treatments in the literature have suggested that, beginning in adolescence, females are particularly vulnerable to suppression of their true selves. Our findings reveal, however, that the field needs to guard against such generalizations. The data show that those adolescent females who adopt a highly feminine gender-role orientation, coupled with lack of support, are most at risk for lack of voice. In contrast, androgynous females who also report support, have very high levels of voice. Similarly, those women who adopt an other-focused style in which their own needs are denied report low levels of validation and authentic self-behavior, in contrast to those identifying with the mutual style. These findings suggest a refinement of Gilligan's position in that it is only that subset of females who buy into the "good woman" stereotype who exhibit serious suppression of self.

Lack of authenticity is cause for concern since theory and our own research reveal that it is associated with low self-esteem (both global and relational), hopelessness, and depressed effect, a constellation that in turn not only interferes with the ability to achieve one's potential but can lead to self-destructive behaviors as well. Among adolescents, the liabilities are greatest for those females who endorse feminine sex-role stereotypes, including the importance of appearance.

It should be noted that constructs such as self-esteem have fallen from grace in the eyes of some contemporary theorists—for example, Damon (1995) and Seligman (1993). Damon contends that self-esteem has been overrated as a commodity, and that the effusive praise that parents or teachers heap on children to make them feel good is often viewed with suspicion by children and interferes with the goal of building specific skills in the service of genuine achievement. Seligman further argues that self-esteem is merely an epiphenomenon, a reflection that one's commerce with the world is going badly, with little explanatory power in and of itself.

At one level, self-esteem would appear to have little explanatory power since, as a mediator, self-esteem has been casually implicated in numerous problem behaviors, including depression and suicide, eating disorders, antisocial behaviors (most recently gang activity), as well as teen pregnancy. Thus, we do not know what specific forces lead one individual with low self-esteem to terminate his or her *own* life; another with low self-esteem to put his or her life at risk, through eating disordered behavior; still another to terminate someone else's life; and yet another, through pregnancy, to create a new life. Self-esteem, therefore, has little explanatory power in predicting which particular outcome will ensue. In our zeal for parsimonious explanatory models we must not ignore the fact that the phenomenological self experienced by children, adolescents, and adults is not necessarily parsimonious. Self-representations, self-evaluations, self-authenticity or self-distortions, self-esteem—all appear as very salient constructs in an individual's working model of self. As such, they wield powerful influences on affective and behavioral outcomes. Thus, the challenge is to develop models that not only seek to identity the specific antecedents of different outcomes, but that preserve self-representations as critical, phenomenological mediators.

References

Allen, J. P., Hauser, S. T., Bell, K. L., & O'Connor, T. G. (in press). Longitudinal assessment of autonomy and relatedness in adolescent-family interactions as predictors of adolescent ego development and self-esteem. *Child Development*.

Baldwin, J. M. (1897). *Social and ethical interpretations in mental development.* New York: Macmillan.

Baumeister, R. F. (1987). How the self became a problem: A psychological review of historical research. *Journal of Personality and Social Psychology, 52,* 163–176.

Bem, S. (1985). Androgyny and gender schema theory. Nebraska Symposium on Motivation. Lincoln, NE: University of Nebraska Press.

Bleiberg, E. (1984). Narcissistic disorders in children. *Bulletin of the Menninger Clinic, 48,* 501–517.

Boldizar, J. P. (1991). Assessing sex-typing and androgyny in children: The children's sex-role inventory. *Developmental Psychology, 27,* 505–515.

Bowlby, J. (1980). *Attachment and loss: Vol. 3, Loss, sadness, and depression.* New York: Basic Books.

Bretherton, I. (1991). Pouring new wine into old bottles: The social self as internal working model. In M. R. Gunnar & L. A. Sroufe (Eds.), *The Minnesota Symposia on Child Development: Vol. 23. Self processes and development* (pp. 1–42). Hillsdale, NJ: Erlbaum.

Broughton, J. (1981). The divided self in adolescence. *Human Development, 24,* 13–32.

Case, R. (1991). Stages in the development of the young child's first sense of self. *Developmental Review, 11,* 210–230.

Chodorow, N. (1978). *The reproduction of mothering.* Berkeley and Los Angeles: University of California Press.

Cicchetti, D. (1990). The organization and coherence of socioemotional, cognitive, and representational development. In R. Thompson (Ed.), *Nebraska Symposium on Motivation: Vol. 36. Socioemotional development* (pp. 266–375). Lincoln, NE: University of Nebraska Press.

Cooley, C. H. (1902). *Human nature and the social order.* New York: Scribner's.

Cooper, C. R., Grotevant, H. D., & Condon, S. M. (1983). Individuality and connectedness both foster adolescent identity formation and role taking skills. In H. D. Grotevant & C. R. Cooper (Eds.), *Adolescent development in the family. New directions for child development* (pp. 43–59). San Francisco: Jossey-Bass.

Crittenden, P. M. (1994). Peering into the black box. An exploratory treatise on the development of self in young children. In D. Cicchetti & Sheree L. Toth (Eds.), *Rochester Symposium on Developmental Psychopathology: Vol. 5. Disorders and dysfunctions of the self* (pp. 79–148). Rochester, NY: University of Rochester Press.

Damon, W. (1995). *Greater expectations: Overcoming the culture of indulgence in America's homes and schools.* New York: Free Press.

Deci, E. L., & Ryan, R. M. (1995). Human autonomy: The basis for true self-esteem. In M. H. Kernis (Ed.), *Efficacy, agency, and self-esteem: Vol. 2* (pp. 31–46). New York: Plenum.

Deutsch, H. (1955). The imposter: Contribution to ego psychology of a type of psychopath. *Psychoanalytic Quarterly, 24,* 483–505.

Dunn, J., Brown, J., & Beardsall, L. (1991). Family talk about feeling states and children's later understanding of others' emotions. *Developmental Psychology, 27,* 445–448.

Eisenberg, A. (1985). Learning to describe past experiences in conversation. *Discourse Processes, 8,* 177–204.

Elkind, D. (1967). Egocentrism in adolescence. *Child Development, 38,* 1025–1031.

Emde, R. N. (1988). Developmental terminable and interminable: Innate and motivational factors from infancy. *International Journal of Psychoanalysis, 69,* 23–42.

Erikson, E. H. (1950). *Childhood and society.* New York: Norton.

Fivush, R., & Hudson, J. A. (Eds.). (1990). *Knowing and remembering in young children.* New York: Cambridge University Press.

Garner, D. M., & Garfinkel, P. E., Schwartz, D., & Thompson, M. (1980). Cultural expectations of thinness in women. *Psychological Reports, 47,* 483–491.

Gergen, K. J. (1991). *The saturated self: Dilemmas of Identity in modern life.* New York: Basic Books.

Gilligan, C. (1982). *In a different voice: Psychological theory and women's development.* Cambridge, MA: Harvard University Press.

Gilligan, C., Lyons, N., & Hammer, T. J. (1989). *Making connections.* Cambridge, MA: Harvard University Press.

Goffman, E. (1959). *The presentation of self in everyday life.* Garden City, NY: Doubleday.

Griffin, N., Chassin, L., & Young, R. D. (1981). Measurement of global self-concept versus multiple role-specific self-concepts in adolescents. *Adolescence, 16,* 49–56.

Guisinger, S., & Blatt, S. J. (1993). Individuality and relatedness: Evolution of a fundamental dialectic. *American Psychologist, 49,* 104–111.

Harter, S. (in press-a). The effects of child abuse on the self-system. In B. B. Rossman & M. S. Rosenberg (Eds.), *Multiple victimization of children: Conceptual, developmental, research, and treatment issues.* New York: Haworth.

Harter, S. (in press-b). The development of self-representations. In N. Eisenberg (Ed.), *Social and personality development: Handbook of child psychology.* New York: Wiley.

Harter, S. (1993). Causes and consequences of low self-esteem in children and adolescence. In R. F. Baumeister (Ed.), *Self-esteem: The puzzle of low self-regard* (pp. 87–116). New York: Plenum.

Harter, S., Marold, D. B., & Whitesell, N. R. (1991). A model of psychosocial risk factors leading to suicidal ideation in young adolescents. *Development and Psychopathology, 4.* 167–188.

Harter, S., Marold, D. B., Whitesell, N. R., & Cobbs, G. (1996). A model of the effects of parent and peer support on adolescent false self-behavior. *Child Development, 67,* 360–374.

Harter, S., & Monsour, A. (1992). Developmental analysis of opposing self-attributes in the adolescent self-portrait. *Developmental Psychology, 28,* 251–260.

Harter, S., Waters, P. L., Pettitt, L., Whitesell, N. R., Kofkin, J., & Jordan, J. (in press). Autonomy and connectedness as dimensions of relationship styles in adult men and women. *Journal of Social and Personal Relationships.*

Heatherton, T. F., & Baumeister, R. F. (1991). Binge eating as escape from self-awareness. *Psychological Bulletin, 110,* 86–108.

Herman, J. (1992). *Trauma and recovery.* New York: Basic Books.

Hill, J. P., & Holmbeck, G. N. (1986). Attachment and autonomy during adolescence. In G. J. Whitehurst (Ed.), *Annals of Child Development: Vol. 3* (pp. 145–189). Greenwich, CT: JAI Press.

Horney, K. (1950). *Neurosis and human growth.* New York: Norton.

Hudson, J. A. (1990). The emergence of autobiographical memory in mother-child conversation. In R. Fivush & J. A. Hudson (Eds.), *Knowing and remembering in young children* (pp. 166–196). New York: Cambridge University Press.

Jordan, J. V. (1991). The relational self: A new perspective for understanding women's development. In J. Strauss & G. Goethals (Eds.), *The self: Interdisciplinary approaches.* New York: Springer-Verlag.

Jordan, J. V., Kaplan, A. G., Miller, J. B., Stiver, L. P., & Stiver, J. L. (Eds.). (1991). *Women's growth in connection.* New York: Guilford.

Kohut, H. (1984). *How does analysis cure?* Chicago: University of Chicago Press.

Kolligian, J., Jr. (1990). Perceived Fraudulence as a Dimension of Perceived Incompetence. In R. J. Sternberg and J. Kolligian, Jr. (Eds.), *Competence Considered: Vol. 12* (pp. 261–285). New Haven, CT: Yale University Press.

Lerner, H. G. (1993). *The dance of deception.* New York: HarperCollins.

Lifton, R. J. (1993). *The protean self.* New York: Basic Books.

Markus, H. R., & Kitayama, S. (1991). Culture and the self: Implications for cognition, emotion, and motivation. *Psychological Review, 98,* 224–253.

Mead, G. H. (1934). *Mind, self, and society from the standpoint of a social behaviorist.* Chicago: University of Chicago Press.

Miller, J. B. (1986). *Toward a new psychology of women* (2nd ed.). Boston: Beacon.

Nelson, K. (1986). *Event knowledge: Structure and function in development.* Hillsdale, NJ: Erlbaum.

Nelson, K. (1993). Events, narratives, memory: What develops? In C. A. Nelson (Ed.), *Minnesota symposium on child psychology: Vol. 26. Memory and affect* (pp. 1–24). Hillsdale, NJ: Erlbaum.

Powers, S., Hauser, S. T., & Kilner, L. (1989). Adolescent mental health. *American Psychologist, 44,* 200–208.

Riesman, D. (1950). *The lonely crowd.* New Haven, CT: Yale University Press.

Rogers, C. R. (1951). *Client-centered therapy.* Boston: Houghton Mifflin.

Ryan, R. M., & Lynch, J. H. (1989). Emotional autonomy versus detachment: Revisiting the vicissitudes of adolescence and young adulthood. *Child Development, 60,* 340–356.

Seligman, M. E. P. (1993). *What you can change and what you can't.* New York: Fawcett Columbine.

Selman, R. (1980). *The growth of interpersonal understanding.* New York: Academic Press.

Smollnar, J., & Youniss, J. (1985). Adolescent self-concept development. In R. L. Leahy (Ed.), *The development of self.* New York: Academic Press.

Snow, K. (1990). Building memories: The ontogeny of autobiography. In D. Cicchetti & M. Beeghly (Eds.), *The self in transition: Infancy to childhood* (pp. 213–242). Chicago: University of Chicago Press.

Snyder, M. (1987). *Public appearances, private realities: The psychology of self-monitoring*. New York: Freeman.

Spence, J. T., Helmreich, R., & Stapp, J. (1974). The Personal Attributes Questionnaire: A measure of sex role stereotypes and masculinity-femininity. *JSAS Catalog of Selected Documents in Psychology, 4*, 43–44.

Sroufe, L. A. (1990). An organizational perspective on the self. In D. Cicchetti & M. Beeghly (Eds.), *The self in transition: Infancy to childhood* (pp. 281–307). Chicago: University of Chicago Press.

Stern, D. (1985). *The interpersonal world of the infant*. New York: Basic Books.

Stiver, I. P., & Miller, J. B. (1988). From depression to sadness in the psychotherapy of women. *Work in Progress, No. 36*. Wellesley, MA: Stone Center Working Paper Series.

Sullivan, H. (1953). *The interpersonal theory of psychiatry*. New York: Norton.

Trilling, L. (1971). *Sincerity and authenticity*. Cambridge, MA: Harvard University Press.

Winnicott, D. W. (1965). *The maturational processes and the facilitating environment*. New York: International Universities Press.

Peggy A. Thoits
Lauren K. Virshup

5

Me's and We's

*Forms and Functions
of Social Identities*

While the concept of "social self" or "social identity" has always had multiple meanings, two predominant conceptions of social identity can be found in the social psychological literature. For simplicity, we will term these two conceptions "me's" and "we's," or for variety, "individual-level" and "collective-level" identities, or more briefly, "individual" and "collective" identities. Individual-level me's are identifications of the self as a certain kind of person, using broad social categories to describe "who I am." Collective-level we's are identifications of the self with a group as a whole, using broad social categories to describe "who we are."[1] Because, as will be seen, both types of identity are social in origin, we must use terms other than "social identity" to distinguish between them.

Our primary goal is to delineate me's and we's and their theoretical functions. To this end we examine four major social-identity theories, two from sociologists that develop the "me" concept (McCall & Simmons, 1966/1978; Stryker, 1980) and two from psychologists producing the "we" concept (Tajfel, 1981; Turner, Hogg, Oakes, Reicher, & Blackwell, 1987). We will also point to unresolved problems in each approach and raise questions about the relationships between individual-level and collective-level identities.

A brief summary of our general terminology and underlying assumptions is in order. Consistent with most theorists, we view "social identities" (or "social selves") as socially-constructed and socially meaningful categories that are accepted by individuals as descriptive of themselves or their group. In essence, social identities are answers to the questions "Who am I?" or "Who are we?" when those answers refer to socio-demographic characteristics (e.g., male, African-American), group/organizational memberships (Little League member, church member), social roles (stepfather, attorney), social types of person (intellectual, leader), and, in some cases, personality or character traits (optimist, caring). As we will show, all of these social categories can serve as the basis of both individual and collective identities. "Personal identities," in contrast, are self-descriptions referring to unique or highly specific details of biography and idiosyncratic experiences (e.g., "I am Jane Doe, from Crossville, Tennessee; I graduated from Duke; I had polio as a child; I moved around a lot because my father was in the military") (Goffman, 1963; McCall & Simmons, 1966/1978). The term "personal identity" will be used throughout this chapter to refer to unique or idiosyncratic self-understandings, whereas "individual identity" will refer to self-conceptions in terms of broader social categories (for example, Jane Doe might abstract from her biographical details self-categorizations as a Southerner, a college graduate, physically handicapped, and a military brat). Our focus here will be only on categories that refer more generally to types of people or to social groups.

Like most theorists, we assume that identity categories are socially produced and culturally variable. Societies may just as easily classify and imbue with meaning differences between brown-eyed and blue-eyed people, as between heterosexuals and homosexuals or Americans and Chinese. We further assume that societies construct multiple categorization schemes to classify people and that individuals therefore acquire multiple social identities. In William James's famous words, "*a man has as many social selves as there are individuals who recognize him and carry an image of him in their mind. . . .* But as the individuals who carry the images fall naturally into classes, we may practically say that he has as many different social selves as there are distinct *groups* of persons about whose opinion he cares" (1890/1990, p. 294, emphases in the original). In sum, our focus is on the multiplicity of ways that individuals may define themselves with broad, socially derived categories and the implications these multiple self-conceptions have for social psychological theory and research.

Me's—Individual-Level Identities

Sociologists have primarily examined individual-level social identities while psychologists have tended in recent years to pursue collective-level social identities.[2] Consequently, we will begin with two sociological approaches, George McCall and J. L. Simmons's (1966/1978) role-identity theory and Sheldon Stryker's (1980) identity theory. These two approaches are based in symbolic interactionism and this underlying perspective is the foundation for almost all sociological thinking about the self (e.g., Alexander & Wiley, 1981; Burke & Reitzes, 1991; Callero, 1985; Heise, 1988; Rosenberg, 1981; Thoits, 1992; R. Turner, 1978; Weigert, Teitge, & Teitge, 1986).

Symbolic Interactionist Underpinnings

Very generally speaking, symbolic interactionism sees both self and society as created, sustained, and changed through the process of symbolic communication. In this approach, shared meaningful symbols are the keys to the emergence of self or identity (Blumer, 1969; Cooley, 1902; Mead, 1934). The symbolic meaning of a word or gesture lies in the response of an audience. To borrow an example from McCall and Simmons (1978, p. 51), when a cowboy reaches for his gun, a sheriff may react to this act by grabbing for his own. The meaning of the cowboy's gesture is found in the sheriff's reaction. An unthinking or poorly socialized cowboy quickly grasps the symbolic message of his own move by observing the sheriff's response (or, if the cowboy is truly unsocialized, he learns the full meaning of his gesture from the sheriff's completed response to his act—being shot). When the meaning of reaching for a gun is shared, however, both the cowboy and the sheriff understand the cowboy's gesture symbolically as a threat—the gesture is a mutually understood, shorthand indication (a symbol) of an act as yet uncompleted. The cowboy can intentionally use his symbolic gesture to elicit the sheriff's response; the sheriff reacts as the cowboy expects because he has interpreted the meaning of the gesture in (roughly) the same way.

Crucially, because shared symbols have the same meaning (i.e., evoke the same anticipated response) in both ego and alter, they enable individuals to "take the role of the other" (Mead, 1934). That is, one can imagine the responses of others to one's own use of words and gestures, and thus one can shift perspectives. Using symbols (language), one is able not only to classify, think about, and act toward meaningful social objects, but also to reflect on oneself as a meaningful social object from the perspective of others. An internal, silent "conversation of gestures" (Mead, 1934, p. 43) becomes possible, as the self privately considers performing a behavior, for example, then imaginatively anticipates other people's reactions to that behavior, then responds to their expected reactions, and so on. In James's (1890/1950) terms, one shifts from the self as subject to the self as object and back again. Mead (1934) called these two aspects of the self the "I" and the "me," where the I is the active, creative agent doing the experiencing, thinking, and acting, and the me is the perspective or "attitude" toward oneself that one assumes when taking the role of specific others or the generalized community.[3] In the symbolic interactionist approach, these me's, or perspectives on the self, are one's social selves/identities: who I am in my own and others' eyes.[4]

Not surprisingly, symbolic interactionists stress the mutual interdependence of self and society. Selves cannot exist without society and society cannot exist without selves. A society provides shared language and meanings, which enable taking the role of the other, which in turn results in the acquisition of a variety of social self-conceptions. But individuals also tend to recreate the social order as they enact their social identities. This is because people can imaginatively anticipate others' evaluations of their identities and identity performances (Cooley, 1902). Because the positive regard of others is rewarding, individuals are motivated to modify their thoughts, feelings, and behaviors to conform. Thus, social control (or the social order) is partially a product of self-control. Lest this suggest an "oversocialized conception" of human beings (Wrong, 1961), symbolic interactionists also stress the indeterminacy in human behavior implied by the basic duality of the self: the I is the source of spontaneous, novel thought and action that cannot be predicted (Blumer, 1969). When new ideas or behaviors generated by the I are adopted by others and become widespread in a community or society, then social change on a larger scale is occurring. This understanding of the mutual interdependence of self and society underlies both McCall and Simmons's and Stryker's theories of social identity.

McCall and Simmons' Role-Identity Theory

McCall and Simmons's central concept, role identity, incorporates both the I and the me aspects of the self. They define a role identity as "the character and the role that an individual devises for himself as an occupant of a particular social position" (1978, p. 65). They stress that individuals carry out the broad dictates of social positions (the *role* part of role identity, reflecting the me) but do so with improvisations and flourishes that make role performances expressive of personal character and idiosyncrasies (for them, the *identity* part of role identity, reflecting the I). Individuals are able to improvise and embellish their me's because most social positions or roles only loosely prescribe appropriate behavior, allowing considerable latitude for creative, individualized performance.

For McCall and Simmons, social positions that can form the basis for identities include sociodemographic characteristics (e.g., race, gender, ethnicity), social roles (conventional and deviant, such as father and alcoholic), and positions defined by characteristic activities (e.g., hostess, thinker, golfer, opera lover). Because people usually have many role identities, McCall and Simmons's central theoretical problem is explaining which role identities individuals will value most and attempt to perform.

McCall and Simmons argue that people organize their multiple role identities in a "prominence" hierarchy that reflects the "ideal self." The prominence of any one role identity depends on its reward value, which is a complex weighted sum of various sources of reward—for example, the degree to which others positively support the identity, the degree to which one is personally committed to and invested in the identity, and the intrinsic and extrinsic gratifications gained through competent performance. When situations permit a choice among alternative lines of action, individuals will attempt to enact the more prominent or valued role identities. McCall and Simmons note, however, that situational contingencies also constrain choices among role-identity performances. Some situations are more likely to yield rewards for one identity enactment than another (e.g., enacting one's professor identity in the classroom is likely to gain more approval and support from students than enacting one's theatergoer identity). The demands of the situation, other people's role-identity needs or intentions, and their probability of supporting one's own must always be taken into account. Thus, identities of lower prominence may become situationally salient and performed. McCall and Simmons point out that one often experiences discrepancies between one's ideal self and one's situational self, producing pressures to validate, eventually, those valued role identities that have been neglected in social interaction. Alternatively, one may reorganize one's prominence hierarchy so that frequently performed situational identities become more important.

McCall and Simmons argue that legitimating and maintaining identities is a need and a never-ending process. They liken it to dusting a huge old house: by the time one gets to the upstairs, the downstairs is badly in need of dusting again (1978, p. 163). An efficient means of meeting this need for identity legitimation is through establishing durable interpersonal relationships: finding role-identity partners who can be relied upon for dependable mutual exchanges of support and rewards. More and more of one's self-structure can be incorporated into these relationships. For example, over time, a married couple does an increasing number of activities together—going to movies, playing cards with friends, going to church or synagogue, visiting family, having children—incorporating into and efficiently sustaining several role identities within the bounds of their relationship. Durable, multiplex interpersonal relationships tend to stabilize the prominence hierarchy, since the costs of giving them up increase as more aspects of the self become assimilated. Nevertheless, the individual's prominence hierarchy is still likely to change over time. Some role identities are devalued and sloughed off (due to lack of rewards, identity support, or situational opportunities to enact them), and other identities are made prominent or added to the hierarchy as the life course unfolds.

McCall and Simmons add that the broader social structure and cultural expectations also constrain the identity structure: "human beings are not socially equal but are ascribed and committed to a set of relative positions in the society, so that social opportunities for legitimating and enacting role-identities are limited, scarce, and differentially available" (1978, p. 233). In other words, broader social structural forces strongly influence the content and range of people's ideal and situational selves.

McCall and Simmons devote considerable theoretical attention to the intricacies of obtaining role-identity support from alters who are also attempting to sustain their own valued role identities; ego's and alter's identities may not match, and working compromises must be negotiated. Thus, these theorists focus primarily on the individual-level functions of role-identity enactment: sustaining and validating valuable (i.e., rewarding) aspects of the social self. Although not spelled out, one implication of their overall argument is that most individuals and their role partners will behave in ways that largely (but never exactly) recreate the existing social structure. Despite the potential for novelty built into the very nature of the self and the unconventional "role bargains" that may be struck with willing partners, the realities of differential power, status, and opportunity cannot easily be ignored. Although recognizing the possibilities of change always inherent in individuals and negotiable in social interaction, symbolic interactionists generally tend to explain more adequately how regularities in social behavior occur than how large-scale social change is brought about. This tendency can also be seen in Stryker's identity theory, to which we turn next.

Stryker's Identity Theory

Like McCall and Simmons, Stryker's central problem is explaining why individuals choose to enact certain roles among the many available in their identity repertoires. Stryker defines social identities as "reflexively applied cognitions in the form of answers to the question 'Who am I?'" (Stryker & Serpe, 1982, p. 206). Identity answers refer to positions in organized structures of relationships, to which are attached sets of behavioral expectations or roles. "Thus, a person may hold the identities of doctor, mother, churchgoer, friend, skier, etc., all of which collectively make up her self" (p. 206). Although Stryker's definition (and most of his empirical work) seems to equate social identities only with social roles, he has expanded this conception in subsequent discussions: "There is nothing in the essentials of [identity theory] that demands that self-concepts be limited to role-linked identities per se, in the sense of narrowly defined organizational roles" (Stryker & Statham, 1985, p. 357). He notes that the term social "position" refers more broadly to the types of person it is possible to be in a given society. Thus, social selves might also include "divorcee," "rebel," "fat person," and "shy person," as well as age, gender, race/ethnicity, and social-class statuses. Stryker's broader conception of identity, then, encompasses not only social roles but sociodemographic characteristics, social types of person, and personality traits—although his focus remains on roles.

Stryker's primary goal is to build social structure more explicitly into symbolic-interactionist explanations of the self-structure. Social structural influences were more an afterthought than central in McCall and Simmons's theory; neglect of structure is a recurrent criticism of symbolic interactionism in general (Stryker & Statham, 1985). Stryker reasons that because selves reflect society, and society is complexly differentiated and yet organized, selves must be complexly differentiated and organized, too (Stryker & Serpe, 1982; Stryker & Statham, 1985).

To incorporate social structure theoretically, Stryker develops the notion of identity commitment. In contrast to most conceptions that refer to subjective commitment, Stryker defines commitment in terms of the number of social ties or the affective importance of the social ties upon which each identity is predicated. "A man is committed to the role of 'husband' in the degree that the number of persons and the importance to him of those persons requires his being in the position of husband and playing that role" (Stryker & Serpe, 1982, p. 207). Identities that are based on more relationships or intense, emotionally positive relationships will be placed higher in the commitment hierarchy. Commitment hierarchies reflect the social structure, Stryker suggests, because gender, age, race/ethnicity, and social class largely determine the social networks into which people are born or may enter (Stryker & Serpe, 1982). For example, white middle-class adolescents are more likely than black working-class adolescents to be tracked into college-preparatory courses and are thus more likely to form many friendships and positive teacher-student relationships based upon a "good student" identity. Moreover, the costs of giving up any one identity depend upon the number or the affective intensity of the social ties on which it is based (Stryker & Statham, 1985). Thus, the higher in the commitment hierarchy, the more stable an identity is likely to be.

According to Stryker, identity commitment in turn strongly influences identity salience. He defines salience again not in subjective terms but as the probability of invoking an identity across a variety of situations (Stryker & Serpe, 1982). That is, salience refers to the likelihood that a person will enact a particular identity when given an opportunity to do so or when lines of possible action are open. Identity salience in turn influences the actual enactment of social roles: the higher the salience of a particular identity, the more time and effort one will invest in its enactment, the more one will attempt to perform well, the more one's self-esteem will depend on that identity, and the more one's identity performance will reflect generally shared values and norms.

Although the primary goal of Stryker's theoretical work is to explain the differential investment of people's time and effort in various social roles at the individual level, it is clear, given the origins of his theory in symbolic-interactionist thought, that the theory helps link identity performances to the maintenance of the social order. Because role identities are embedded in networks of relationships, people are (presumably) motivated to carry out the behavioral expectations attached to their role identities. Meeting others' expectations simultaneously maintains these interpersonal relationships and fulfills behavioral norms, thus sustaining the broader social order from which these identities were initially derived. Like all symbolic interactionists, Stryker also emphasizes that people may deviate from or renegotiate the norms governing identity behavior, due to the creativity and initiative of the I aspect of the self (Stryker, 1987). Ordinarily, however, structural constraints are sufficiently strong that deviations are empirically less frequent than behavior that conforms to broad social norms (Stryker, 1994).

Role-Identity Theory and Identity Theory Compared

Stryker places much less emphasis than McCall and Simmons do on the nuanced and tentative identity negotiations that occur between and among individuals. Stryker also deemphasizes the various rewards obtained through successful identity performances. Individual free will or agency (the I) is much less featured and the influence of social structure (through social me's) is much more highlighted in Stryker's approach than in McCall and Simmons's. Probably because Stryker is developing a deductive, testable theory of identity processes his approach is more deterministic than McCall and Simmons's.

Nevertheless, certain points of similarity between role-identity theory and identity theory should be readily apparent. First, both sets of theorists focus on social roles as the key bases of social identity (me's), although they acknowledge other bases (sociodemographic characteristics, social types of person, personality traits). Second, both rely on positive reflected appraisals from other people as motives for identity performance, although this motivation is much more clearly stated in McCall and Simmons's work than in Stryker's. Third, for both, identity hierarchies formed through rewarding social interactions predict the performance of certain role identities over others. Finally, despite individual-level analyses, both theories can be extended to explain the maintenance of the broader social order. This is because both theories stress the performance of roles, and roles are the basic building blocks of all social institutions (families, schools, government, the courts, etc.). It is the centrality of social roles in sociological conceptions of social identity that distinguishes them from psychological approaches, to which we now turn.

We's—Collective-Level Identities

Tajfel's Social Identity Theory

European psychologist Henri Tajfel developed social identity theory in deliberate contrast to what he saw as an individualist bias in American psychology. Tajfel argued for a more *social* social psychology—one that emphasized the wider social context within which individuals interact (Tajfel, 1981). A survivor of the dislocations of World War II, his goal was to understand prejudice and social conflict. He sought the explanation not in intra-individual or interpersonal processes, but in inter*group* psychological processes.

Social identity theory begins with categorization, the cognitive process that allows humans to streamline perception by separately grouping like and unlike stimuli. Tajfel demonstrated that people categorize social as well as nonsocial stimuli and that people use social categories to identify themselves and others. He defined social identity as "that part of an individual's self-concept which derives from his knowledge of his membership of a social group (or groups) together with the value and emotional significance attached to that membership" (Tajfel, 1981, p. 255). Research in this tradition has focused on such categories as race, ethnicity, class, and nationality; Tajfel illustrated his work with examples such as blacks and whites, Jews, Pakistanis, and French- and English-speaking Canadians. Importantly, Tajfel did not distinguish between these larger sociodemographic classifications and more structured, face-to-face groups such as clubs, sororities, and teams. For Tajfel, what defined a group was not its structure, function, or size, but its social reality; that is, a group exists insofar as its members "categorize themselves with a high degree of consensus in the appropriate manner, and are consensually categorized in the same manner by others" (Tajfel, 1981, p. 229). (As his well-known "minimal group" experiments showed, an identity can form on the basis of nothing more than a preference for the art of Klee as opposed to Kandinsky (Tajfel, 1981].) Note that when individuals identify with members of categories or groups, they posses "we" social identities (who we are), rather than "me" social identities (who I am).

Tajfel argued that because social categories are differentially valued within cultures, social identities also carry varying degrees of positive and negative value for the self. Individuals obtain an assessment of their in-group's value relative to an out-group through social comparison processes. Tajfel assumed that humans need positive and distinctive group identities, from which individual self-esteem and a sense of personal value can be derived (Hogg & Abrams, 1990). It is this need that motivates intergroup behavior. If the group with which an individual identifies is less highly valued than relevant out-groups, the individual becomes motivated to improve the group's standing. A variety of strategies are available (Tajfel & Turner, 1986). Those who perceive differential group evaluations as legitimate and group boundaries as permeable may try to move into the higher-status group. Where group boundaries are perceived as illegitimate and impermeable, collective strategies come into play, with group members jointly seeking (1) to change the evaluation of the comparison criterion, (2) to make a different positive and distinctive criterion salient, or (3) to shift comparisons to a different out-group. Finally, when boundaries appear to be illegitimate but changeable, lower-status groups will challenge the hierarchical structure itself, initiating direct social competition with the higher-status group. Regardless of the strategy selected, the dominant group is likely to resist, thus creating intergroup conflicts and competition.

Social Identity Theory and Role-Based Theories Compared

Clearly, sociologists' role identities and Tajfel's social identities are quite different psychological phenomena. Role-based identities are individual-level self-conceptions; they are identifications of the self *as* a certain kind of person in relation to particular role partners ("who I am"). Group- or category-based identities are collective-level self-conceptions; they are identifications of the self *with* a collectivity, claimed and enacted with or for other members ("who we are"). Because both types of identity are fundamentally social (one derived from role relationships with others, the other from memberships in collectivities or groups), we have persistently used terms other than "social identity" to distinguish between them. We shall continue to distinguish between "me's" and "we's," "individual" and "collective" identities, or for further variety now, "role-based" and "collectivity-based" identities.

These self-conceptions also serve very different functions on a theoretical level. Role-based identities provide individuals with senses of meaningful self, and identity performances are ways to garner self-validation, positive reflected appraisals, and perceptions of competence. In contrast, Tajfel's collectivity-based identity theory focuses on relations within and between groups—psychological affiliation within in-groups and collective competition and/or conflict with out-groups. The two types of identity also imply different large-scale consequences of identity-related behavior. Sociological identity theories help explain the perpetuation of the existing social order and therefore are more structural-functional in orientation, although interactionists also insist on the potential for indeterminacy and change built into the duality of the self. Tajfel's theory focuses on intergroup competition and social change as consequences of identity-related behavior and thus comes from a conflict orientation.

Three important issues crop up at this point. First, how frequent or enduring are experiences of "we" compared to experiences of "me"? Tajfel himself stated that "much (if not most) of our social behaviour in many circumstances may have very little to do with group membership" (1981, p. 242), a point with which we tend to agree. He suggested that there is an "interpersonal-intergroup continuum," with interpersonal behavior at one end based on actors' highly unique characteristics and intergroup behavior at the other (Tajfel, 1981, p. 238). Clearly, most daily interaction occurs at many points in between. Tajfel included in this midrange "professional" 'role' encounters—as between patient and doctor, student and teacher, car owner and mechanic" (Tajfel, 1981, p. 240). In other words, role relationships (me's) fall into the midrange.

Second, the conditions under which uniquely personal, role-based, and collectivity-based identities become salient or activated have not been well specified. Tajfel argued that collective identities become salient and influence group behavior only when situations stimulate intergroup categorizations and comparisons. But what are the key stimuli? Abrams (1992, p. 61) has criticized social identity theory for its tautological reasoning on this issue: "When social identity is salient individuals are said to act as group members (and should they fail to, the explanation is that social identity is not salient *enough*)."

Third, while Tajfel acknowledged the difference between role identities and collective identities, he was quite uncertain how these two types of self-conception relate to one another. He suggested (1981, p. 240) that all social interactions, including role-based interactions, are colored to some extent by the expectations and definitions associated with categorical memberships. This is an interesting but unelaborated idea in Tajfel's work. If the suggestion is valid, theory will need to specify in what ways and under what conditions such coloring occurs. We will return to how individual and collective identities might relate to one another after we discuss Turner's self-categorization theory, an outgrowth of Turner's earlier work with Tajfel.

Turner's Self-Categorization Theory

John C. Turner's self-categorization theory (Turner et al., 1987; Turner, Oakes, Haslam, & McGarty, 1994) seeks to understand further our psychological capacity for collective behavior. Whereas Tajfel's primary concern was intergroup relations, especially group conflict and competition, Turner focuses on the cognitive processes that create a collective sense of self and make possible such group-level phenomena as "social stereotyping, group cohesiveness, ethnocentrism, co-operation and altruism, emotional contagion and empathy, collective action, shared norms and social influence processes, etc." (Turner et al., 1987, p. 50). Generally, Tajfel's and Turner's theories are complementary; Tajfel's emphasizes *inter*group relations as a product of social identity, while Turner's emphasizes *intra*group behavior.

Turner and his colleagues define social identity as "self-categories that define the individual in terms of his or her shared similarities with members of certain social categories in contrast to other social categories" (Turner et al., 1994, p. 454). In other words, social identities are in-group versus out-group categorizations, employed "when we think of and perceive ourselves as 'we' and 'us' . . . as opposed to 'I' and 'me'" (Turner et al., 1994, p. 454). Turner uses as examples sociodemographic groupings by gender, race, social class, religion, and nationality. Like Tajfel, he does not distinguish theoretically between these larger classifications and organized groups as bases of social identity because members of each "develop a shared social categorization of themselves in contrast to others, which, in a given situation, becomes the basis of their attitudes and behaviour" (Turner et al., 1987, p. 203).

It is important to note that for Turner all identities are self-categorizations, differing only in their content and their level of abstraction or inclusiveness. The sense of oneself as human, what Turner calls the "superordinate" level (Turner et al., 1987, p. 45), is a more inclusive self-categorization than a collective identity, which is in turn more inclusive than a personal-level identity based on one's sense of uniqueness. (Turner does not mention or include role identities as part of this continuum, a deliberate omission to which we will return.) According to Turner, regardless of the level of abstraction, how self and other are categorized is always determined by their relative similarity or difference compared with other stimuli in the situation. Self-categorization theory is therefore both comparative and contextual in emphasis.

A key question for Turner is how one shifts from a personal to a collective identity. He argues that the cognitive process of *depersonalization* enables the shift, where one's unique characteristics fade from awareness and one defines oneself in terms of stereotypical group characteristics (Turner et al., 1987). Depersonalization in turn produces intragroup behavior. Cohesiveness occurs because individuals perceive similarity between themselves and others in the in-group; positive self-sentiments are extended to other members of the in-group as interpersonal attraction and liking. Group cooperation occurs because identifying oneself with others leads to a perceived similarity of interests and goals; concurrently, conformity takes hold because one adopts the stereotypical traits, attitudes, and behavioral norms of the group. In short, intragroup behaviors are consequences of depersonalization—perceiving the self as part of "we" or "us."

If collective identification and group behavior are the outcomes of depersonalization, what are its causes? According to Turner, the emergence of any self-categorization—superordinate, collective, or personal—is a result of the interaction of three factors: the relative accessibility of a category, its normative fit, and its comparative fit. Relative accessibility is the individual's "readiness" to use the category, based on "past experience, present expectations, and current motives, values, goals, and needs" (Turner et al., 1994, p. 455). Comparative fit reflects the degree to which the individual perceives fewer differences on relevant categorical characteristics *among* "us" than *between* "us" and others (Turner et al., 1987); this is also called "the principal of meta-contrast." Normative fit is the degree to which the stimuli in the context match normative stereotypes or beliefs about the comparison criterion or category that is being applied (Turner et al., 1994). These three factors together determine whether a self-categorization will become a psychologically active or salient influence in a particular situation. To revisit an earlier example, a cowboy is more likely to perceive and relate to another as a sheriff to the degree that his cowboy identity is readily accessible, the cowboy and sheriff each fit normative, stereotypical conceptions of cowboys and sheriffs, and the metacontrast between cowboys and sheriffs is contextually more relevant than that between, say, human beings (cowboy *and* sheriff) and stampeding buffalo.[5]

Turner and colleagues (1994) stress that self-categorizations are inherently fluid, variable, flexible, and context dependent. When the context changes (for example, when the local madam joins the cowboy and the sheriff), self-categorizations are also likely to change (male versus female may become more salient). Turner asserts that there is no stable self-categorization or self-concept except to the degree that the social structure itself generates stable contexts or social norms, values, and motives (Turner et al., 1994), making some social identities relatively more accessible and therefore more likely to be applied in a given setting.

Tajfel's Social-Identity Theory and Turner's Self-Categorization Theory Compared

Not surprisingly, given their earlier extensive work together (e.g., Tajfel & Turner, 1986), Tajfel's and Turner's conceptions of identity are highly similar. Both focus on "we" identities, where individuals perceive themselves as the in-group: identical to other in-group members and maximally different from out-group members (Turner & Oakes, 1986). Both rely heavily on social comparison and categorization processes in the formation of collective identities. Finally, both theorists view memberships in large-scale social categories and in face-to-face groups as bases for collective identities.

There are notable differences as well. As pointed out earlier, while Tajfel focuses more on *inter*group relations as a product of social identity, Turner's emphasis is on *intra*group relations as a product of self categorization. In contrast to Tajfel, whose primary purpose is to explain the dynamics of intergroup relationships, Turner's main goal is to explain how collective identification occurs. Finally, the two theories differ in the motivational bases for group behavior. Tajfel's more proximate explanatory mechanisms for collective behavior are needs for positive group distinctiveness and individual self-esteem, although evidence suggests that the central role given to self-esteem in the theory may need to be reevaluated (e.g., Abrams & Hogg, 1988; Deaux forthcoming; Hogg & Abrams, 1990). Turner posits depersonalization as the cognitive mechanism through which people become a psychological group. Individuals think and act in group-characteristic ways less because of human needs or motivations and more because they are cognitively identified with the group. Abrams (1994) argues, however, that self-categorization theory views people as motivated to reduce subjective uncertainty. Conformity to the prototypical positions of the category or group reduces disagreements and thus uncertainty among members (Hogg & Abrams, 1993).

Both theories leave certain problems unresolved. In both, interpersonal attraction and group cohesion are treated only at the cognitive level. Turner sees cohesion as a product of depersonalization: positive self-evaluations are simply generalized to other members of the ingroup. Although Tajfel includes the emotional significance of the group in his definition of social identity, like Turner he does not capitalize on the emotional (as opposed to cognitive) causes or consequences of collective identification. In fact, Tajfel rebuts claims that in-groups form due to emotional attachments among members, arguing instead that identification with a group as a whole accounts for in-group formation and cohesion (see Prentice, Miller, & Lightdale, 1994, for a detailed discussion and examination). Whether emotional antecedents and consequences of collective identification are as important as cognitive ones needs further theoretical (and empirical) consideration.

Another problem involves the theories' treatment of sociodemographic collectivities as just as determinant of group behavior as organizations in which members are closer in proximity, share common goals, and perceive common fate. Gender, race and ethnicity, and class identities are presumed to lead to in-group cooperation and out-group competition. Yet in practice, activists have found it notoriously difficult to develop political consciousness and concerted action within such collectivities. Members of sociodemographic groups such as "women" often vary dramatically on other social characteristics (e.g., African-

American women, lesbian women) as well as in their values, attitudes, and behaviors (e.g., women who are prolife versus those who are pro-choice). Self-categorization theory does, of course, expect variation in group formation as a function of perceived similarity on such dimensions as adherence to normative values, attitudes, and behavior (Turner et al., 1987, p. 61). But collective identification may be produced less often by a knowledge of shared category membership per se and more often by similarities in normative beliefs and behaviors within more delimited subgroups (Gurin & Markus, 1989; Skevington & Baker, 1989). In short, similarity on one social characteristic may be insufficient to generate the full range of intra- and intergroup behaviors described by Tajfel and Turner. At the very least, the conditions under which collectivities become able to act as groups need further specification (Deaux forthcoming).

Self-Categorization Theory and Role-Based Theories Compared

Like Tajfel's theory, Turner's approach to identity differs from sociological role-based identity approaches in several ways. Most obviously, Turner's theory emphasizes "we" states; sociological theories focus on "me" states. Beyond this, the two approaches differ regarding the presumed stability of social self-conceptions. McCall and Simmons and Stryker have suggested fairly stable and organized self-conceptions, embedded as these are in enduring social relationships, themselves broadly patterned by the social structure. In contrast, Turner et al. (1994, p. 458) "doubt whether the idea of self as a relatively fixed mental structure is meaningful or necessary." In fact, Turner argues against conceptualizing the self (whether it be at the individual or collective level) as a set of stored constructs, calling it instead "a flexible, constructive process of judgment and meaningful inference in which varying self-categories are created to fit the perceiver's relationship to social reality" (Turner et al., 1994, p. 458). Turner implies that identities are essentially fleeting phenomena, assembled anew every time relevant stimuli are present in a situation.[6] In our view, it seems inconsistent to argue, as Turner does, that all the components of self-relevant information, such as values, motives, and goals, are stored in memory as "cognitive resources" (Turner et al., 1994, p. 455) while representations of personal and collective selves are not. Moreover, it seems cognitively inefficient for individuals to construct or reconstruct whole identities each time relevant categorical stimuli appear. Turner also ignores research in the self-schema tradition that indicates that stable self-conceptions exist and that schemas not only heighten the speed and accuracy of information processing but increase selective attention to self-relevant cues (Gurin & Markus, 1989; Markus, 1977; Markus, Crane, Bernstein, & Siladi, 1982; Markus, Smith, & Moreland, 1985).

As Deaux (forthcoming) notes, identities generally have a persistent quality that makes them less context dependent than self-categorization theory may recognize or allow. Clearly, the degree to which individual-level and collective-level identities are fleeting and unstable or persistent and stable is a point of major disagreement requiring resolution.

Turner has explicitly distinguished self-categorization theory from some of the precepts of symbolic interactionism upon which role-based identity theories are founded. He views the self as a product of social comparison and categorization processes "in which the perceiver appraises the self *in relation to* others, not *from* the perspective of others" (Turner et al., 1994, p. 460, emphasis added). This assertion touches on a fundamental difference between Turner and Tajfel and the symbolic interactionists. McCall and Simmons and Stryker stress the causal importance of interpersonal processes in the development and maintenance of identities, while Turner and Tajfel give causal priority to cognitive processes. In sociological approaches, individuals apprehend and actively incorporate the evaluations, expectations, and behaviors of other people into their self-understandings. Moreover, interdependent behavior is required for identity maintenance; role partners mutually legitimate and sustain each other's identities. For Turner and Tajfel the processes of grouping self with others and of distinguishing "us" from "them" are solely cognitive.

Turner rejects role-taking processes as vaguely specified and without clear explanatory power. Although we agree that the dynamics of taking the role of the other have not been thoroughly explicated, evidence shows that individuals' self-evaluations *are* influenced by their perceptions of others' appraisals (e.g., Webster & Sobieszek, 1974). Moreover, in our view, processes of social comparison are equally underspecified. Although social comparisons do occur and have demonstrable effects on self-esteem and conformity (Suls & Wills, 1991), the conditions under which comparisons are made and the factors predicting the selection of comparison groups have yet to be systematized (Singer, 1981; Wills & Suls, 1991). Consequently, outside of laboratory experiments, where relative accessibility and the degree of comparative and normative fit can be manipulated, we suspect that Abrams's (1992, p. 61) wry comment would again apply, modified here to fit self-categorization theory: When a social self-categorization is salient, individuals are said to act as group members—and should they fail to, the explanation is that factors producing social self-categorization are not salient *enough*. We believe it inappropriate for Turner to dismiss role-taking processes out of hand, while sociologists should not ignore social-comparison processes. Whether role-based identities might spring (at least in part) from social comparisons and collectivity-based identities might derive (at least in part) from role-taking (for example, through taking the role of the *collective* other) should be explored both theoretically and empirically.

Individual-Level and Collective-Level Identities Contrasted

At this point we are able to summarize a number of gross contrasts between me states and we states. It should be clear by now that individual and collective identities tap very different aspects of self-understanding. "Me's" are identifications of the self *as an X* ("I am a mother"), while "we's" are identifications of the self *with other X's* ("We are Muslims"), where "X" in both cases refers to socially recognized types or groups of people. The processes that produce these two kinds of identity also differ, at least theoretically. Individual-level me's are derived from taking the role of the other and from responding to others' expectations and reflected appraisals, while collective-level we's are derived from cognitive processes of group social comparison, group categorization, and group evaluation. Further, individual and collective identities serve very different social functions. Me's provide the person with meaningful, usually positive self-conceptions, and the enactment of these identities helps to maintain the normative social order at the macro level (although the individual may always choose to deviate). We's serve to foster intragroup cohesion and conformity, thus promoting the status quo, or function to spark intergroup competition and conflict, thus potentially producing macrolevel social change.

One of our goals in distinguishing clearly between individual and collective identities is to challenge certain assumptions implicit in the social-identity literature. McCall and Simmons and Stryker (and those who draw from their work) generally tend to presume that social roles are the primary bases for "me" states; Tajfel and Turner (and those who draw from their work) generally presume that large-scale social categories and groups are the primary bases for "we" states. The social psychological literature has often equated social roles with me's and large-scale group categories with we's. To avoid creating confusion, we have not disputed these equations, though we can now argue that the implicit equivalences often found in the literature are limiting and unnecessary.

These common correspondences can be traced to uncertainties within the theories themselves. Tajfel was unsure how role identities "fit" within the broad confines of social identity theory. (Turner and his colleagues have more definite ideas.) In ironic contrast, role-identity theorists have been uncertain how broad sociodemographic characteristics fit within their own perspectives. We will argue that these difficulties can be resolved within each identity tradition by recognizing that social roles and sociodemographic categories (e.g., mother and Muslim) can be the basis of individual *or* collective identities (Deaux, Reid, Mizrahi, & Ethier, 1995).

Large-scale social categories have often presented a problem in symbolic interactionist approaches to the self. Theoretically, because societies are organized by gender, age, race and ethnicity, and so forth, and because selves reflect society, such sociodemographic characteristics should be important aspects of individual-level self-definition. In other words, a person may self-identity as a women or as Jewish, as opposed to identifying *with* other women or Jews. Indeed, analyses of answers to the Twenty Statements Test ("Who am I?") indicate that people routinely use these social categories self-descriptively (Gordon, 1968). Despite their potential importance and their empirical recurrence as individual-level identities, however, such self-definitions have usually been relegated by symbolic interactionists to secondary status in favor of identities based on roles (although see Burke & Tully, 1977).

We believe this secondary status can be explained by contrasting the ways that sociodemographic attributes and social roles organize society. Sociodemographic attributes divide people into broad social groupings or strata, regardless of roles: men and women; lower, middle, and upper class; and so forth. A key feature of these social attributes is that they are transsituational—"carried" by individuals into every situation (though they may not always be salient or activated). In contrast, social roles organize society by structuring relationships within particular institutions or systems; roles are not transsituational but situationally specific.[7] Psychology departments, for example, are small systems (within larger institutions) made up of the positions of chair, director of graduate studies, faculty, graduate students, and undergraduate majors. Incumbents enact the behavioral expectations (roles) attached to these positions when two or more department members are together actually or imaginatively.

Crucially, the hierarchical organization of positions within a system or institution is in part determined by the sociodemographic attributes of conventional incumbents. For example, faculty members are usually older and have more years of education than graduate or undergraduate students; these characteristics give faculty greater power, status, and authority over students and shape faculty and students' reciprocal rights and obligations. Indeed, broad social categories penetrate or permeate most social roles. In a very real sense, most roles are gendered, racialized, age-specific, and classed (e.g., fathers are always male; housecleaners are usually female and poor; bank presidents are usually male, white, older, and well-to-do). Househusbands, male nurses, and African-American physicians are treated as special cases of marginality or status inconsistency because they violate stereotypes about the auxiliary characteristics of typical role incumbents (Hughes, 1944; Kanter, 1977). Because most daily interaction occurs in role relationships (rather than purely on the basis of sociodemographic attributes), and because many, if not most, social roles imply auxiliary or embedded social characteristics, role identities have tended to become the central focus of sociological attention, with large-scale social attributes almost necessarily treated as secondary, auxiliary, or embedded features (see also Stryker, 1987).

Some sociologists who focus on role identities have gone so far as to argue that sociodemographic attributes influence the positions people hold and the style or quality of their social relations, but these attributes are not important bases for identities in themselves (e.g., Thoits, 1991). Other sociologists disagree, maintaining that sociodemographic characteristics serve as important role identities in their own right (e.g., Burke & Tully, 1977; McCall & Simmons, 1966/1978; Stryker, 1987). This seems justified because, as pointed out earlier, people in fact describe and think of themselves as individuals by using large-scale social attributes. The disagreement, we believe, stems from different usages of the term "role." It can be resolved by viewing sociodemographic characteristics as important (and understudied) sources of individual-level identities but analytically distinguishable from other individual-level identities based on social roles.

A narrow definition of "role" refers to two or more individuals in a specifiable relationship in which the role partners have reciprocal rights and obligations to one another (e.g., teacher-student, parent-child, employer-employee). A much looser meaning of the term refers to the types of people that it is possible to be in a given society (Stryker & Statham, 1985). This looser sense of "role" requires neither an interpersonal relationship nor normative behaviors to be performed vis-à-vis particular others. It is in this looser sense that we speak of "sex roles" or "gender roles"—ways in which males and females are expected to appear, believe, and act in general, regardless of the specific others with whom they are interacting. In this much looser sense "roles" encompass not only sociodemographic attributes but also types of people classified by their leisure activities (e.g., jogger, stamp collector), by their interpersonal styles (playboy, clown), by their dress, appearance, or physical characteristics (fat person, homeless person, disabled), by their personal preferences or values (pacifist, conservative), and by their role histories (unemployed, divorced, ex-con). Even personality traits (honest, extroverted) can be viewed as socially recognized ways of behaving in general (Stryker, 1987). We prefer to limit the term "role" to its narrower meaning and to understand individuals' sociodemographic (and other) self-descriptions as depicting the social types of people they are ("I am middle-aged, white, an atheist, a feminist"). When understood in this way, sociodemographic attributes used to describe the self are indeed individual identities but are not individual *role* identities in the narrower sense of the term "role." In short, individual-level identities (me's) can be based on social roles *or* sociodemographic characteristics *or* other types of person that it is socially possible to be (see also Stryker, 1987).

Tajfel's and Turner's quite brilliant sociological insight was that individuals think and act on occasion as members of a group or collectivity; that is, they think of themselves in terms of "us" and "we" instead of "I" and "me." How frequently and for how long individuals shift into "we" is a matter for debate, probably resolvable only through empirical observation. (We believe that we states are usually transitory since the bulk of daily behavior occurs within family and work relationships.) Nevertheless, Tajfel and Turner saw that we states are possible and have important group-level and societal-level consequences. They then grappled with how personal and especially role-based identities might fit within their theoretical frameworks (here again "role" is used in the narrower sense).

Tajfel viewed role identities and collective identities as different phenomena and suggested that roles might fall somewhere in the middle on a continuum from interpersonal to intergroup behavior. Nevertheless, he remained vague about these issues. In contrast, Turner and his colleagues explicitly subsumed role-related behaviors under collective phenomena, viewing social roles as simple enactments or fulfillments of in-group norms and responsibilities (Turner et al., 1994, p. 460).[8] They reasoned that roles are properties of groups because roles emerge from the behavioral similarities among and the functional interchangeability of in-group members.

We believe it is a mistake to treat individual role identities as by-products of collective identification, as Turner does. Although, for example, family members may occasionally think of themselves as a collective unit and behave similarly and interchangeably on its behalf, roles within the family are not performed by similar and interchangeable members. Rather, family roles are enacted by reciprocal, complementary, and socially dissimilar members such as parent and child. Further, role and collective identities involve different psychological states: in one, the person is psychologically merged with the role (this is who I am with respect to specific role partners); in the other, the person is psychologically merged with the group (this is who we are, including me). Finally, these identities serve different social functions (individual-level versus group-level functions). In short, role identities cannot be treated as derivative aspects of collective identification because they are qualitatively distinct psychological phenomena with different origins and consequences.

We do *not* preclude social roles as the basis for collective identification. By the logic of collective-identity theories, people may group themselves psychologically not only with others who share the same sociodemographic attribute or the same group membership but also with others who possess the same social role or even the same personality trait, since any and all of these social classifications are available for self-categorization at the collective level. For example, nurse practitioners may normally view themselves in terms of their occupational identity as individuals ("I am a nurse practitioner"), but may shift to a collective identity ("we nurse practitioners") when their abilities, status, or functions related to physicians are in question. Smokers (as a social type) might unite in opposition to lawmakers who restrict their freedom to smoke in restaurants or public buildings. Even workaholics might become "we" in reaction to social devaluation or a generalized threat from the medical establishment directed at people with their trait. The point is that social roles (*as well as* sociodemographic characteristics, other social types of persons, and personality traits) may serve as individual-level identities *or* as collective-level identities, depending on the context or situational contingencies.

Sociologists have had trouble with sociodemographic characteristics and psychologists have had trouble with social roles in developing their respective social-identity theories. In contrast to the limiting equivalences often drawn in the social psychological literature, however, sociodemographic characteristics can be treated as individual *or* collective identities and social roles can be treated as individual *or* collective identities. Similarly, group memberships, social types of persons, and personality traits also can be individual *or* collective identifications. The content of a self-categorization (i.e., whether it is a sociodemographic characteristic, social role, etc.) is less relevant than the psychological state (me versus we) and the social functions (ego- and societal-maintenance versus inter- and intragroup dynamics) of interest to the analyst. The central psychological difference is between "me" and "we," not among more specific identity contents.

Future Directions

When me states and we states are kept distinct, it is possible to raise additional questions about the relationships between them. Most obviously, what are the triggers for shifts from one psychological state to another? Turner and his colleagues (1994, p. 456) reply, "Fundamentally, it is where intergroup differences tend to be perceived as larger than intragroup differences that we tend to categorize self as 'we' instead of 'I.'" Conversely, people are more likely to switch from collective to role-based (or perhaps to personal) identities when perceived differences among in-group members outweigh their similarities.

However, Brewer's (1991; Brewer, Manzi, & Shaw, 1993) very interesting extensions of social identity theory suggest that collective identification itself can be a double-edged sword, motivating individuals to change their self-categorizations. She argues that people's needs to belong to a valued group can conflict with their needs for personal and group distinctiveness. She shows that when a group is large and highly inclusive (e.g., all college students), subjects' needs for differentiation cause them to align themselves with a minority group within the collectivity—even a low-status minority. By the same logic, identification with an in-group that is large and highly homogeneous on several positive attributes may stimulate needs for *individual-level* distinctiveness, producing a shift to a role-based or perhaps even a unique personal identity. Note that by positing needs for both individual and group distinctiveness, Brewer has added new conditions under which people may shift from "me" to "we" or vice versa.

A less obvious question is whether me states and we states can exist simultaneously. Turner contends that when depersonalization occurs, social role and social status differences within a group fade from awareness and differences between groups become salient. Thus, he would argue that these types of identity are mutually exclusive. Yet group behavior (decision making, cooperative action toward shared goals) often requires differentiated activities among members—some lead, some follow; some prepare speeches, others design pamphlets, still others keep track of the treasury or serve on subcommittees. Since divisions of tasks implies that various formal or informal roles are performed in the group, it seems possible that people may be simultaneously aware of themselves as, say, officers or committee members (role identities within the group) and as group members working together for the whole (collective identity). If simultaneous awareness can occur, then needs for positive individual distinctiveness may be satisfied at the same time as needs for positive group distinctiveness. We raise these possibilities because the lack of differentiation among members that theoretically accompanies depersonalization seems inconsistent with actual group behavior over time, at least for groups which have face-to-face interaction, shared goals, and perceptions of shared fate. (These observations highlight again the problems that stem from treating large-scale collectivities, such as those based in race, class, or gender, as theoretically equivalent to organized groups. Organized groups are by definition composed of roles, which in turn can engender me states.)

There are a variety of other unresolved issues about me states and we states, such as the conditions under which they are activated, whether one state is more frequent or enduring than another, how they are organized or structured, and how they may relate to one another. It is on this last issue that further theoretical steps should be taken.

Although it is generally understood that people have multiple selves or identities, theorists typically do not ask whether and how various me identities or we identities influence one another when they are combined (although see Heise, 1988; Simon, 1995). That people do see themselves in complex ways is clear from spontaneous answers to the "Who am I?" test. Respondents frequently add identity qualifiers (e.g., I am a working mother, a teenage tennis champion, an Hispanic college student). As Griffin and Korstad (1995) have observed, people normally hold combinations of social identities that taken together, interactively, should affect their social experiences, actions, and reactions.

We suggest that there are at least two ways that multiple identities might combine: through modifying one another or through merging with one another. First, the meaning and the enactment of a social identity that is situationally salient might be modified by other visible or known social identities. Heise (1988) provides empirical evidence that perceptions of the goodness, powerfulness, and liveliness of a social identity (e.g., "doctor") change significantly when observers acquire additional identity information (e.g., the doctor is "young" or "female"). Expectation-states studies (Webster & Foschi, 1988) also show that individuals' dominance and deference behaviors in groups depend on the combination of positive and negative social statuses that they hold relative to other group members. In short, the meaning and the enactment of salient social identities may be altered or modified by the presence of other identity information.

Alternatively, multiple identities may merge or fuse into one entity. For example, a woman may come to think of herself not only as a wife or a traditional woman but as a homemaker. Her gender-role orientation may shape her enactment of the wife identity to such an extent that the two become inseparable and are experienced—and perhaps even cognitively processed—in a unitary manner. When multiple identities are conjoined (e.g., student activist) or are fused within a single self-descriptive term (e.g., breadwinner = adult, parent, gainfully employed), their meaning and behavioral consequences may reside in the amalgamation itself. Such merged or fused identities may also be more resistant to change.

Just as multiple me's may modify or may merge with one another, so might multiple we's. At a World Conference on the Status of Women, for example, participant's might see themselves as "we women," but this dominant collective identity might be modified by various levels of collective identification: "we Ghanian women," "we African women," "we women from nonindustrialized countries," and so forth. Such qualified or modified collective identifications may influence which women's issues are perceived as most important and how various policy proposals are evaluated (see Griffin & Korstad, 1995). Alternatively, some we's may merge. Newsome (1995) points out that African-Americans' racial-ethnic identity often fuses pannationalism (identification with Africans in their homeland) with transethnicity (identification with oppressed peoples in general). She shows that international events (e.g., Israel's attacks on Egypt in the 1967 Arab-Israeli war) can sometimes create conflict between collective identifications that were merged, pitting African-Americans' loyalties to others of their homeland (Egypt) against loyalties to others with similar histories of oppression (Israel).

The above examples suggest how multiple me's or multiple we's might combine to affect meaning and behavior. Earlier we raised the possibility that people may be simultaneously aware of, say, a role-based identity ("I'm a volunteer for the Republican Party") and a collectivity-based identity ("I'm calling on behalf of the Republican Party—we need your vote"). How might me-we combinations operate? We have argued that me's and we's are qualitatively different states, so it follows that they probably do not merge. However, concurrent awareness of "me" and "we" may modify the way each identity is enacted. For example, members may devote more or less time and energy to their roles within the group (as "me") depending on the strength of their collective identification. Conversely, leaders may more strongly profess and abide by a group's ideology than followers (acting as or for "us") because leaders are aware of the importance of their own roles within the group.

There likely are other ways that multiple identities combine in form and function that we have not anticipated. In future work, more detailed examinations of identity combinations will better capture the complexities of social reality and social experience.

Acknowledgments: We are grateful for the very helpful comments of Richard Ashmore, Kay Deaux, Lee Jussim, and Sheldon Stryker on an earlier version of this chapter.

Notes

1. We do not use the term "group-level" identity because "group" is a more restrictive concept signifying face-to-face relationships, boundaries, bonds that endure, and usually some internal structure (minimally, a leader and followers). "Collective-level" or "collective" identity is more inclusive than "group." Throughout this chapter, "collectivities" denote either aggregates or face-to-face groups in which members have at least one large-scale social attribute in common.

2. An important exception within psychology is Markus's (1977) self-schema theory, which has focused mainly on individual-level self-conceptions (although see Gurin & Markus, 1989, for an application to collective schemas). We do not consider self-schema theory in this chapter because the theory's primary purpose is to describe the information-processing functions of identities rather than explicate their social origins and consequences.

3. *The* self (the "I") is that aspect of the person that experiences, reflects on experience, and acts upon self-understandings that are derived from experience (Gecas & Burke, 1995; McCall & Simmons, 1966/1978; Weigert et al., 1986). The self is aware of and can behave in terms of *a* self or *an* identity (the "me"—a more specific understanding of oneself as a women or a professor, for example).

4. For many theorists (e.g., Gecas & Burke, 1995; McCall & Simmons,

1966/1978; Weigart et al., 1986), social selves refer to private self-definitions, while social identities refer to who or what one is in the eyes of others—i.e., to public selves. We employ the terms "self" and "identity" interchangeably because people usually invest themselves in (identity with, internalize) their public identities. However, the distinction can be useful when private and public definitions of self do not correspond (for example, when one has been erroneously labeled by others, or when one has imaginatively taken on an identity of which others are unaware).

5. According to Turner et al. (1987), social self-categorizations do not depend on the number of people in a context. A lone cowboy and sheriff may shift into collective identities on the basis of their perceived differences just as easily as might numerous cowboys and lawmen on encountering each other.

6. Although Turner et al. (1994) say that collective identities are stable only when social structures are stable, they seem to mean that roughly the same collective identity will be constructed each time structurally recurrent contextual cues stimulate the self-categorization.

7. Roles are situationally specific but role *identities* may be transsituational. For example, one may carry one's "father" identity into a variety of nonfamilial situations.

8. This point may best apply to organized groups that have internal structures, rather than to collectivities or classes.

References

Abrams, D. (1992). Processes of social identification. In G. M. Breakwell, (Ed.), *Social psychology of identity and the self concept* (pp. 57–99). London: Academic/Surrey University Press.

Abrams, D. (1994). Social self-regulation. *Personality and Social Psychology Bulletin, 20*, 5, 473–483.

Abrams, D., & Hogg, M. S. (1988). Comments on the motivational status of self-esteem in social identity and intergroup discrimination. *European Journal of Social Psychology, 18*, 317–334.

Alexander, C. N., Jr., & Wiley, M. G. (1981). Situated activity and identity formation. In M. Rosenberg & R. H. Turner (Eds.), *Social psychology: Sociological perspectives* (pp. 269–289). New York: Basic Books.

Blumer, H. (1969). *Symbolic interactionism: Perspective and method.* Englewood Cliffs, NJ: Prentice-Hall.

Brewer, M. B. (1991). The social self: On being the same and different at the same time. *Personality and Social Psychology Bulletin, 17*, 475–482.

Brewer, M. B., Manzi, J. M., & Shaw, J. S. (1993). In-group identification as a function of depersonalization, distinctiveness, and status. *Psychological Science, 4*, 88–92.

Burke, P. J., & Reitzes, D. C. (1991). An identity theory approach to commitment. *Social Psychology Quarterly, 54*, 239–251.

Burke, P. J., & Tully, J. C. (1977). The measurement of role identity. *Social Forces, 55*, 881–897.

Callero, P. L. (1985). Role-identity salience. *Social Psychology Quarterly, 48*, 203–215.

Cooley, C. H. (1902). *Human nature and the social order*. New York: Scribner's.

Deaux, K. (forthcoming). Social identification. In T. Higgins & A. Kruglanski (Eds.), *Social Psychology: Handbook of basic mechanisms and processes*. New York: Guilford.

Deaux, K., Reid, A., Mizrahi, K., & Ethier, K. A. (1995). Parameters of social identity. *Journal of Personality and Social Psychology, 68*, 280–291.

Gecas, V., & Burke, P. J. (1995). Self and identity. In K. S. Cook, G. A. Fine, & J. S. House (Eds.), *Sociological perspectives on social psychology* (pp. 41–67). Boston: Allyn and Bacon.

Goffman, E. (1963). *Stigma: Notes on the management of spoiled identity*. Englewood Cliffs, NJ: Prentice-Hall.

Gordon, C. (1968). Self-conceptions: Configurations of content. In C. Gordon & K. Gergen (Eds.), *The self in social interaction: Vol. I. Classic and contemporary perspectives* (pp. 115–136). New York: Wiley.

Griffin, L. J., & Korstad, R. R. (1995). Class as race and gender: Making and breaking of a labor union in the Jim Crow South. *Social Science History, 19*, 425–454.

Gurin, P., & Markus, H. (1989). Cognitive consequences of gender identity. In S. Skevington & D. Baker (Eds.), *The social identity of women* (pp. 152–172). London: Sage.

Heise, D. R. (1988). Affect control theory: Concepts and model. In L. Smith-Lovin & D. R. Heise (Eds.), *Analyzing social interaction: Advances in affect control theory* (pp. 1–33). New York: Gordon and Breach.

Hogg, M. A., & Abrams, D. (1990). *Social identifications*. London: Routledge and Kegan Paul.

Hogg, M. A., & Abrams, D. (1993). Towards a single-process uncertainty-reduction model of social motivation in groups. In M. A. Hogg & D. Abrams (Eds.), *Group motivation: Social psychological perspectives*. Englewood Cliffs, NJ: Prentice-Hall.

Hughes, E. C. (1944). Dilemmas and contradictions of status. *American Journal of Sociology, 50*, 353–359.

James, W. (1950). *The principles of psychology* (Vol. 1). New York: Dover. (Original work published 1890).

Kanter, R. M. (1977). Some effects of proportions on group life: Skewed sex ratios and responses to token women. *American Journal of Sociology, 82*, 965–990.

Markus, H. (1977). Self-schemata and processing information about the self. *Journal of Personality and Social Psychology, 35*, 63–78.

Markus, H., Crane, M., Bernstein, S., & Siladi, M. (1982). Self-schemas and gender. *Journal of Personality and Social Psychology, 42*, 38–50.

Markus, H., Smith, J., & Moreland, R. L. (1985). Role of the self-concept in the perception of others. *Journal of Personality and Social Psychology, 49*, 1494–1512.

McCall, G. J., & Simmons, J. L. (1966/1978). *Identities and interactions*. New York: Free Press.

Mead, G. H. (1934). *Mind, self, and society from the standpoint of a social behaviorist*. Chicago: University of Chicago Press.

Newsome, Y. D. (1995). Middle East Enigma: Transnationalism in Black-

Jewish Conflict. Unpublished paper, Department of Sociology, Vanderbilt University, Nashville.

Prentice, D. A., Miller, D. T., & Lightdale, J. R. (1994). Asymmetries in attachments to groups and to their members: Distinguishing between common-identity and common-bond groups. *Personality and Social Psychology Bulletin, 20,* 484–493.

Rosenberg, M. (1981). The self-concept: Social product and social force. In M. Rosenberg & R. Turner (Eds.), *Social psychology: Sociological perspectives* (pp. 593–624). New York: Basic Books.

Simon, R. W. (1995). Gender, multiple roles, role meaning, and mental health. *Journal of Health and Social Behavior, 36,* 182–194.

Singer, E. (1981). Reference groups and social evaluations. In M. Rosenberg & R. Turner (Eds.), *Social psychology: Sociological perspectives* (pp. 66–93). New York: Basic Books.

Skevington, S., & Baker, D. (1989). *The social identity of women.* London: Sage.

Stryker, S. (1980). *Symbolic interactionism: A social structural version.* Menlo Park, CA: Benjamin/Cummings.

Stryker, S. (1987). Identity theory: Developments and extensions. In K. Yardley & T. Honess (Eds.), *Self and identity: Psychosocial perspectives* (pp. 89–103). New York: Wiley.

Stryker, S. (1994). Freedom and constraint in social and personal life: Toward resolving the paradox of self. In G. Platt & C. Gordon (Eds.), *Self, collective behavior and society: Essays honoring the contribution of Ralph H. Turner* (pp. 119–138). Greenwich, CT: JAI Press.

Stryker, S., & Serpe, R. T. (1982). Commitment, identity salience, and role behavior: Theory and research example. In W. Ickes and E. Knowles (Eds.), *Personality, roles, and social behavior* (pp. 199–218). New York: Springer-Verlag.

Stryker, S., & Statham, A. (1985). Symbolic interaction and role theory. In G. Lindzey & E. Aronson (Eds.), *Handbook of social psychology* (3rd ed., pp. 311–378). New York: Random House.

Suls, J., & Wills, T. A. (1991). *Social comparison: Contemporary theory and research.* Hillsdale, NJ: Erlbaum.

Tajfel, H. (1981). *Human groups and social categories: Studies in social psychology.* Cambridge: Cambridge University Press.

Tajfel, H., & Turner, J. C. (1986). The social identity theory of intergroup behavior. In S. Worchel & W. G. Austin (Eds.), *Psychology of intergroup relations* (2nd ed., pp. 7–24). Chicago: Nelson-Hall.

Thoits, P. A. (1991). On merging identity theory and stress research. *Social Psychology Quarterly, 54,* 101–112.

Thoits, P. A. (1992). Identity structures and psychological well-being: Gender and marital status comparisons. *Social Psychology Quarterly, 55,* 236–256.

Turner, J. C., with Hogg, M. A., Oakes, P. J., Reicher, S. D., & Blackwell, M. S. (1987). *Rediscovering the social group: A self-categorization theory.* Oxford: Basil Blackwell.

Turner, J. C., & Oakes, P. J. (1986). The significance of the social identity concept for social psychology with reference to individualism, interactionism, and social influence. *British Journal of Social Psychology, 25,* 237–252.

Turner, J. C., Oakes, P. J., Haslam, S. A., & McGarty, C. (1994). Self and collective: Cognition and social context. *Personality and Social Psychology Bulletin, 20,* 454–463.

Turner, R. H. (1978). The role and the person. *American Journal of Sociology, 84,* 1–23.

Webster, M., Jr., & Foschi, M. (Eds.). (1988). *Status generalization: New theory and research.* Stanford, CA: Stanford University Press.

Webster, M., Jr., & Sobieszek, B. (1974). *Sources of self-evaluation: A formal theory of significant others and social influence.* New York: Wiley.

Weigert, A. J., Teitge, J. S., & Teitge, D. W. (1986). *Society and identity.* Cambridge: Cambridge University Press.

Wills, T. A., & Suls, J. (1991). Commentary: Neo-social comparison theory and beyond. In J. Suls & T. A. Wills (Eds.), *Social comparison: Contemporary theory and research* (pp. 395–411). Hillsdale, NJ: Erlbaum.

Wrong, D. (1961). The oversocialized conception of man in modern sociology. *American Sociological Review, 26,* 183–193.

CRITICAL CONTEXTS

PART III

STATISTICAL METHODS

The Historical Formation of Selves

The topic of the self is different from many other psychological topics in that psychology has to share it with a number of other disciplines, sociology and psychiatry, to mention only the most obvious ones. In that way "self" differs from "intelligence," for example, which became an almost uncontested psychological category many years ago. That had a lot to do with psychologists' early production of a specific technology that they very successfully marketed as a socially useful way of measuring intelligence. Having no rivals in the scientific study of intelligence, psychologists rapidly became the recognized experts. They could get away with saying that intelligence was what intelligence tests measured because they controlled the only viable technology in the area. Similar things happened in connection with other categories, such as perception and learning, where psychologists were able to decide among themselves what these terms referred to because they had the field pretty much to themselves.

But in regard to the self, psychologists are not in such a fortunate position. This is a term that has long been in vogue, not only in neighboring disciplines, but in fields such as philosophy, literary studies, and history. Moreover, psychologists are the latecomers here. For several decades, while the self was virtually a taboo topic in psychology, other disciplines were producing a stream of intellectually challenging, and often conceptually subtle, studies of this topic. The chances of "self" becoming essentially a technical psychological term in the way that "intelligence" has do not seem high. Nevertheless, psychological interest in the self has taken a sharp upswing in recent times (see chapter 1).

What Kind of History?

This situation presents the historian of the psychological self with some special problems. A literature review of recent work, though extremely useful, would have too shallow a time perspective to constitute a historical study. Going further back, there is much of historical interest in the ideas of self psychologists like G. W. Allport and C. R. Rogers, not to speak of William James and James Mark Baldwin. But within the discipline there is little genuine historical continuity when it comes to the topic of the self. As has been pointed out before (Rosenberg, 1988), the very promising opening represented by the writings of James and Baldwin was not followed up within psychology. With certain exceptions, much of the more recent work is in no sense a continuation of the work of the handful of psychologists of the self who flourished around mid-century. This absence of a coherent intradisciplinary tradition of psychology of the self suggests that a broader historical approach is likely to be more rewarding than one limited to the discipline of psychology. Furthermore, this sharing of the topic between several disciplines also indicates that a historical approach to the self ought to transcend disciplinary boundaries.

But the most important argument in favor of painting a broad historical canvas derives from the fact that the impulses for much psychological work do not originate solely within the discipline of psychology. This is particularly true for the topic of the self, which psychology is obliged to share with many other, more venerable, stakeholders. There may have been little empirical work on the psychology of the self until quite recently, but there were certainly ideas about the self, some of them within psychology and some outside it. Several of these ideas even form part of the taken for granted, unexamined, cultural assumptions that psychologists share with other members of their culture. Before empirical hypotheses can be put to the test they must be formulated, and they can only be formulated by drawing on the repertoire of culturally given categories that are available to the investigator. This is all the more true when we are dealing with a concept such as the self, which is still the focus of broad cultural, rather than narrow technical, meanings. It is at this broader level that we are likely to find the historical continuities that are so elusive at the disciplinary level.

But there is still the question of the connection, if any, between these broader cultural continuities and the dicipline of psychology. A British historian of psychology, Graham Richards (1989), points out that people began to address psychological topics in a relatively systematic way and developed a range of psychological concepts long before the advent of the modern discipline of psychology. Accordingly, he makes a distinction between the history of what he calls Psychology with a capital P, which is disciplinary history, and the history of small-p psychology, which deals with the emergence and transformation of specifically psychological ways of interpreting everyday life and its problems.

Does this differ from Ebbinghaus's oft-repeated distinction between psychology's long past and short history? Yes, because what Ebbinghaus, and those who thought like him, had in mind was a distinction between a relatively recent scientific study of psychological phenomena and an ancient tradition of prescientific speculation about those phenomena. The assumption was that what changed historically were not the psychological phenomena themselves but only our way of studying and thinking about them. Like the objects studied by physical science, the objects studied by psychological science had no history— they were natural objects, not historically constituted objects.

Quite to the contrary, the distinction between capital-p and small-p psychology implies that the phenomena studied are not natural objects at all but historically constituted objects. Before there could be anything for the discipline of psychology to study, people had to develop a psychological way of understanding themselves, their conduct, and their experiences. They had to develop specifically psychological concepts and categories for making themselves intelligible to themselves. Only then did aspects of people's lives present themselves as potential objects of psychological study, rather than, say, objects for religious meditation or moral disputation. The history of small-p psychology, therefore, is not the history of primitive "anticipations" of later scientific formulations but the history of the emergence of those discursive objects without which the science of psychology would have had nothing to study.

"Nothing to study" is a pretty radical formulation, and I am quite prepared to leave open the question of whether the science of psychology can lay claim to any objects of study that are "natural" in the way that the objects of physics are. That is not an issue that requires an answer here. What does need to be addressed is the status of the self. And to the self, as understood in present-day psychological discourse, we must surely assign a historical rather than a natural status. Assigning it a natural status would imply that, like the objects of the physical world, the self always remains the same, irrespective of how we think and talk about it. This is not plausible. The self's features cannot be independent of historically changing ways of describing and relating to it. Much of the evidence for this has already been marshaled by psychologists such as Baumeister (1986, 1987), Cushman (1990), Gergen (1991), Sampson (1989), Verhave and van Hoorn (1984).

Here I want to supplement this literature in two ways: First, I want to focus on a specific form of small-p psychology that has played a foundational role for the conceptualization of the self in twentieth-century social science. That line of development is closely associated with the emerging project of philosophical empiricism. Its concepts regarding the self can, however, be seen as the product of constructive processes whose significance transcends this specific historical case. Therefore, in the second part of this chapter, I want to switch to a more general level of analysis in order to discuss the way in which the historical formation and reconstruction of the self was actually accomplished. Here I will focus on two crucial factors to which recent work has drawn attention: first, so-called "technologies of the self," as discussed by Michel Foucault; and second, the central role of language in the articulation of a psychological conception of the self.

The Empiricist Self

Philosophical Background

Within the network of small-p psychological conceptions about the self there is a historically formed kernel that provides the key to understanding the whole. That kernel has to do with the way we regard the self as an object of knowledge. All attempts at investigating the self in the social sciences are based on the assumption that the self can be known empirically. In most cases, the assumption is that it can be known empirically in much the same way as other natural objects, that its separate features can be systematically observed, described, and studied, as one would study any other natural phenomenon. This implies that the self exists as a phenomenon, quite independently of the methods we use to observe it and the language we use to describe it. In this conception, the way we obtain knowledge about the external world becomes the model for the way we are thought to obtain knowledge of the self (Toulmin, 1977).

Historically, this is a relatively recent conception whose origins are closely connected to the rise of empiricism and its brand of mental philosophy. When this conception was first explicitly formulated, three hundred years ago, it was widely regarded as not only contrary to common sense, but as distinctly shocking. That was because the self was being put forward as providing a new basis for the unity of the human individual, one that could be empirically known like any other natural object. But, as everyone knew at that time, the real basis for the unity of the human individual was the immortal soul, and that was not another object of empirical knowledge.

To understand the implications of the empiricist turn from soul to self, we need to look at it a little more closely. Although this kind of historical turn is usually based on slow changes, it is sometimes possible to pinpoint a particular text in which a new way of talking about a topic emerges with such force and clarity that it directs subsequent discourse into new channels. The watershed for the concept of the self is John Locke's *Essay Concerning Human Understanding*, or, more precisely, the second edition of that work, published in 1694, to which Locke added a chapter that discussed the nature of personal identity in entirely secular terms (Locke, 1694/1959). It is no exaggeration to say that this chapter dominated English-language discussions of the self for at least two centuries. In 1890 William James still refers to the "uproar" caused by Locke's views (James, 1890, 1:349). "Uproar" was not too strong a word (Fox, 1988); in 1714, twenty years after the appearance of Locke's chapter, the topic of personal identity made the pages of *The Spectator*, and in the years that followed virtually all the major figures of eighteenth-century British philosophy—Berkeley, Butler, Hume, Reid—had their say on the matter.

Locke had obviously touched a nerve by treating the core of the human individual as an observable natural phenomenon. He accomplished this by raising the question of personal identity. How do I establish that I am now the same person I was last year? Although the question was new, it was both meaningful and unsettling for his audience. It was meaningful because in the increasingly commercialized society of post-Revolutionary England social identities conferred by birth—such as class, kinship, and occupation—were no longer immutable. Not only were individuals becoming separated from their social identities, but that separation was accelerating at a time when the hold of theologically based notions of personal identity was also beginning to weaken. Where neither social identity by descent nor the immortality of the soul provided a sufficient guarantee of permanence and stability, personal identity had to come into question.

Locke's solution to the problem was to base it on a continuity of consciousness of self. This consciousness of self accompanies all our experiences as a kind of shadow, "it being impossible for anyone to perceive without *perceiving* that he does perceive." He explains that "since consciousness always accompanies thinking, and it is that which makes everyone to be what he calls self, and thereby distinguishes himself from all other thinking beings, in this alone consists personal identity" (Locke, 1694/1959, p. 449).

This argument depended on the use of two crucial terms—"consciousness" and "self"—in what was then quite a novel manner. "Consciousness" seems to have been virtually a neologism whose first recorded occurrence hardly antedated Locke's *Essay* (*Oxford English Dictionary*, 1989, 3:756). Locke had invented a way of describing what was then a new way of experiencing the world by separating the sense of self from the experience of one's inner and outer actions. In this world one never just lives or acts; one is always "conscious" of one's self living and acting. This Lockean self has been rather aptly named the punctual self (Taylor, 1989), for it is conceived as a point within experience or a focus of concern that is "disengaged" and quite separate from any specific actions and experiences. Such a view forms the psychological counter-part to Locke's political doctrines, which were based on a model of society as an aggregate of strictly separate individuals, rather than a collective entity.

In the course of the eighteenth century, the Lockean conception of the self replaced the older notions and provided the basis for a new, empiricist, tradition that is still powerful. Later Anglo-Saxon texts on mental and moral philosophy were usually based on the assumption of a profound distinction between persons on the one hand and their acts and experiences on the other. People did not live in, were not manifest in, their acts and experiences—they *owned* them, stood behind them as their proprietors. Therefore, reflexive actions—actions that take other actions as their objects—were now increasingly conceived as also directed at a separate entity, the self, as the owner of the actions. In Alexander Bain's words: "there is a tendency in men. . . . to look with a warm eye upon some portion of their activity, and ac-quire a tenderness for that as for another person" (Bain, 1859/1977, p. 131).

What were the psychological consequences of this relentless process of self-objectification? One was the foundation of the belief that the self is composed of empirical phenomena that can be observed, analyzed, and known, just like other worldly phenomena. This leads to a descrip-tively analytic literature on the psychology of the self that differs from recent work only because of its lack of a quantitative and experimental technology. Bain's mid-nineteenth century work is a prime example of this older literature.

Authors in the empiricist tradition did not make their contributions independently of one another. They participated in a discourse of texts that spanned long periods of time and relatively large distances. Indi-vidual authors took positions with regard to each other's work, and, while they sometimes disagreed with each other, they shared a basic outlook. In their contributions they gradually developed a new set of terms and concepts that elaborated the basic empiricist scheme. At times, they picked up these terms from everyday use but gave them a place in the network of concepts that constituted empiricist mental philosophy. In doing so, they invested them with the authority ac-corded to terms of scholarly discourse. More than everyday lay terms, such terms were generally assumed to be more than mere rhetorical inventions and to refer to real entities. In the course of time, such entities could be appealed to for explanations of human conduct.

Motivational Implications

The conception of an empirical self as a distinct object of regard made it possible to reformulate some fundamental principles of human conduct in a recognizably modern way. When the English word "self" first appeared as a noun, around 1300, it has the negative connotations derived from a long tradition of seeing the individual primarily as a sinner. The *Oxford English Dictionary* (1989, 14:906) quotes an early example: "Oure awn self we sal deny, And folow oure lord god al-myghty." This opposition between the self as an incarnation of wickedness and divine goodness survives for several centuries. An example from 1680 declares that "Self is the great Anti-Christ and Anti-God in the world" (*Oxford English Dictionary*, 1989, 14:907).

By contrast, the empiricist scheme made it possible to endow the self with a much more positive value. The self became a term used to describe those observable phenomena that defined an individual's unity and identity. This observation was, however, private and introspective. The self was a private possession that each individual discovered in him or herself, which meant that it could become an object of concern as well as an object of knowledge. Indeed, Locke had anticipated this by making the self the locus of experiences of pleasure and pain. But soon this was generalized to positing the self as the object of a special class of praiseworthy motives.

We see this in the writings of many eighteenth-century British moralists. An early example is provided by Bishop Butler, a prominent Anglican divine who makes a fundamental distinction between two kinds of selfishness, namely, "cool or settled selfishness" and "passionate or sensual selfishness" (Butler, 1726/1950). What he had in mind was the difference between the feelings of the moment and long-term self-interest. This latter Butler referred to as "the cool principle of self-love or general desire of our happiness" manifested by "a regard to our own interest, happiness and private good" (Butler, 1726/1950: 52). The trouble with humanity, the good bishop proclaimed, was not that people had too much self-love but too little. This was the beginning of a modern tradition that distinguishes motives that take the self as their object from other kinds of motives and that treats the self as an essentially motivational concept.

Butler's principle of self-love marks the beginning of a long discursive tradition in which the self is conceptualized as a self-reflective monitoring agent oriented to the maximizing of its own overall advantage. From the beginning, this functioned both as a supposed description of how human beings actually conducted themselves and as a prescription for how they ought to conduct themselves. It was a normative concept developed by the moral philosophers of a commercial civilization, but it was also presented as a factual account of something called "human nature." Monitoring one's actions with regard to "one's good on the whole" (Reid, 1788/1969) was something that was normal for all humankind, in both the statistical and the prescriptive senses of "normal." Increasingly, deviance came to be ascribed to a failure in this monitoring mechanism and hence to a weakness in the self.

Self-monitoring and Social Control

The idea of the self as the core of a monitoring mechanism introduces an aspect of the empiricist conception of the self that was to assume foundational importance for the social sciences. Most of the questions about the self posed and investigated by twentieth-century social science depend upon a certain way of conceiving the origins of prosocial action. To put it crudely, individuals learn how important the good opinion of others is to their welfare and therefore seek to influence that opinion by appropriate conduct. This implies a process of social learning in which the self features as an object of social control. But this notion is already found in Locke's educational writings where parents are advised not to reward children for specific behaviors but to supply them with signs of their general esteem for their "carriage," or style of good conduct (Locke, 1693/1968). In other words, it is the person, not the specific action, that forms the appropriate object of social control. Those who followed on the path that Locke had indicated soon elaborated on a clear implication of his analysis—namely, that a psychology of self-monitoring was the necessary complement of a political theory that regarded society as an aggregate of individuals.

This line of development first becomes apparent in the early work of Adam Smith, better known for his construction of a system of political economy based on the assumption of the existence of an entrepreneurial self. His prominence as an economist has tended to overshadow his role in the prehistory of other social sciences, though that role was by no means a minor one. His earlier work on "The Theory of Moral Sentiments" (Smith, 1813) introduces certain conceptualizations regarding the self whose echoes are still detectable more than two centuries later. The subtitle of this work provides a clue to its importance: "An analysis of the principles by which men naturally judge concerning the conduct and character, first of their neighbours, and afterwards of themselves." What we find here is a clear recognition of the dependence of people's relationship to themselves on their relationship to others.

This insight marks an important development in the conceptualization of the Lockean "punctual" self. As we have seen, the idea of such a self had depended on the distancing of the self from its objects and from the actions of the individual. Persons no longer lived in their actions but adopted an observational, monitoring stance towards them. Smith realized that this could only happen through individuals "endeavouring to view them with the eyes of other people, or as people are likely to view them." A solitary individual, according to Smith, would not be concerned with his own character, but "bring him into society, and he is immediately provided with the mirror which he wanted before. It is placed in the countenance and behaviour of those he lives with, which always mark when they enter into, and when they disapprove of his sentiments" (Smith, 1813, 2:251).

In Smith's writing, the basic outline of the modern map of the self, which British moralists had worked on since the closing years of the seventeenth century, is just about complete. The distancing of the self from its incarnations that had been implicit in Locke becomes explicit. Smith advises us to "become the impartial spectators to our own character and conduct." When we observe ourselves in this way we become, in a sense, two people:

> When I endeavour to examine my own conduct, when I endeavour to pass sentence upon it, and either to approve or condemn it, it is evident that, in all such cases, I divide myself, as it were into two persons; and that I, the examiner and judge, represent a different character from that other I, the person whose conduct is examined into and judged of. (Smith, 1813, 2:255)

This is the conceptualization of the self that will come to dominate the emerging discourse of the social and psychological sciences in the nineteenth and twentieth centuries. William James's "social self" (James, 1890) and Charles Horton Cooley's "looking glass self" (Cooley, 1902) could be regarded as variations on a theme composed by Adam Smith, and there are echoes of it in George Herbert Mead's "taking the role of the other" (Mead, 1934).

Beginning in the latter part of the eighteenth century, a new vocabulary of self-evaluation came into being, one very different from the religious vocabulary current until then. A flow of approval or disapproval, directed at the self rather than at specific actions, was now thought to accompany individuals throughout their lives. There were Protestant sources for this belief, but by now self-evaluation had become secularized. The standards and criteria for self-evaluation were no longer derived from absolute religious values but simply from the individual's social environment. Accordingly, the language of self-evaluation changed from that of sin and guilt to that of "blame-worthiness" (Smith, 1813, 2:257) and "self-esteem" (Reid, 1788/1969, p. 238; Bain, 1859/1977, p. 134). The objectified self that persons now harbor within them is above all an object of approval and disapproval, both by others and by the person herself. This self is always conceived as an object of variable worth, and therefore the desire to raise or maintain its worth comes to be regarded as an identifiable human motive.

Again, we find that insidious mixture of the normative and the allegedly factual that is so characteristic of empiricist mental and moral philosophy. The preoccupation with self-worth is presented as a universal feature of "human nature," but this is no neutral fact, like having five toes. It is a feature that is highly applauded, because it is seen as crucial for the achievement of self-improvement, a core cultural value. Preoccupation with self-worth is seen as driving people to better themselves, and, in the process, bringing about social progress as well. Self-esteem is not just something that people happen to have; it is something they *ought* to have.

To the modern reader, however, the earlier psychological literature exudes a certain presumption of worthiness. This is because a particular set of social expectations was assumed to command virtually universal respect. In quite a fundamental way, these expectations were tied to rigid social distinctions of gender, age, social class, race, and so on. Women were not expected to compare themselves to men, the poor not to the rich, and the black not to the white. As long as individuals accepted the validity of these distinctions and applied the corresponding expectations to themselves, anxiety about self-worth was kept within certain limits; this changed with the corrosion of traditional patterns and the fracturing of common standards. Individuals are now on their own, with the result that the assessment of self-worth becomes much more problematic. At the same time, the normative pressure on individuals to engage in self-assessment is stronger than ever. That creates an enormous pool of "low self-esteem" that can always be invoked as an explanation of life's failures. The validity of such explanations depends on the tacit acceptance of a particular philosophical framework with deep historical roots in the culture. Within this framework, the maximization of self-worth is regarded as both potent and beneficial. The possibility that, given different premises, it might be neither is not often considered.

There are, however, two ways of interpreting the image of a self that is constantly assessing its own worth. One can see the person as suffering the results of such a process—as a victim of low self-esteem—or as actively engaged in maximizing the flow of approval from others. Adopting the latter point of view makes salient other possibilities opened up by the loosening and fracturing of social expectations. If individuals are no longer bound by rigidly circumscribed conventions, they are free to maneuver among different patterns of conduct, always intent on choosing the alternative that promises the best returns from others and from one's reflected self-esteem. That leads to the late twentieth-century view of the self as social strategist, a view first given prominence in the writings of Erving Goffman (1959). It is also the view that underlies a great deal of contemporary social psychological work on the self (Banaji and Prentice, 1994).

Common to both the passive and the active interpretation of the empiricist self-image is the assumption of a distancing of the self from itself. Over time, the empiricist way of talking about selves as the observers of their own acts and experiences was extended to the relation of the self to itself. That is, the self's relationship to other people became a model for its relationship to itself: the self knows, evaluates, and controls itself as it knows, evaluates, and controls other people, and, as other people know, evaluate, and control it. Such beliefs provide both a model for how social control works in an antiauthoritarian society and a legitimation of such control.

The Splitting of the Self

Once the self is conceptualized as an entity that observes, evaluates, and controls itself, it is, in principle, a divided entity, unlike the soul, whose indivisibility was of the essence. While the original division was between the self as observer and as observed, in the nineteenth century, with the increasing emphasis on the topic of self-control, the division between ideal self and real self assumed more prominence. From this position it was not a tremendous step to assert that there could be not just two selves in the same person, but many.

That step was indeed taken, in the late nineteenth century, in the context of psychopathology. Ribot, Janet, and others in France, as well as Morton Prince, Putnam, and others in America, began to make sense of certain clinical material by interpreting it in terms of the existence of multiple selves in the same individual. Where previously there had been virtually no psychiatric cases recorded as cases of "multiple personality," they now appeared with some frequency (Hacking, 1992). In making remembered biography the criterion of selfhood, medical investigators were actually reviving the original Lockean definition of the self in terms of the continuity of conscious memory. In France, at least, this was probably a result of an ideological agenda that involved rescuing "the soul" from the obscurantist patronage of clerics and idealist philosophers and transforming it into a natural entity, "the self," that could function as an object for investigation by clinical science (Hacking, 1994). Much of the original controversy about Locke's invention of the modern conception of the self had been due precisely to its provocative replacement of the spiritual soul with an entirely secular and this-worldly entity. By the end of the nineteenth century, however, the leadership in the battle against the soul had passed from philosophers to men of science.

To begin with, the multiply split self only appeared in a pathological context, but its "normalization" followed quite soon. In his treatment of the self, William James (1890) devoted considerable attention to the medical literature on "alternating selves," but his own innovative extension of the basic idea took a very different turn with the assertion that multiple selves were involved in everyday social life. The principle that individuals take their standards for self-evaluation from those with whom they interact had been part of the empiricist scheme from the very beginning. (James actually quotes Locke in this context.) While earlier, it had been tacitly assumed that "civilized" people all shared more or less the same standards, James, writing in late nineteenth-century America, recognized that individuals exposed to varying evaluative standards will apply different standards to themselves in different social situations. Already familiar with the notion of "alternating selves," James declares that individuals have multiple social selves. In fact, he draws the general conclusion that "a man has as many social selves as there are individuals who recognize him and carry an image of him in their mind" (James, 1890, 1:294).

With the exception of Baldwin (1897/1973), American psychologists left the further development of this way of talking about the self to sociologists such as Cooley, Mead, and, later, Goffman. When the concept of the self did make a reappearance in American psychology toward the middle of the twentieth century, it was deployed in a very different way. When Gordon Allport made his classical plea for the readmittance of the self into psychology, he did so on the grounds that this concept was required in order to do justice to the unity and coherence of the human personality (Allport, 1943). It was not the fragmented self, by now identified with the disciplines of psychiatry and sociology, that was to be welcomed in the house of psychology, but a much older and more idealistic version. Much the same can be said of Carl Rogers's notion of a "true self" that is explicitly juxtaposed to the vagaries of social life. Somewhat later, the ideal of wholeness, of coherence, of unity, reappears in psychological "consistency" theories. For a time, it seemed as though there was a tacit division of labor among the disciplines, with psychology seeing only the benign, rationally coherent face of the self, and the others seeing only its unhappy face, riven by division and conflict. More recently, that has begun to change (Markus & Wurf, 1987; see also chapters 2 and 3).

The self may be an example of what some philosophers have called "essentially contested concepts" (Gallie, 1956). Such concepts are not to be confused with mythical or confused concepts. Essentially contested concepts do not refer to matters that cannot be verified in experience, but they are saddled with an inescapable ambiguity—common examples of such concepts are "democracy" and "social justice." Such concepts can function as a focus for different ways of understanding common problems, but the different understandings also reflect the existence of different interests in constituting a field of human experience in one way rather than in another. It is an unfortunate by-product of our high degree of specialization that these interests tend to become identified with specific disciplines and subdisciplines, each laboring to carve out its own distinct territory.

Formative Practices

I have concentrated on the content of a specific conceptual framework that constituted the historical roots of much social-science theorizing about the self in the twentieth century. I want to now shift to another level of analysis and raise some general questions about how this kind of content is produced historically. For there is no doubt that these ideas are the products of some process of thought, discovery, invention, or construction. Therefore, any historical analysis that did not go into the question of how these ideas were produced would at best be seriously incomplete, and probably dangerously misleading.

Better then to confront the question of historical production, even at the risk of stirring up a hornet's nest. I will try to minimize that risk by imposing rather strict limits on what is relevant to the present context. I will not address purely historiographic questions arising from grand theories of history, such as the Great Man theory, the Marxist theory, the Idealist theory, and so on. There is, however, one aspect of the historical production of concepts that has a special relevance for concepts of the self, both past and present. This aspect has to do with the active nature of the process by which concepts are changed and maintained. Obviously, when people change their ideas about something, they are *doing* something, engaging in some action. Constructionists also believe that even when concepts appear to be stable there is constructive work going on to keep them that way (Shotter, 1993). Nowadays, this formative component in the production of concepts is often subsumed under the category of practice, a broad notion that does, however, have the more specific connotation of joint action, collective rather than individual activity. Practice is *not* a psychological concept.

There are two varieties of practice that have played a significant role in the historical formation of selves; one is linguistic practice. I have already mentioned that John Locke's articulation of a new conception of the self depended on the novel deployment of two terms, "self" and "consciousness." I also noted the emergence of a new vocabulary of psychological terms referring to the self, like "self-esteem" and "alternating selves." Before I discuss the more general significance of such linguistic developments for psychological conceptualization, I want to draw attention to another kind of historical practice which the French scholar, Michel Foucault, has labeled "technologies of the self."

Technologies of the Self

Beginning with the 1965 publication of *Madness and Civilization*, a translation of parts of a larger work, the contributions of Michel Foucault have exerted an enormous influence internationally, especially on approaches to the history and philosophy of science and medicine. I am only concerned with one relatively small and rather specific aspect of his work, and the use I make of it differs from that of Foucault himself. His primary interest was in the historical formation of particular kinds of selves as moral subjects, but in pursuing this interest he identified certain self-forming practices (Foucault, 1988) that are important, even when the question of the self as moral agent is not on the agenda.

In his studies of what he calls "The History of Sexuality," Foucault (1986) drew attention to a considerable classical literature on the topic of self-care. This literature is part of, and emerges out of, a more extensive body of writing on the good life, on how to conduct oneself in order to live a life worth living. Such a project entails a systematic reflexive examination of one's own behavior, and this was often accomplished through the medium of specific practices, such as keeping a diary and writing personal letters to friends.

By engaging in these practices individuals learned to examine aspects of themselves in such a way that the results of such an examination would be intelligible to others. This is quite obvious in the case of letter writing, but keeping a diary meant following generally recognized rules regarding its form and content and often engaging in a kind of imaginary or postponed communication with some other. Quite generally, self-reflection relied on the guidance of another person recognized as being specially equipped for this role. An early prototype for such a relationship is presented in those Platonic dialogues (e.g., Alcibiades 1) in which Socrates offers to guide the self-improvement of a younger man.

In drawing attention to the importance of "technologies of the self" in antiquity, Foucault has identified an aspect of historical self-formation whose role is not limited to that period. The most important technology of the self introduced by Christianity is undoubtedly the practice of confession, though it was not until 1215 that an annual confession was demanded as a minimal and universal requirement by the Roman church. Not long before that, the attention of confessors had begun to shift from overt actions to the intentions behind actions, even for the laity (Morris, 1972). Individuals were now held accountable, not only for their overt conduct, but also for their hidden desires. Inevitably, their inner life became an object of increasingly intensive self-scrutiny.

During the Renaissance and the Reformation, the practice of confession became gradually more systematized through the multiplication of manuals for the guidance of confessors and through the institution of a general confession that addressed not just specific sins but an entire life of sin (Hahn, 1990). With the Reformation came a decisive shift of attention from specific acts and specific penances to the individual's life as a whole. What had previously been practiced only in monastic institutions now became an everyday expectation: individuals are held accountable for the entire pattern of their lives. Self-monitoring now becomes highly systematizd. A regular, often daily, examination of one's conscience is now expected, and this encourages the keeping of diaries among the literate, those of John Evelyn and Samuel Pepys being the best known.

To generalize, the term "technologies of the self" refers to socially sanctioned procedures that encourage or teach people to address themselves systematically to their own feelings, thoughts, and conduct. As this happens, individuals develop particular ways of experiencing, of understanding, themselves. Keeping in mind that these procedures are not idiosyncratic but socially institutionalized, it follows that in societies with significantly different "technologies of the self" people will tend to experience and understand themselves in different ways. As these technologies change historically, there will be corresponding changes in the way individuals relate to themselves. Of coures, this process should not be taken to imply a mechanical kind of causal effect. The point is that self-concepts are not constructed once and for all; they require reconstruction and maintenance through the exercise of specific socially sanctioned "technologies." Systematic changes in the latter will therefore be accompanied by changing self-concepts.

Was the new self-concept of classical empiricism also maintained by new "technologies of the self"? It is not difficult to identify such technologies. Diaries, already mentioned, really come into their own at this time. Even more striking is the proliferation of literary productions whose preoccupation with the inner life of the self differs so much from previous norms that it prompted one well-known literary historian to entitle his study of the period "The Invention of the Self" (Lyons, 1978). It is at this point that autobiographical texts not only become much more numerous but take on what, to the modern reader, comes across as a "genuine" autobiographical quality. Older autobiographical writing, such as it was, almost invariably served didactic, missionary, or polemical purposes (Weintraub, 1978). But now the private rather than the public life of the individual, the idiosyncratic rather than the typical features, became the focus of attention and define the true self.

However, introspection—the practice that underlies these literary productions and that has a particularly intimate connection with the empiricist philosophy of the self—is not itself literary in character. The polemical use and abuse to which the term "introspective psychology" was subjected by the behaviorists should not blind us to the historical specificity of that category. In fact, "introspection" was another new word that appeared in the time of John Locke (*Oxford English Dictionary*, 1989, 8:26). Its origins were theological, and it referred to the systematic examination of one's conscience, a post-Reformation practice. Gradually, the practice of examining the content of one's mind became separated from its origin in moral accounting, and that opened up tremendous possibilities for the elaboration of the self as an object to itself.

Invariably, the empiricist philosophers appealed to the evidence of inner experience to justify their conclusions about the nature of the self. Look inside yourself and you will find what I am describing, was their message, explicitly and implicitly. They assumed consciousness was a phenomenon of nature with definite features that were there to be detected by the use of some "inner sense" and then labeled and described. Nowadays, we would be more inclined to say that they actually constructed most of these features in the act of looking for them and applying verbal labels to them. Without the practice of introspection, Locke's invention of a self based on the continuity of consciousness would have had no basis for existence.

The secular doctrine of classical empiricism introduced a highly analytic type of introspection in which one was directed always to look for the sensory elements that were supposed to form the basis of all mental life. This resulted in two alternative ways of understanding the self, reductionist and skeptical. In the reductionist mode—prominent in British introspectionist psychology right up to its final incarnation in the work of Titchener—consciousness of self was essentially a matter of proprioceptive sensation. In the skeptical mode, famously represented by the philosopher David Hume, the very existence of the self was put in question because one could be certain only of the existence of bodily sensations, and these did not constitute a self. Closer to our own time, the Gestalt psychologists were most explicit in their rejection of the classical introspectionist technology (Köhler, 1929) and were thus able to offer their phenomenal self as a replacement for both reductionism and skepticism (Koffka, 1935).

It is not difficult to identify examples of twentieth-century technologies of the self, two of which have been closely associated with the discipline of psychology. One of these is psychotherapy; the other involves various techniques employed in psychological research. Of course, the term "psychotherapy" covers a multitude of procedures, but many of them do seem to involve precisely the sort of reconstitution of people's understanding of themselves that Foucault regarded as typical for technologies of the self. Psychotherapeutic protocols often read like textbook examples of a class of procedures devoted to the systematic reformation of the self in accordance with a particular image of it. Nikolas Rose (1990) has provided an extensive analysis of current psychotechnologies along lines suggested by the work of Foucault.

Psychological research procedures are less likely to be thought of as technologies of the self, though in many cases they do fit the definition of systematic social procedures that have the effect of constituting selves in a particular way. They do this on two levels. On a more general level, psychological experiments involve a particular type of social situation that demands a certain kind of self-presentation on the part of experimental subjects (and of experimenters, for that matter). Subjects must assume a particular situated identity (Alexander & Knight, 1971; Hales, 1985) that differs in certain respects from the identity conferred on them in other social situations. One cannot investigate the self without constituting the self in a certain way by the very process of investigation. This does not mean that experimental selves are unreal; it means that they are different, and that affects the generalizability of experimental results.

On a more specific level, experimental procedures can be thought of as technologies of the self in the sense that different investigative procedures may well constitute the self in somewhat different ways and therefore provide evidence for different theories of the self. For example, experimental subjects asked to respond to a prepared list of adjectival trait names have to organize their self-reflection in a particular manner if their responses are to count as appropriate. The same goes for subjects asked to tell the experimenter "how I am now," "how I would like to be," and "how I would not like to be" (Rosenberg, 1988). But the organization of their self-reflection is unlikely to be the same in the two cases, if only because in the second case the self is explicitly structured in terms of a distinction between the real and the ideal. This little example, chosen almost at random, must suffice to illustrate a very general point—namely, that different research procedures constitute the object investigated, in this case the self, in often very different ways (Danziger, 1990). Therefore, the evidential value of empirical findings becomes problematic where cross-procedural comparisons are involved (Danziger, 1988).

Languages of the Self

Before one can begin to think of investigating something like the self psychologically one has to encounter such a thing in one's experience. That is the case even if one decides, as a result of one's investigation, that the self is just a label for something else. Without the label there would have been no corresponding discriminable unit of experience, and no empirical hypotheses regarding such a unit could have been formulated. It is language that enables us to do this, and the limits of language also constitute the limits of what we can knowingly investigate. But language is not static—it changes historically, and as it changes the possibilities and directions of our investigations, or of our experiences for that matter, change too.

I have already mentioned the negative connotations that were associated with the word "self," at least until the end of the seventeenth century, and in some circles probably well beyond that. Two other lexical phenomena are also worth noting. First, between the middle of the sixteenth and the middle of the seventeenth century, we can observe the appearance of numerous new compounds of self in the English language: self-praise (1549), self-pride (1586), self-contained (1591), self-regard (1595), self-made (1615), self-interest (1649), and self-confidence (1653). Second, it is of interest that many of these new compounds were often used in a positive or neutral, rather than a negative, sense (Rosenthal, 1984).

This development supplies at least part of the background that makes the nature of John Locke's contribution intelligible. The changes in everyday talk were not deliberately intended by anyone, they just happened, as such changes usually do. Of course, there were reasons for this in the changing everyday life of individuals who were less and less bound by rigid feudal relationships and increasingly free to enter into contractual-type relationships with other individuals. These changes are well known and can simply be accepted as providing the necessary background for other processes that, until recently, have attracted less attention among historians.

Just as changes in everyday social, economic, and religious life provided the background in which linguistic changes were embedded, so the latter should be seen as providing an important part of the background for the more deliberate accomplishments of the philosophers. In this vein, Toulmin (1977) has traced the absence in ancient Greek texts of anything like the modern self-concept to a profound structural difference between their language and ours. In early eighteenth-century Britain, the earlier changes in everyday self-related talk had helped to form an experiental basis that the reflective discourse of the philosophers could appeal to. Once people find themselves using a whole set of self compounds in a secular and positive context, it becomes possible to raise questions about an entity that all these compounds have in common. Such an entity would seem to be something quite different from the soul. It was an object, not for moral judgment or theological doctrine, but for analytic dissection and rational investigation.

The invention of the empiricist self should therefore be seen as part of a specific cultural history, ultimately depending on particular changes in social relations and language. The aspect of specificity is worth noting: other cultures have had a different historical experience, and this is reflected both in their language and their philosophical tradition. As has recently been pointed out in the psychological literature, the English word "self" cannot be translated into Spanish, or even into French, without undergoing a significant change of meaning (Harré & Gillett, 1994; Muhlhausler & Harré, 1991). Had I chosen to base this history of the self on German-language texts, the results would have been very different. In fact, it could not have been a history of the *self* at all, because the German equivalent of that substantive never achieved any prominence in either everyday or reflective discourse. I would have had to write about another entity, the *Ich*, conventionally translated as "ego," whose properties only partially coincide with those of the Anglo-Saxon self.

But it was the empiricist, Anglo-Saxon self that American social science inherited and that has helped to shape its taken-for-granted background knowledge. That has had consequences, not only for American social science itself but also for social scientists in other countries who have been exposed to American influence. So we now get a certain amount of European psychological literature that is beginning to join in the discourse about the self, and because this literature affects what is said in counseling sessions and in popular psychological texts, we can no doubt expect a gradual internationalization of the empiricist self. This illustrates a very important aspect of the link between everyday and reflective discourse. The formative linguistic influences flow in both directions. Historically, significant changes in everyday language may have had their effect on philosophical, and ultimately on scientific, conceptualizations, but over time the latter act back on everyday use and understanding. This circle makes it possible to verify empirically, among culturally selected populations, what social scientists think about the self.

In conclusion, I need to make explicit a certain view of the role of language that has formed the basis for these remarks. In treating language as a formative practice, I am obviously departing radically from a tradition that regarded language as essentially representational. It used to be believed that, for clear thinking, words had to mirror a totally independent nonlinguistic reality. Sometimes words could also be used to do other things, such as command or persuade, but that was not legitimate in science or in any rational discussion, for that matter. Words as representations were regarded as completely separable both from what they represented and from their nonrepresentational function.

Applying this view to language about the self leads to the idea that there is something inside a person that remains the same no matter how we describe it, but that happens to be accurately represented by the word "self." If that were the case, the empiricist belief that we know the self in the same manner as we know other things would be correct; the self is there, we observe it, we label it, and it is still there, unaffected by our activity. In other words, the self would be a natural object, in the same way that flowers or stomachs are natural objects. Like a stomach, it would be inside us but in our minds rather than in our bodies.

Nowadays, few would be prepared to defend this view of the self, but the alternative is to accept the consequences of the recognition that talk about the self cannot be separated from what the self is. There are two levels on which the inseparability of the self and its representation operates. First, there is the intrapersonal level. Here, John Locke got it right. The self *is* a matter of personal experience, though in the light of later philosophizing we might want to add, "whatever else it might be." Locke overlooked what we all tend to overlook: our own role in shaping the things we investigate and discuss. In using words such as "consciousness" and "self" in novel ways, he was encouraging his readers to make discriminations they would not otherwise have made, to reorganize their map of their own experience, to shift the distribution of their attention. But because the targets of these changes were also the very persons who were performing them, the object of those changes was not the same before and after the change. In the case of the self, the referent cannot maintain the same kind of independence from the representation that occurs with natural objects in everyday life (Taylor, 1985).

But talk about the self also operates on the interpersonal level. No sane person wishes their talk about the self, or their writing, or their research to be simply a monologic act of representation. In their self-directed actions people commonly also address themselves to an actual or potential audience. They expect to have some effect, and sometimes of course, they produce effects they did not anticipate. As one modern philosopher put it in a famous phrase, we do things with words (Austin, 1962). In the case of self words, what we do with them in some sense affects who we are, for the self is not just a private secret but also something on public display. This accounts for the "uproar" that Locke's views about the self caused. In presenting these views, he was *doing* something historically (see Skinner, 1988): he was putting a new kind of person on view. After that, it became possible for others to articulate and proclaim their own identification with that kind of person, and, in their everyday social life, this made a difference to who they were.

Language is indeed a formative practice. That is something that has been maintained by a theoretical tradition that for about two centuries has provided an alternative to the mirror theory of language (Taylor, 1985). The Sapir-Whorf hypothesis represents a relatively recent and relatively familiar contribution to this tradition. But one does not need to accept this radical version of the tradition to appreciate the formative role of language in concepts of the self, for the self is by definition a reflexive concept. It is both the subject and the object of verbal description and therefore has a capacity for self-definition. Unless, like some philosophers, we assign to the self as subject a metaphysical status, beyond this-worldly influences, the verbal description of itself as object must affect the self as subject. That means that the kinds of self-descriptions available to it will determine the boundaries of the kind of self it can be. But the categories of self-description, as I have tried to show, are historically constituted and culturally variable, making the self a historical, rather than a natural, object.

This does not mean that we should never study the self with methods developed for the study of natural objects. For producing knowledge that is of practical use within a culture marked by the pervasiveness of naturalistic assumptions, such methods have their place. What is questionable is the implication that this kind of knowledge can ever transcend its inevitable cultural myopia. To do that, we have to break down the protective boundaries that the naturalistic discipline of psychology erected around itself when it was young but which have now become counterproductive. Disciplinary isolation is not good for our understanding of the self. It makes it too easy to go for the little problems and label the big problems someone else's business. To get somewhere with the bigger problems, psychologists, sociologists, psychiatrists, historians, and a few others need to talk to each other more than they have been. The present volume represents a significant step in this direction.

References

Alexander, C. N., Jr., and Knight, G. W. (1971). Situated identities and social psychological experimentation. *Sociometry, 34*, 65–82.

Allport, G. W. (1943). The ego in contemporary psychology. *Psychological Review, 50*, 451–478.

Austin, J. L. (1962). *How to do things with words*. New York: Oxford University Press.

Bain, A. (1977). *The emotions and the will* (D. N. Robinson, Ed.). Washington, D.C.: University Publications of America. (Originally published 1859.)

Baldwin, J. M. (1973). *Social and ethical interpretations in mental development*. New York: Arno. (Originally published 1897.)

Banaji, M. R., and Prentice, D. A. (1994). The self in social contexts. *Annual Review of Psychology, 45*, 297–332.

Baumeister, R. F. (1986). *Identity: Cultural change and the struggle for self*. New York: Oxford University Press.

Baumeister, R. F. (1987). How the self became a problem: A psychological review of historical research. *Journal of Personality and Social Psychology, 52*, 163–176.

Butler, J. (1950). *Five sermons preached at the Rolls Chapel and a dissertation upon the nature of virtue*. Indianapolis: Bobbs-Merrill. (Originally published 1726.)

Cooley, C. H. (1902). *Human nature and the social order*. New York: Scribner's.

Cushman, P. (1990). Why the self is empty: Toward a historically situated psychology. *American Psychologist, 45,* 599–611.

Danziger, K. (1988). On theory and method in psychology. In W. J. Baker, L. P. Mos, H. V. Rappard, and H. J. Stam (Eds.), *Recent trends in theoretical psychology.* New York: Springer.

Danziger, K. (1990). *Constructing the subject: Historical origins of psychological research.* New York: Cambridge University Press.

Foucault, M. (1965). *Madness and civilization.* New York: Random House.

Foucault, M. (1986). *The care of the self: The history of sexuality* (Vol. 3). New York: Pantheon.

Foucault, M. (1988). *Technologies of the self.* Boston: University of Massachusetts Press.

Fox, C. (1988). *Locke and the Scriblerians: Identity and consciousness in early eighteenth-century Britain.* Berkeley and Los Angeles: University of California Press.

Gallie, W. B. (1956). Essentially contested concepts. *Proceedings of the Aristotelian Society, 56,* 167–198.

Gergen, K. J. (1991). *The saturated self: Dilemmas of identity in modern life.* New York: Basic Books.

Goffman, E. (1959). *The presentation of self in everyday life.* Garden City, NY: Doubleday.

Hacking, I. (1992). Multiple personality disorder and its hosts. *History of the Human Sciences, 5,* 3–31.

Hacking, I. (1994). Memoro-politics, trauma and the soul. *History of the Human Sciences, 7,* 29–52.

Hahn, A. (1990). Beichte und Biographie. In M. Sonntag (Ed.), *Von der Machbarkeit des Psychischen.* Pfaffenweiler: Centaurus.

Hales, S. (1985). The inadvertent rediscovery of self in social psychology. *Journal for the Theory of Social Behavior, 15,* 237–281.

Harré, R., and Gillett, G. (1994). *The discursive mind.* London: Sage.

James, W. (1890). *Principles of psychology.* New York: Holt.

Koffka, K. (1935). *Principles of Gestalt psychology.* New York: Harcourt, Brace.

Köhler, W. (1929). *Gestalt psychology.* New York: Liveright.

Locke, J. (1959). *An essay concerning human understanding.* New York: Dover. (Second edition originally published 1694.)

Locke, J. (1968). Some thoughts concerning education. In J. Axtell (Ed.), *The educational writings of John Locke.* New York: Cambridge University Press, pp. 109–325. (Originally published 1693.)

Lyons, J. O. (1978). *The invention of the self: The hinge of consciousness in the eighteenth century.* Carbondale, IL: Southern Illinois University Press.

Markus, H., and Wurf, E. (1987). The dynamic self-concept: A social psychological perspective. *Annual Review of Psychology, 38,* 299–337.

Mead, G. H. (1934). *Mind, self and society from the standpoint of a social behaviorist.* Chicago: University of Chicago Press.

Morris, C. (1972). *The discovery of the individual 1050–1200.* London: SPCK.

Muhlhausler, P., and Harré, R. (1991). *Pronouns and people.* Oxford: Blackwell.

Oxford English Dictionary (2nd ed.) (1989). London: Oxford University Press.

Reid, T. (1969). *Essays on the Active Powers of the Human Mind.* Cambridge, MA: MIT Press. (Originally published 1788.)

Richards, G. (1989). *On psychological language.* London: Routledge.

Rose, N. (1990). *Governing the soul: The shaping of the private self.* London: Routledge.

Rosenberg, S. (1988). Self and others: Studies in social personality and autobiography. In L. Berkowitz (Ed.), *Advances in experimental social psychology,* (Vol. 21, pp. 57–95). New York: Academic Press.

Rosenthal, P. (1984). *Words and values: Some leading words and where they lead us.* New York: Oxford University Press.

Sampson, E. E. (1989). The deconstruction of the self. In J. Shotter, and K. J. Gergen (Eds.), *Texts of identity* (pp. 1–19). Newbury Park, CA: Sage.

Shotter, J. (1993). *Conversational realities: Constructing life through language.* Thousand Oaks, CA: Sage.

Skinner, Q. (1988). Meaning and understanding in the history of ideas. In J. Tully (Ed.), *Meaning and context: Quentin Skinner and his critics.* Princeton: Princeton University Press.

Smith, A. (1813). *The theory of moral sentiments.* Edinburgh: Hay. (Originally published 1759.)

Taylor, C. (1985). *Human agency and language.* New York: Cambridge University Press.

Taylor, C. (1989). *Sources of the self: The making of the modern identity.* Cambridge, MA: Harvard University Press.

Toulmin, S. (1977). Self-knowledge and knowledge of the "self." In T. Mischel (Ed.), *The self: Psychological and philosophical issues.* Oxford: Blackwell.

Verhave, T., and van Hoorn, W. (1984). The temporalization of the self. In K. J. Gergen, and M. M. Gergen (Eds.), *Historical social psychology.* Hillsdale, NJ: Erlbaum.

Weintraub, K. J. (1978). *The value of the individual: Self and circumstance in autobiography.* Chicago: University of Chicago Press.

Dorothy Holland

Selves as Cultured

As Told by an Anthropologist
Who Lacks a Soul

This chapter tells my version of the story of anthropological studies of self.[1] It begins with the culturalist versus universalist debate and ends with an emerging "practice theory" of self. Between these conceptualizations falls "the critical disruption," the intrusion of issues of power, hegemony, and history into anthropology in general and psychological anthropology in particular. Foucauldian, feminist, and other critical approaches not only undermined the older conceptualization of cultures as discrete, coherent, systems of meaning, common to all members, but also popularized a social-constructivist view of self. In the last section, I discuss the varieties of anthropological research undertaken in the wake of the critical disruption. Their commonalities reveal the possibilities of a practice theory of self, a theory that bears the strong marks of social constructivism, yet, because of its grounding in ethnographic research, avoids the extreme versions of constructivism. This emerging practice theory recognizes plural sites of self-making, focuses on mediational processes of the self, insists on embodiment, and gives culturally specific discourses and practices a pivotal role in constituting the self. My review is organized around the significance of culturally constructed, socially (dis)empowered languages and practices of the self, which constitutes one of the major points of disagreement in the literature.

Some years ago, I had a close encounter with the crossing of the cultural boundaries of the self. It happened in a café in Seoul, South Korea. I was drinking tea with several Korean women when one of them turned toward me, looked directly across the table and asked: "What does it feel like not to have a soul?" She and the others at the table were interviewers on a research team that I had recently joined. I had been traveling around the country with them and knew that they had trouble understanding the upsetting and crude ways in which American soldiers and tourists behaved. I also knew that they considered the United States to be a country with little historical depth. Still I was unprepared when the shortcomings of my home country turned out to have implications for my self. "What does it feel like not to have a soul?" she asked me.

My friend's stark cross-cultural inquiry raises both my anxiety and important issues in contemporary anthropology and so is a useful starting point for a review of the anthropological and other cross-cultural literatures on self and identity. Her question depended on a particular cultural idiom whose dimensions I was then only beginning to glimpse. It came across a gulf of meaning surely similar to those that often separate us self-researchers from those we study. What should we researchers make of these discourses about souls and other self-related concepts that we come across in fieldwork? The soul question had another disturbing aspect: it cast me as someone who had no soul, a presumably unflattering position, at least as far as my fellow tea drinkers were concerned. What difference should it make in our theories of self that discourses about the self, including our own disciplinary inquiries, position the subjects of the discourse and so become implicated in issues of interpersonal influence and other forms of power?

Discourses and Practices of the Self

Because my knowledge of the meaning and significance of souls in that part of the world is limited, allow me to move away from South Korea. I can easily imagine similarly perplexing questions arising in other places where I have done longer term fieldwork—in Nepal, for example, or in American Samoa. In both places there are ways of talking about what we might take to be a person's self or selves. In both there are conventional ways—ways that leave many assumptions implicit—for talking about the capacities and processes intrinsic to a person that shape his or her actions. Further, these intrinsic entities or processes are implicated in the reflexive mediation of behavior, the objectifying, monitoring, and evaluating stances that a person sometimes takes toward his or her own behavior. This discourse about what I will call "selves" takes many forms. It may consist of expressions implying a subjective sense of oneself as an actor or subject; it may be embedded in claims about others or expressed directly in pontifications about the self on the part of specialists. Nepalis and Samoans have ways of talking about selves, but their discourses differ from those familiar in the United States. They also engage in "practices of the self" that are not necessarily common in the United States (e.g., Clement's 1982 description of Samoan therapeutic procedures for mental disorders).[2]

Parish (1991, 1994) has written about people living in the Kathmandu valley of Nepal who identify themselves as members of an ethnic group, the Newars. At the time of his fieldwork in the 1980s the Newar people he met did not use any term that might be easily glossed in English as "self," but they talked about the heart in ways akin to our talk about the self. Memories, thoughts, and feelings were stored in the heart (nuga); willful actions came from the heart. English speakers in the United States sometimes say things such as "Who knows what's in his heart?" but the Newar talked about the heart in ways that would not be readily understood in English. They spoke, for example, of someone with no ability to commit himself or follow through on moral action as lacking "heart blood." Furthermore, the self/heart was an abode of the sacred. They spoke of a deity residing in their hearts and dictating morally commendable actions.

Shore (1982), Mageo (1989), and others have systematically studied Samoan concepts of the person and the self. Although the Samoans that the researchers consulted did talk about subjectivity and even used a Samoan concept, the loto, that some anthropologists have translated as a quasi-bodily organ of subjectivity (Mageo, 1989, p. 197, n. 34), they showed only a limited interest in subjective aspects of self either as concepts to be elaborated or as a feature of others that is discussed. In comparison to the immense popularity and intense seriousness of self-discourses in the United States, conventionalized discourses about inner selves, such as those found in therapists' offices and innumerable self-help books, simply were not greatly elaborated in Samoa.

Furthermore, a person's acts tended not to be read by Samoans as signs of the person's self, but rather read as indicators of the state of relationships between the person and the recipient of his act and among members of the group as a whole. Few cared, at least at the level of discourse, what, if any, aspect of self—what personality trait, what psychodynamic impasse—might have led Chief So and So to behave as he did in the village council. What people talked about was the social import of what he said—its social effects, in other words (Duranti, 1992).

Similar points can be made about cross-cultural differences regarding the term "identity," which can be defined roughly as a self-understanding or self-objectification to which one is emotionally attached. Discourses, means, and modalities of identities vary.[3] Rosaldo (1980), for example, argues forcefully that Ilongot masculine identity— Ilongot men's understandings of themselves as masculine—in the days before headhunting was stopped, and even for a long period after, was organized around the key experience of taking, or failing to take, a human head. Readers who have a sense of being masculine, what does it feel like not to have taken a head?

Fifty years of research by anthropologists and other cross-cultural researchers contain many further examples. It is now absolutely clear that there exists a huge variety of discourses, practices, concepts, means, and modalities of the self.[4] The question now is not so much whether there are differences, but rather what they signify. My Korean friend's question about my soul, or lack thereof, startled me because I was suddenly designated as an object of cross-cultural inquiry and faced with an idiom that was none of my own. Her question reminds us, indeed forces us, to notice that in asking questions about the self we are frequently crossing the boundaries of collectively generated interpretations of the self. Do we cross such boundaries confident that our own discourses have universal value, as my friend seemed to do, or do we cross with trepidation? I hope she will forgive me for using her question to ask what the existence of the range of self-discourses and practices signifies. Of what are they a sign? A larger issue, of course, is the role of these historical, social, and cultural phenomena in constituting the self. How, if at all, are they significant in forming the self that is their object? Stances toward the ontological status of these self-discourses and practices demarcate the literature and lie at the heart of successive debates.

It should be noted that in reviewing these debates, I emphasize and sometimes speak from extreme positions in the debates. My purpose is less to create straw men for merciless slaughter than to throw into relief the major dimensions of the dialogues that frame the production of knowledge about the self during the different periods I describe.

The Universal versus the Culturally Specific Self

Before the 1970s, anthropological work on culture and the self, as with other cross-cultural inquiries, developed primarily through a dialogue, sometimes implicit, sometimes explicit, between universalist and culturalist perspectives. The oft-remarked division of labor between anthropology and psychology (e.g., Bloch, 1985; Miller, 1988) cast psychology and psychologists as the champions of universalist perspectives and anthropology as the bastion of culturalist positions, but the dialogue was also conducted within anthropology.

The universalist versus culturalist debate is very familiar and can be recounted quickly. The point of particular importance here is the status attributed to specific discourses and practices of the self. For those who embrace the theoretical priority of the "natural self," culture is subordinate to universal properties of human psychology. The human self is, first and foremost, a complex of natural, species-given, structures and processes. The selves found in Samoa are simply refractions of an underlying natural self; those in the Kathmandu Valley of Nepal show other possible refractions; and so on. Pliant to scientific probing, the natural self exists beneath the sometimes dazzling, but always thin, cultural overlay—much as the species-given human body exists beneath our easily discarded clothing.

In this view, the natural self is akin to the heart or the liver. Although we might not want to go so far as the Newar and talk about an actual organ as though it were the self, we still might draw an analogy. Suppose the self around the world is as invariant as the human kidney and for the same reasons: its ontology is that of a natural phenomenon. From such a perspective, culturally distinct discourses of the self are simply more or less correct, more or less productive of scientifically sound interventions, but scarcely significant in any other way. Even in the field we could often amalgamate the understandings of different groups to our own. So the Newar talk about a deity in their hearts: Could we not simply say that they have a metaphorical way of talking about the superego? And what of practices? Misguided practices of child rearing, say, may lead to pathologies of the natural self just as poor eating habits affect whether the heart becomes diseased, but the relationship is the same no matter what the culture. One's "cultural background" may affect such things as whether one's self-esteem is high or low, yet self-esteem remains not only ascertainable but also a significant correlate of other aspects of the person, no matter what the culture. How, or even whether, there exists a comparable concept, a similar discourse about the importance of self-esteem in a given culture, is irrelevant.

Countervailing, more culturalist positions, of course, cannot be captured by the clothing/body analogy. For them, culturally specific concepts—the Samoan notion of loto, for example—are not mildly interesting but mostly inconvenient coverings of the universal self. Instead, they, along with other important self-discourses and practices, are indicators of important contours of Samoan culture that shape the self in profound ways. South Asian religious and philosophical writings and pronouncements on the self, for example, have been read by anthropologists such as Dumont (1966/1980) and Marriott (1976a, 1976b) as signs or indicators of a culture deeply at odds with Western culture. These anthropologists argue that South Asian cultures, especially dominant Hindu forms, grant value to the collective while ignoring and devaluing the individual. The culture derogates individuals to the point that, especially for Dumont, the Western concept of the "individual" is not very helpful, to say the least, in the study of Indian societies. They have little relevance to behavior and events in those societies.

The culturally variable discourses and concepts of the self, from such a view, are not simply more, or less, accurate maps of the same territory, but different maps that bespeak a difference in the territory. For example, Shweder and Bourne (1984), summarizing a large amount of cross-cultural literature, identify two ideal types of self: the Western concept of person that is autonomous, acontextual, abstract, and independent opposed to a non-Western self that is context dependent, concrete, and socially defined. They write: "To the question 'Does the concept of the person vary cross-culturally?' our answer is obviously 'yes'; we have tried to identify two major alternative conceptualizations of the individual-social relationship, viz., the 'egocentric contractual' and the 'sociocentric organic'" (p. 193).

For many anthropologists, this research implies the proposition that culture profoundly shapes selves, a proposition psychologists such as Markus and Kitayama (1991; Kitayama, Markus, & Lieberman, 1995) and Miller (1988) have set out to test through quasi-experimental designs. Different cultural conceptions of the self are treated as indicators of underlying cultural themes that affect not only conceptions of the self but also conceptions of emotion, child development, and mental disorders, as well as individuals' patterns of cognition and affect. As Miller (1988) puts it: "the studies imply that cultural content must be regarded as an essential influence on the patterning of psychological structures and processes" (p. 280). The differences in collective meaning systems, in other words, are productive, and therefore indicative, of profound and thoroughgoing differences in the selves of those who are cultured in these systems. These cultural discourses and their relationship to the self are not like the relation of the clothes to the body, but more like that of a bottle to the liquid it contains. Self-discourses and practices must be scrutinized, for they are clues to the contours of the bottle—the culture—that shapes the malleable self.

Few anthropologists, if any, fully embrace the extremes of either the universalist or culturalist position. Rather, they try to reconcile the tensions between universalism and cultural specificity. For example, Hallowell (1955a, 1955b), an anthropologist who pioneered anthropological theories of the self (Fogelson, 1979; Robbins, 1973; Whittaker, 1992; Marcus & Fischer, 1986), argued that every person anywhere had a sense of him- or herself as a separate being and could thus become an object to him- or herself. For Hallowell, self-awareness and self-reflexivity were universal, species-given characteristics. He pointed out other invariant aspects of selves as well, yet at the same time he argued that many seemingly natural aspects of the self are, in fact, culturally shaped to the extent that they cannot be universally interpreted. For instance, in a culture where demons are taken seriously, a feeling that one is being threatened by demons is indicative of culture, not of pathology as it probably would be in a demonless culture. More recent approaches to the problem of articulating the universal with the cultural include the work of the anthropologist Gananath Obeyesekere (1981) who builds upon psychodynamic theories an account of important, universal structures and processes that, at the same time, emphasizes cultural symbols. In his view, cultural symbols are appropriated by individuals to assuage and manage the psychodynamically generated dilemmas that face all of us. The medical anthropologist Thomas Csordas has more recently (1994) drawn upon the phenomenological psychology of Merleau-Ponty in order to articulate a notion of the self embodied within—i.e., universally oriented to—an experiential world that remains deeply and inevitably informed by its particular cultural environment. He, too, seeks to reconcile, albeit in ways very different from Obeyesekere, the universal and culturally specific aspects of self (see also Ewing, 1990; Scheper-Hughes & Lock, 1987; Shweder, 1991, pp. 346–347; and Spiro, 1993).

In this debate, then, we see broad differences in the assessment of culturally specific discourses and practices of the self. From the universalist position, these discourses are largely irrelevant; from the culturalist, they are indicative of key contours of cultures. In the more recent debates, these discourses are certainly considered relevant, but they are not considered to be indicators of an underlying, pervasive culture. Rather, they are considered to be what I will call "living tools." Obeyesekere's conceptualization of cultural symbols as taken up by individuals faced with psychodynamic dilemmas hints at this direction, but the new development moves outside of the old issues.

The Critical Disruption

Roughly two decades ago, powerful cross-currents began to disrupt the universalist-culturalist debate. Anthropology entered into a period of critical examination of its relations with its subjects. The discipline came under sustained criticism from within, and the critics were, and continue to be, many. They reflected upon the collaboration of anthropologists with colonial powers (e.g., Asad, 1973), for example, and upon the tendency of anthropological fieldwork to focus myopically on males and male activities (e.g., Weiner, 1976; Reiter, 1975). Somewhat later, anthropologists began asking questions about their representation of others. What messages were conveyed by anthropological writing practices? Clifford (1988), Fabian (1983), and others harshly judged devices such as use of the ethnographic present (the use of the present tense) to describe peoples who were actually studied during a particular, historical period. Such use suspended the Samoans, or whomever, in time, removed them from history, and treated them as though they were simply pliable specimens of science.

In a move critical to our discussion here, anthropologists also, along with some psychologists (e.g., Henriques, Hollway, Urwin, Venn, &

Walkerdine, 1984), adopted Foucault's work, especially his formulation of power and knowledge, as an impetus for critical reflection. Foucault's histories of post-Enlightenment disciplines depicted social and psychological sciences as constructing, rather than objectively studying, their subjects. In the post-Enlightenment West, the scientific management of populations places people in categories that determine the treatment they receive in such centralized institutions as mental institutions, prisons, and schools. Scientific categories—such as "schizophrenic" or, more recently, "at risk" children—the argument goes, also enter into, or return to, everyday discourse, and are used as well in schools and other institutions. People treat each other and themselves according to these categories. This traffic between the scientific and the institutional, between the scientific and the popular, of course, belies the possibility that social scientists could be what they claim to be: noninterfering, truth-telling observers. Instead, scientists, most obviously those whose "findings" enter directly into institutional treatments, become implicated in a kind of forced reductionism. The knowledge that the objects of study have generated to live under the conditions that they do is (at least partly) disregarded and replaced with scientific categories imposed by those with power. No matter how scrupulous the attempts of individual scientists to be objective, social scientists, today as in the past, are, in effect, studying what their field of study has helped to create. In this Foucauldian vision, unreflexive claims to "objectivity" become hollow, at best; at worst, they are a self-serving means by which science rhetorically claims authority.[5]

In anthropology, this critical stance has had a number of ramifications. For one, anthropological descriptions of cultures came under scrutiny and were seen to be suspiciously entangled with systems of power/knowledge, such as Foucault described. Looking back to past collaborations with colonial governments, for example, contemporary anthropologists analyzed how anthropological constructions of the colonized informed governmental actions. Governments' efforts to subjugate their colonized populations in turn powerfully constrained these peoples to reconstruct themselves either in embrace of or in opposition to the categories used to describe them.[6] The guise of scientist has thus become suspect to the point that, now, a good number of anthropologists will meet unreflexive claims to scientific objectivity and authority with incredulity if not antagonism.

Feminists rigorously critiqued past representations of culture as well, claiming that anthropologists had often put forward a patriarchal and thus myopic account of other ways of life. Twenty years of detailed and persuasive feminist scrutiny have made it impossible to ignore the importance of gender in all societies and to avoid the recognition that what males may take to be important and sacrosanct may well be experienced in quite different ways by females. Twenty years ago, Geertz (1973) could get by analyzing the cockfight in Bali, a solely masculine activity, without paying particular attention to the social significance of its gendered quality, of who participated and who did not. It has become clear, even to those who are not particularly engaged by feminist theory, that women have a different perspective on the apparatuses of male privilege—such as men's houses in Amazonian cultures, for example—than men do; that their perspectives are not, in other words, necessarily those that men wish them to adopt (Gregor, 1977). Clearly a person's social position—defined by gender, race, class, and any other social division that is structurally significant—potentially affects one's perspective on cultural institutions and the ardor of one's subscription to the values and interpretations that are promoted in rituals and other socially produced cultural forms.

These feminist critiques, attuned to Foucault's work, but more often attending to resistance than Foucault himself, see cultural discourses that privilege males, for example, as impositions, pushing women and men to behavior that is compatible with the structures and institutions that favor members of one social category over another. Feminists then provide yet another basis for suspecting descriptions of seemingly holistic, coherent, integrated cultures. They object when it is taken for granted that everyone subscribes equally, despite their social position, to cultural tenets. "Whose account is being privileged?" they ask. Whose view is being constructed as though it were the only one? And they answer, "Probably not the view of those who are in positions of restricted privilege." Accounts of culture that ignore the importance of social position, in other words, surreptitiously participate in the silencing of those who lack privilege and power.

The critical disruption has further affected the writing of ethnographies across cultural boundaries. Consistent with a Foucauldian logic, texts, including ethnographic ones, predicate positions for the reader— i.e., they invite the reader to regard anthropological subjects from a certain perspective. Thus, the writings of contemporary ethnographers, as well as those of researchers in other fields (see, for example, with reference to psychology, Parker, 1992), are now vulnerable to criticism of their "textual strategies." Textual strategies include more than theories about significant structures and processes important to the question at hand; they also include the text's implications about the position of the researcher, relative to the people being studied and relative to the reader. Ethnographic accounts are now critically read for their portrayal of the relationship between anthropologist and subject and many texts now include explicit sections that problematize that relationship (for early examples, see Favret-Saada, 1980, and Crapanzano, 1980b). It is now commonplace for writers to consider critically the perspective that they convey.

Clearly this critical disruption has a number of implications for comparison across cultural boundaries. The very conceptions of culture have changed drastically. Anthropology no longer endeavors to describe cultures as though they were coherent, integrated, timeless wholes. The object of study has shifted, away from Samoan culture, say, or American culture, or any culture taken as a whole. Anthropology no longer treats the cultural discourses and practices of a group of people as though they were indicators of an underlying cultural logic or essence equally compelling to all those raised in its folds. Instead, contest, struggle, and power have been brought to the foreground. Culture as an integrated, coherent entity that can be considered apart from issues of power and contestation is no longer a taken-for-granted core concept in anthropology and, in fact, is opposed by most.

Instead, in anthropology, the cultural objects of study are now particular, circumscribed, historically and socially situated "texts" or "forms" and the processes through which they are negotiated, resisted, institutionalized, and internalized. Significant for the study of culture and self, "cultural forms" are presumed to affect and shape subjectivity, and these cultural forms come in great variety. They include, for example, images of the other in *National Geographic* (Lutz & Collins, 1993), life-story genres in Alcoholics Anonymous (Cain, 1991), specialist discourses on the self in the anthropology and psychology of the 1950s, and performances such as the Balinese cockfight made famous by Geertz (1973). But, to qualify as "cultural studies," a name given both to the new cultural anthropology and to an interdisciplinary approach, these forms must be analyzed in relation to the social and material conditions in which they are produced and appropriated. In cultural studies, whose roots lie in the critical disruption I have just described, analytic questions often concern the politics—the oppressive or liberatory potential—of cultural forms for subjectivities. Moreover, cultural forms are recognized to be the products of particular groups within a population, created under and in response to their social position and condition. This latter point definitively sets cultural studies off from, say, Geertz's (1973) analysis of the Balinese cockfight, in which the cockfight is presented as though it were produced from no particular social position and without reference to its historically changing circumstances (see Roseberry, 1982).

The Socially Constructed, Ephemeral Self

In addition to bringing about a refiguring of culture as an object of study and of the scientist's position with regard to those being studied, the critical disruption in anthropology and other fields has also had a powerful impact on dialogues about the self per se. Discourse (or discursive) theory, as Foucauldian understandings are sometimes called, has provoked a new concept of the self as socially constructed. The discourses and categories dominant in a society, the argument goes, are imposed upon people, both interpersonally and institutionally. Eventually, the imposition comes to be self-administered. Selves, in short, are socially constructed through the mediation of powerful discourses and their artifacts—tax forms, census categories, curriculum vitae, and the like.

Social constructivists emphasize that our communications with one another not only convey messages, but also always make claims about who we are relative to one another and the nature of our relationship. When we speak, we "afford"—i.e., we make available and seek to attribute—subject positions to one another. My Korean friend afforded me the position of a person who lacked a soul. This chapter affords certain positions to anthropologists and others to psychologists, certain positions to women, others to men, certain positions to those who identify themselves as scientists, certain positions to those who suspect scientific representations, and so on. Genres such as censuses or curriculum vitae require us to present ourselves according to categories obligatory to the form. Resistance to such affordances is possible, if not likely. All the same, for example, the text I have created here nonetheless constrains, according to the social constructivist, my readers to two choices: to comply or resist. Perhaps the discourses I use are not hegemonic and perhaps I lack even momentary power to make the constraints chafe, nonetheless, there exist other texts and other discourses that cannot be similarly put aside. The "subject" of the self is always open to the power of the discourses and practices that describe it.

In their zeal to communicate the importance of powerful, socially administered constraints on subjectivity (e.g., Davies & Harré, 1990; Harré & Van Langenhove, 1991; Kondo, 1990), some social constructivists seem to offer up the image of a fleeting, fragmentary self, buffeted here and there by powerful social currents. In the strong version of this view, selves become virtually ephemeral, leaving the selves described in the universalist-culturalist debate with far too much "essence." They are much too substantial, whether envisioned as made up of a natural or a cultural essence, and have too much durability, stability, and coherence. To the ephemeralist, such selves, whether natural or cultural, are of little moment and are overwhelmed by the positioning continually imposed upon them. Even if a historically particular set of selves persist for a long time, say during feudalism in Europe, their staying power comes from social and material circumstances, not from any impetus for continuity from within. As seen from the extreme ephemeralist position, daily life, especially in the postmodern era, is a movement from self to self—at one moment a self resists or is successfully positioned as lacking a soul; the next, it is an emotional woman; the next, an organ donor; two minutes later, a high-risk driver; and then, later in the day, "a bad neighbor" (see also Smith, 1988).

Viewed from a strong social-constructivist position, then, all the phenomena addressed by the universalist-culturalist debate might as well be collapsed into one "embodied" self. This embodied self is peren-

nially suspected as a product of "essentialist" thinking, while the socially constructed self remains a paragon of antiessentialism. Concepts
of selves created by culture especially are subjected to criticism by social
constructivists. Embodied selves formed by culture have, after all, been
envisioned as stable, enduring, and manifesting the core values of what
were assumed to be pervasive cultures—a case of double essentialism.
Once created, by the end of childhood (or shortly thereafter), through
the rituals and other socializing practices that distill cultural principles
for the neophyte, they persist through time, regardless of change in
social and material conditions. Socially constructed selves, in sharp
contrast, are subject to positioning by whatever powerful discourses
they encounter. Perhaps they are resistant. Nonetheless, they remain
provisionally at the mercy of social forces, of changes in the policies of
the state (which dictate new ways of categorizing people in the census),
of diagnostics in school that label some children "at risk," or of new
forms of racist discourse, taken up from right-wing talk shows by a boss
at work. In the case where culture is emphasized, constant, stable,
interpretations of the world and values—of interdependence, say, deriving from the core of the culture—become embodied in mind/body
and inform culturally specific behavior. For the socially constructed
self, in contrast, discourses and practices are tools, and the self an object
of such tools. In the new debates, in other words, socially empowered
discourses and practices of the self appear in a different light. They are
tools of construction—perhaps tools of oppression, perhaps tools of
liberation.

The social-constructivist position cannot be contained by the terms
of the old universalist/culturalist debate. The heated dialogue now concerns the degree to which the embodied self is important at all. And,
again, this time, as with the universalist/culturalist debate, I depict a
continuum running between two poles: an extreme essentialist view
that pays no attention to the socially positioning power of discourses,
and an extreme ephemeralist position that has no interest in the embodied self. Most, if not all, actual statements, of course, lie somewhere
along the continuum and seek to reconcile the tensions between what
can be depicted as incompatible views. We can find social constructivists, such as Hollway (1984), for example, who, despite their emphasis
on discursive positioning, consider Lacanian concepts useful to delineate parts of the embodied self that endure and make a difference in
capitulation or resistance to social positioning.

Emerging Directions in the Anthropological Study of the Self and Subjectivity

This critical disruption has, to put it mildly, interfered with the kind of
questions posed by Shweder and Bourne's (1984) summary of cross-

cultural variation in concepts of the person. The intellectual and political climate within anthropology, writ large, has decisively changed, affecting the questions that studies of self and identity are now pursuing.

Perhaps the most obvious new studies are those critical of psychology and psychological anthropology themselves. Works by psychologists, such as *Changing the Subject* (Henriques, et al., 1984) and the writings of the "critical psychologists" (Tolman & Maiers, 1991) parallel "critical" works by anthropologists. Scheper-Hughes's (1992) analysis of the folk idiom of *nervios* and its appropriation and use by clinic physicians in Brazil against the sick-poor, provides a good example, as do Lutz's (e.g., 1988) critiques of scientific discourses on emotion and her research (in press) on the effects of U.S. military funding in the 1950s on subsequent directions of psychological research (see also the long-standing cultural and social criticism of psychiatric practice—e.g., Kleinman, 1988). "Critical psychological anthropology" and its correspondents, critical psychology and "critical social psychology" (Wexler, 1983), are important in general because they disallow innocent-seeming and apolitical views of the conceptual tools and discourses that researchers and practioners use. At the same time, they have a more specific import for theories of the self. They suggest a revised theoretical orientation that admits power relations. Although as Scheper-Hughes (1992, p. 222) points out, such theory mostly awaits invention, the newer research provides, in combination with past work, a basis for a practice theory of self, one fundamentally reformed and informed but not determined by the extreme versions of the critiques mounted in the last twenty years.

The more recent inquiries, though not necessarily undertaken in the name of critical psychological anthropology, nonetheless reflect dimensions of the critical disruption. Perhaps they are especially sensitive to the ways in which respondent and informant texts are a matter of coproduction with the researcher (e.g., see Crapanzano, 1980a, 1980b), or perhaps they participate in the deconstruction of received notions of culture units such as "the West," or perhaps they pay special attention to the power of cultural discourses and practices to position, and so socially shape, others (see Kondo, 1990). Whatever the particular effect, we can discern at least three interrelated components of a theoretical refiguring of the relationship between culture and self. First, culturally and socially constructed discourses and practices of the self, differentiated by relations of power and the institutional infrastructure associated with them, are recognized by latter-day research as living tools of the self—as media that figure the self constitutively, in open-ended ways. Second, the self is treated as process. Third, "sites of self" are recognized as plural.

The idea of plural, competing sites of the self is now common to a variety of disciplines (see, e.g., Smith, 1988). In anthropology, the demise of the privileged concept of bounded, discrete, coherent cultures has made room for the recognition that people are commonly exposed to competing and differentially powerful and authoritative discourses and practices of the self. A recent series of articles in the journal *Ethos* makes this point.

This series challenges Shweder and Bourne's claim that Western culture produces egocentric or independent selves that are stable and perduring, while non-Western cultures promote sociocentric or interdependent selves. The articles particularly attack the monolithic, essentialist version of the "Western" self (Ewing, 1990; Holland & Kipnis, 1994; Murray, 1993; Spiro, 1993). While they take us through some of the same terrain already explored, they do so specifically with respect to culture and self and with a common, conceptual move to plural sites of self.

Both Ewing (1990) and Murray (1993) argue against the past tendencies among anthropologists to write as though cultural discourses and practices of the self could be taken as indicators of core cultural themes whose internalization, in turn, yielded "culturalized" selves. They call instead for the disambiguation—i.e., the distinction—of the sites or sources of the self. They imply that there are different "production sites" of self-discourses and practices, whose works are not necessarily complementary.

Ewing (1990), for example, argues that the authoritative discourses on the self found in religious and philosophical texts hardly exhaust the sites of self-production. Popular discourses about the self comprise another important locus. Anthropologists such as Marriott and Dumont, Ewing argues, have failed to take account of the self as it is expressed by individuals in their everyday talk and action. Hence their "self," derived from analyses of the talk and texts of specialists, is always partial and may not coincide with the self construed by popular genres of speaking and acting (see also McHugh, 1989; Mines, 1988). In particular, Ewing turns her criticism to the depiction of the Western self. Although Western representations of the self found in philosophical and psychological texts may indeed bespeak a person who is autonomous, bounded, and transcontextual, peoples' representations of themselves in the stream of everyday life reveal a multitude of selves that are not bounded, stable, perduring, or impermeable. Spiro (1993), speaking to a broader set of topics, makes some of the same points to support his thesis that the differences between the West and the non-West have been greatly exaggerated (see also Hollan, 1992).

Murray (1993), another contributor to the debate, speaks to a different point of criticism. His argument has to do not so much with discrepancies between selves founded in authoritative discourses and selves depicted in everyday talk as with discrepant characterizations within

Western authoritative discourse on the self. He finds fault, in other words, with Ewing's and others' summations of these authoritative treatments. Western philosophy, Western psychology, and Western religion do not, he argues, present a unified conception of the self. He cites David Hume as a major philosophical figure whose depictions of the self were quite at odds with those that supposedly characterize the West. Murray's point is that even authoritative sources are far from being in monolithic agreement with one another and are instead diverse and stand in profound contest.

Holland and Kipnis (1994) moves to yet another venue. Kipnis and I describe everyday discourses on embarrassment in the United States and analyze the cultural model of self that underlies this talk. The self that gets embarrassed is a "sociocentric" or, to use Markus and Kitayama's (1991; see also Kitayama, et al., 1995) terms, an "interdependent" self. Western ethnopsychologies, we conclude, like Murray's formal psychologies and philosophies, do not uniformly posit an egocentric self. Americans engage in discourses that are not consistent on the subject of sociocentrism or egocentrism. Some posit a sociocentric or interdependent self; others, an egocentric or independent self.

The upshot of these articles is not that differences we think of as cultural are insignificant or insignificant for people's lives. Nor is the point one that denies the utility of the sociocentric/egocentric distinction. Self-discourses and practices do vary cross-culturally in ways that are, perhaps for some purposes, usefully glossed as sociocentric and egocentric. Markus and Kitayama, for example, are convincing in their argument that accommodating one's self to others is important in Japan. Dorrine Kondo's (1990) ethnography, situated in Japan, vividly communicates the same sense of the valuing of accommodation. My own research in American Samoa on interpretations and treatments of mental disorders (Clement, 1982) found, for example, that Samoan cultural models of mental problems rested upon a notion of persons affected more by their social situation than by their enduring intrapersonal conflicts or tendencies. As Miller (1988) points out in her concise and helpful review of the anthropological literature on concepts of self, these findings fit the generalization that some groups emphasize more relational notions of the self while others, such as those of the West, emphasize more individualistic ones. The caveat, of course, is that such characterizations lend themselves to reification. We must take care that American culture and Americans, for example, are not construed in our specialist discourses (the metadiscourse on self, so to speak) as inherently egocentric or independent, or that Samoans' culture and Samoans are not treated as though they were, in essence, sociocentric or interdependent. Behavior is better viewed as a sign of self in practice, not a sign of self in essence (see also White, 1993). It is certainly possible, and sometimes useful, to extract from the flow of events and discourses in a particular locale important conceits or concepts—i.e., recurring conventions of thinking and behaving—and constantly defended values. But the further step—assuming that this abstraction, this "culture" or "the self" associated with it, has an essence, an impetus of its own that will continue through time, absent any social machinations—has been decisively challenged.

Reification of this sort not only creates an essence, a timelessness, an immunity to social and historical change that cannot be supported, it also overlooks a heterogeneity that is crucial. Reification obviates the recognition that social conditions themselves may be changing. Markus and Kitayama (1991) point out, for example, that scientific terms for independent self-processes, such as self-disclosure, are recent (see also chapter 1). They interpret this as a simple matter of delayed discovery. My guess is that the creation of more and more terms that assume independent selves is both responsive to and—because of their recirculation to the public through stories and articles in the popular media, and to practitioners in schools—creative of historical conditions. The discourses and practices that construct selves as independent, in other words, may be more powerful and dominant in the United States now than they were fifty or so years ago. Kipnis and I argue that both sociocentric and egocentric modes of self-organization are evident in the discourses and practices of American society. Perhaps independence is a more pervasive mode at present, but to read pervasiveness falsely as essence obscures recognition that the relative worth of the two modes is a matter of tension, if not struggle. Certainly, there are those who argue that Americans should pay more attention to community and less to themselves.

A final line of research moves yet more broadly to a reconceptualization of the relationship between culture and self. In 1992, Elvi Whittaker claimed that the anthropological self—that is, anthropology's theorizing about the self—is a scant ten years old. The youth of the anthropological self is debatable. It is unclear, for example, why Whittaker deems anthropology's earlier students of the self, Hallowell (1955a, 1955b) or Sapir (1934/1949), whom she credits with early interests, not to have produced a live birth. Nonetheless, her sense of a renewed interest in the self and in subjectivity is accurate.

Given the critical climate of the last twenty years, this new interest in the self seems, at first glance, counterintuitive. For those wedded to extreme positions in the debate, whether essentialist or ephemeralist, the dialogue over culture and the self need go no further. We have arrived at a pair of mutually exclusive positions; the task is simply to decide which will prevail. From the midst of these struggles, it is difficult to be a noncombatant or, in the terms of another metaphor, to steer between the Scylla of essentialism and the Charybdis of ephemeralism. In particular, the language that we have for talking about the self is burdened with the baggage of past, and now passé, reifications, an overemphasis on essence. Nonetheless, as pointed out by Marcus and Fischer (1986), the demise of the older paradigms of culture, while making the self a risky topic, also make it an intriguing one.

The older, functionalist paradigms of culture encouraged a seamless view of the relation of culture to self, especially for preindustrial societies that organized relatively small numbers of people. Personal experience and subjectivity were expected to be managed so that most members of a culture would, in the end, embrace and enact the cultural principles that ruled their lives. A prototypical study of this kind was that of Dorothy Eggan (1974). She argued skillfully that Hopis' experiences, even though they initially produced great discomfort and anxiety, were eventually revealed to be worthwhile means of conveying the wisdom of particular cultural practices. She described, for instance, Hopi children's discontent upon learning that the gods who punished them in their initiation rites were actually their uncles and fathers. As they matured, however, they came to apprehend the logic of the practice; their anger dissipated, turning into a greater respect for, and commitment to, the Hopi way.

Eggan's study, despite its appeal, was relatively unusual in addressing the details of enculturation. The assumption that rituals and other cultural forms powerfully encultured malleable individuals remained for the most part unexamined. Rituals were considered to distill and enact important cultural themes to which, it was assumed, everyone related in virtually the same way. Thus, for all practical purposes, there was little reason to investigate what was then called intracultural variation or even to examine closely processes by which children became enculturated. Twenty years ago, and even more recently, an anthropologist could study a public ritual, take for granted the claim that public rituals effectively encultured children growing up in the culture, and not expect to be challenged.

A divergent position began to take shape in the 1970s and continues to the present day (see Henry, 1963 for a precursor). The cultural critics who first articulated this opposition were much more likely to find in cultural practices and discourses a source of problems and difficulties that people tried to relieve. Crapanzano (1980a), for example, published an early article, a study of circumcision in Morocco, in which he challenged functionalist notions. His interviews, concerning the experiences of boys undergoing circumcision and of men of all ages, led him to argue that the ritual was indeed very frightening and threatening, and that the anxieties provoked by it were never reconciled and, in fact, remained with the men for the rest of their lives.

Whether subject to direct criticism or not, any anthropological idea of an unproblematic relation between culture and self would have no doubt eroded on its own.[7] Its close tie to the older, integral ideas of culture has made it, too, a victim of the critical disruption. The relationship between cultural forms and personhood is no longer taken for granted and, as a result, subjectivity has become both more significant and more interesting. Persons are now recognized to have perspectives on their cultural worlds that are likely to differ, at least by gender and by other markers of social position.[8] They are no longer considered to be unproblematically instructed by rituals and the other key events of an enculturation that solely reflects cultural ideology. If public institutions and the rituals they stage are important but not determinant of subjectivity, then research needs to address personhood directly. If people are not to be seen simply as living enactments of core cultural themes, then anthropologists are free, indeed pushed, to ask a broader range of questions about experience and subjectivity and the role of cultural resources in the constitution of this experience.

What has ensued are several innovative ethnographic studies of self and personhood (for earlier precursors, see Peacock & Holland, 1993). Although these ethnographic studies are not themselves always in theoretical accord, they do agree that discourses and practices of the self are significant in the constitution of selves. They share points of commonality that offer themselves as a basis for an emerging theory that takes social constructivism seriously but tempers its extreme versions with contrary indications from ethnographic study. The first commonality concerns the "living tools of the self."

Michelle Rosaldo's *Knowledge and Passion: Ilongot Notions of Self and Social Life* (1980) provides a good example of these new ethnographies of experience and subjectivity. The book is, in part, a description of Rosaldo's attempt to understand Ilongot men's motivation for headhunting, or, differently stated, an effort to understand Ilongot masculine identities and the ways in which taking a human head was for them a key event in becoming a man. Rosaldo refused to short-circuit her process of understanding by reducing the activities of headhunting to a utilitarian logic. Such a logic, counting the worth of action according to its utility in obtaining socially defined goods, would have explained headhunting as an effort to achieve status. Rosaldo also refused to reduce the Ilongot perspective to a Freudian logic, say, or to any scheme that demanded that she ignore the particular Ilongot discourses and practices that had to do with headhunting. Similarly, she was determined not to follow the more accustomed anthropological route, devoting herself solely to a semiotic analysis of the symbols used in rituals and myths. She wanted instead to know the things important to the Ilongot themselves: why, for instance, men told her, in a matter-of-fact manner, that *liget*, an emotion word sometimes translated into English as anger, is the reason for beheadings (p. 24). She could not, in pursuit of such questions, bypass Ilongot talk about headhunting because those were the practices and discourses that people used both to understand their own experiences and to communicate them to others (e.g., p. 36).

The same year, Crapanzano (1980b) published *Tuhami*, the life story of a Moroccan tile maker. The book tells, often in his own words, of Tuhami's experience as a man of precarious position in his society. He lacked inherited wealth, had no secure means of employment, and so lacked material resources. Since he had never had the wherewithal to marry, he lacked any family. Tuhami was hardly presented as a revelation of Moroccan culture and, in fact, readers sometimes criticize the book for telling them so little about "Moroccan culture." Rather we, through Crapanzano, are confronted with Tuhami's understanding of himself and his precarious existence, an understanding that Tuhami created, partially in response to Crapanzano's questions, out of elements of Moroccan culture that he himself had put together. Tuhami's subjectivity was not presented as a manifestation of his culture but rather as a subjectivity formed and reformed in response to his specific predicaments.

Dorrine Kondo's *Crafting Selves: Power, Gender, and Discourses of Identity in a Japanese Workplace* (1990), provides an even more recent example of the newer sort of ethnography of personhood and self. Kondo's main point is a social-constructivist one. She emphasizes that Japanese women, both in the workplace and community, and she herself—a Japanese-American who grew up in the United States—were always positioned and powerfully shaped by self-forming discourses and practices. She tells the story of an incident that happened to her, after a period of fieldwork in Japan where she immersed herself in the daily lives of people in her neighborhood. She went shopping one day:

> Promptly at four P.M., the hour when most Japanese housewives do their shopping for the evening meal, I lifted the baby into her stroller and pushed her along ahead of me as I inspected the fish, selected the freshest looking vegetables, and mentally planned the meal for the evening. As I glanced into the shiny metal surface of the butcher's display case, I noticed someone who looked terribly familiar: a typical young housewife, clad in slip-on sandals and the loose, cotton shift called "home wear," a woman walking with a characteristically Japanese bend to the knees and a sliding of the feet. Suddenly, I clutched the handle of the stroller to steady myself as a wave of dizziness washed over me, for I realized I had caught a glimpse of nothing less than my own reflection. (pp. 16–17)

She had acquired the dress, posture, and habits that she, if not her Japanese colleagues, identified as those of a young Japanese housewife. She had formed these ways of being simply by immersing herself in social activity from the position that her gender and her associates assigned her. Her acquisition of the bodily dispositions that marked a particular, gendered identity had occurred without her awareness, and the moment of recognition was disorienting. Despite Kondo's rhetorical fascination with the (social-constructivist) power of discourses and practices, which brings her almost to the point of an ephemeralist position, her ethnographic description shows Japanese women to be something more than "constructed" subjects. They bring past histories of at least some durability to the discourses and practices in which they participate. However much they remain positioned by these discourses and practices and powerfully shaped by them, they are not totally determined. Moments of recognition like hers are indicative of the women's remediation of discursive power, of their possibilities of self-fashioning. As Kondo's title suggests, they craft identities out of the cultural resources available to them.

My own research with Debra Skinner in Central Nepal focused on another source, another "living tool," of the self: songs that the women of the area composed collaboratively for a festival called *Tij*. These songs criticized many patriarchal features of Nepalese community life: the patterns of inheritance that favored men, men's practice of bringing in or threatening to bring in cowives, and the tendency of families to give more material wealth and educational opportunities to sons. We argue not only the evident point—that these Tij songs are and, for a long time, have been an important medium for women's criticisms of their position in Nepalese society—but also that they are an important source of women's gender identities and subjectivities. The songs were taken up by the women as a means of understanding their society and their place as women in it. Girls and women, we learned, used these songs as a means of expressing to themselves both their sense of what it means to be a woman and their feelings about the social position accorded them (Skinner, Holland, & Adhikari, 1994; Holland & Skinner, 1995).

Carole Cain (1991) has given the same kind of attention to the life stories told by American members of Alcoholics Anonymous (AA). Cain's study combined participant observation with ethnographic interviews of AA participants, both newcomers and old hands. She is able to document the increasing familiarity of neophytes with the genre of life story peculiar to AA and their progress in interpreting segments of their lives according to the genre. The intricate development of life stories and of the skills and dispositions necessary for members to subject their lives to the genre's discipline convinced Cain that these stories were a key means by which an "AA identity" became an integral part of the member's self-understanding and, thereby, of the member's daily life.

These ethnographers of personhood and subjectivity do not seek to parse other's—Ilongot men's or Tuhami's or Nepalese women's—experience into categories of cultural essence or into grand conceptual frameworks that presumably cross cultures. They avoid the readily available universalizing moves, not only because they find these discourses and practices intrinsically interesting, but also because they see these discourses and cultural artifacts as the media, the tools that men and women use in the continuing process of constructing and representing self (and others) in response to the situations they encounter. Rosaldo directs her energy to understanding liget better because "liget" was a key term in the talk that Ilongot men did about headhunting, not because liget was possibly a transformed kind of aggression, which figures in our own metapsychologies. She writes, "To comprehend these [discourses], we must ask not if 'anger' and 'lightness' are in fact things that a headhunter is apt to 'feel,' but rather how such terms inform his recollections and accounts and so provide him with a way of understanding the significance of disturbing feats of force for daily interactions" (Rosaldo, 1980, p. 27). Crapanzano, for his part, ends up crossing boundaries to learn about the experience of a man in an extremely difficult social and emotional position. Although frequently tempted by his own proclivities to reduce Tuhami's talk about his demon wife to symptoms of psychodynamic distress, Crapanzano tries to stay with Tuhami's meanings in order to learn more about Tuhami's use of cultural resources for self-creation in response to his dilemmas.

What these new ethnographies of personhood share, in short, is some implicit, if not explicit, components of a theory of the relationship between culture and self.[9] All of these ethnographies emphasize specific cultural discourses and practices. All of them show interest in the plurality of sites of the self. They regard these discourses and practices not as indicators of essential features or themes of Ilongot, Moroccan, or Nepalese culture, but rather as the media around which subjectivities form. More particularly—and these particulars are important—they treat these discourses as the media around which socially and historically positioned persons construct their subjectivities. Rosaldo writes in particular about young adult men among the Ilongot who were still oriented to headhunting; Crapanzano, the socially precarious Tuhami; Kondo, women in a Japanese suburb; Holland and Skinner, Hindu women of higher castes in rural Nepal; and Cain, initiates to Alcoholics Anonymous.

Moreover, in contradistinction to older views of culture as timeless, these are people, dilemmas, and cultural forms that are expected to change over time. The cultural discourses and practices examined by these ethnographies come into play at different historical and biographical points. Subjectivities of the sort described by Rosaldo, for example, clearly form and change over the life span. Older Ilongot men told how their sense of headhunting and the emotions relating to headhunting changed as they took on the social roles and responsibilities of family life. And the practices themselves are subject to change and challenge from within and without. Even while Rosaldo was carrying out her fieldwork, the Ilongot were split between those who had joined Christian congregations and forsaken headhunting and those whose masculine identities were still organized in part around the activity of headhunting. The latter orientation persisted even though the government had disrupted these activities and many young men had never had the opportunity to participate in them. Even so, they understood their masculinity in relation to a felt lack of not having taken a head. Historical time was also vitally significant in Skinner and Holland's study of the critical commentary of Tij songs. The authors show how the content of songs changed markedly following a successful people's movement that brought about a new government. Before the movement, women created songs that mostly depicted women's identities in relation to domestic or familial affairs. After the democracy movement, songs stressed women's sense of themselves in relation to the government and to the political parties then vying for election. The songs both mark and, in their performance, re-create a new venue of women's self-conceptions.

A final example comes from Jane Hill's (1985) research in the Malinche Volcano region of Mexico. It demonstrates not only that discourses and practices of the self are objects of struggle and change, but also the reason why I refer to "living" tools. "Tool" is not exactly the appropriate word, as it implies the notion that it is under the control of the user.[10] Instead, we need a concept that conveys the "indeterminacy" (see Smolka, de Góes, & Pino, in press) and polysemous nature of tools. Even though tools carry with them a collective theory of the task to which they are to be put and of the people who are to use them (Holland & Cole, 1995), they also carry possibilities and consequences that the user may not imagine and, at times, a liberatory potential that a would-be shaper of others might miss. Hill's research addresses language as a living tool, one that is not quite manageable. She takes as her problem the changing consciousness of the proletarianizing peasant groups of the Malinche area. Are people there identifying with and maintaining a style of life associated with a more or less distinct Mexicano community? Or, are they developing a consciousness of themselves that looks outside the community, to the factories, for example, where many hold jobs and where Spanish is the valued language? Hill has studied, with great and greatly necessary analytic subtlety, the speech of area residents. Speakers of Mexicano (Nahuatl) from this area also speak Spanish and they, depending on the speaker's fluency, include Spanish grammatical forms in situations that supposedly demand Mexicano and vice versa. At the time of Hill's field research, several forms had been stigmatized by community members as Spanish and inappropriate for use in the community. When speakers used them, they were criticized for not speaking "pure" Mexicano. Nonetheless, many speakers, even those who presented themselves as purists of Mexicano, were speaking versions highly diluted by Spanish forms. As a result, in a way akin to Kondo's experience in Japan, they were developing out-of-awareness subjectivities in which Spanish "voices" (to use Bakhtin's term) predominated. The living tool of their communal identity, the Mexicano they spoke, itself compromised their intent.

There are several important points to be drawn from these more recent ethnographic studies of self and personhood. Clearly, the critical developments of the past twenty years have not only revived anthropological interest in culture and self, but have also fundamentally shifted anthropologists' view of the relationship between culture and self. What we have seen in these ethnographies is a sensitivity on the parts of ethnographers to the issues of social constructivism and a reformulation of the relation of culture to self. We have seen people, who are their subjects, responding to social constructions and practices that others would impose upon them by drawing upon the historically emerging cultural resources that have, in the past, become subjectively salient—that is, embodied. The new ethnographers of personhood focus on specific, often socially powerful, cultural discourses and practices that both position people and provide them with the resources to respond to problematic situations. Subjectivity in these works is seen to be developing at an interface, within the interplay between the social and embodied sources of the self, in what might be called the "self-in-action," or, to use a label inspired by Bakhtin, the "authoring self" (Bakhtin, 1981). The self-in-action occupies that interface between intimate discourses, inner speaking, and bodily practices formed in the past and the discourses and practices to which people are exposed, willingly or not, in the present. (Others use this concept or emphasize a similar idea, e.g., Ewing, 1990; McHugh, 1989; Miner, 1988; and Parish, 1991.) It authors or orchestrates these sites of self. These ethnographies sidestep a possible impasse between social-constructivist and embodied views of the self and see instead a mediation between them, wrought in part by a developing self-in-action.

What Does It Feel like Not to Have a Soul?

I am able finally to return to the question about my soul, now that I have articulated a position on the sort of culturally specific discourses and practices of the self that this question implied. What the newer studies and developments intimate is that we abandon any detached, impersonal view of the relation of culture to self, whether as clothes to the body or bottle to its contents. Cultural discourses and practices *are* important sources of the self, not so much as indicators of core cultural themes or essences, but as living tools. When used over time, cultural discourses and practices become the media around which one can (be forced to) orchestrate oneself in the context of activity.

Figure 7.1 presents, for heuristic purposes, different sites of the self.

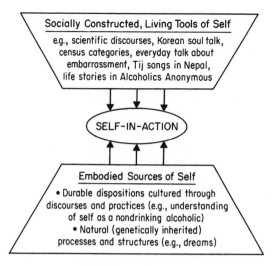

FIGURE 7.1. Sites of self-construction.

The top portion is championed by the social constructivists—the self-in-discourse. These are selves constructed by genres of speech and classification, whether drawn from everyday ways of talking about women as emotional, for example, from the authoritative discourses and texts of Hindu religious and philosophical experts, or from the categorizations of peasants in the state policies of China described by Kipnis (1995; see also Lutz & Abu-Lughod, 1990). These discourses are conventionalized, collective forms and practices that posit a self or selves. The everyday talk about embarrassment, which Kipnis and I studied, for example, implies or presupposes a possible self; it constitutes a self-in-discourse. So, too, do aptitude tests given in counseling offices. Korean discourses on souls and Newari talk about deities in one's heart are examples of self-discourses; Samoan efforts to avoid mental distress, self-practices. Scientific discourses and practices, popular discourses circulated through the media, commonsense talk in the everyday are all sites of the self-in-discourse. Presumably, my Korean friend's question alluded to a Korean way of talking about an aspect of the person that made a difference in her evaluation of different people.

There is no reason to presume, or even expect, that the self-discourses and practices engaged in by a given group of people will all predicate the same sort of self. Nor are the various predications of self of equal potency or value. Some discourses, as the social constructivists point out, are "privileged"; they are the discourses and practices associated with power, the ones that are most highly institutionalized.

Our own academic discourses on the self are implicated, a site of self, as well. We enter a sort of Klein bottle or a Möbius strip, insofar as our theories (including my own) are at the same time a depiction of the self and a discourse about self that participates, to some degree, in self-constitution. That is, even as I describe the self, I create, albeit at a great distance in political space, new means for constructing the selves I depict. My friend's question placed me as a person who lacked a soul. In writing this paper, I position her as someone whose self is constituted, in part, by her experience with Korean talk about and practices of the soul.

Nonetheless, and despite the importance of cultural discourses, it must not be assumed, for a number of reasons, that cultural discourses and practices, even ones imposed on the weak by the socially powerful, unproblematically determine embodied selves—the selves shaped from the past—that people bring to their present circumstances. Societies harbor many cultural discourses and practices of the self. These discourses and practices are neither monolithic nor necessarily coherent; they are contested and often contradictory. No one set can be read as the definitive insight into (or instructions toward) a supposed Samoan self or Western self. Even authoritative and privileged discourses on the self are not necessarily the ones by which people live. Rather, discourses and practices of the self are used and imposed by actors in their attempts to "orchestrate" selves.

The bottom of Figure 7.1 alludes to embodied sources of the self. These might include, depending on one's theoretical proclivities, sources of sensations and feelings related to human psychobiological inheritance—sexual desires, for example—or the roots of psycho-dynamic processes and dilemmas of development, involving, for instance, problematic separation from one's parents. Also relevant to this part of the figure are those embodied dispositions obviously cultivated through cultural discourses and practices. A shaman's sensitivity to inner voices, conceived as the words of deities, would exemplify the latter sort of cultural disposition. Culturally elaborated images that one uses to reconstruct a sense of self—self-images—would be appropriately placed in the bottom triangle as well (see also Scheper-Hughes, 1992, and Scheper-Hughes & Lock, 1987). And so would what I have called our intimate discourses, inwardly spoken memories regarding such things as souls and feelings about accusations that one's soul is deficient or, indeed, lacking.

From the vantage of my Korean friend's question, I made no sense. Not only did I lack a soul, I also lacked any feeling of lacking a soul. In my terms, I had no lived experience of the social and cultural significance of possessing such a soul, nor had I experience of the stigma that might be attached to lacking a soul. I had a very limited sense of the treatment I might receive from other Koreans should the issue of having or lacking a soul become important. I had a faint glimpse of the mysteries she implies that I might be missing, but it was extremely faint. The young Ilongot men who had missed actual headhunting, by contrast, knew how it felt to lack an experience so important to becoming a man. They had grown up surrounded by the discourses and practices organized around that activity. They knew what it meant not to have the opportunity to participate. I had never lived any place where the presence or absence of such a soul was socially or culturally significant. I do believe, however, that had I immigrated to South Korea and lived among my friends and other Koreans, I would have developed a soul or, at least, and more than likely, feelings about lacking one. That is, I would have participated in the discourses and practices that have to do with the soul as a mediator of a person's accumulated experience, present circumstances, and immediate or future social action. I would have become familiar with—probably in the same less-than-conscious way that Kondo acquired the habits of young Japanese women—and become given to representing myself to others and myself in terms of a soul.

The End?

Anthropological interest in selves is presently shaped by broader dialogues that make subjectivities and topics on personhood immensely important and hotly contested. Whittaker (1992), for example, ends that article, in which she announces the recent birth of the anthropological self, with a series of questions, including, "Will the forces of antiessentialist thinking interrupt the construction of a viable self before it can be used and examined?" (p. 211). Will the anthropological self, in other words, be dead on arrival? Marcus and Fischer (1986, p. 65), too, write that anthropology's newfound interest in persons and emotions will perhaps dissipate. The parameters set by the cross-currents in anthropology writ large, as well as by the specific domains which study the self, are exacting. Yet I think they not only can be met, but are also worth meeting, because the work they motivate subsumes much of value. The emerging view of self presented here speaks to at least some of the critical concerns of our postmodern disciplines. It both avoids the error of essentialism, by recognizing that powerful discourses continually shape and reshape human subjectivities, and reflects the gist of anthropological findings about the self—namely, that any self, while it remains a very open system, takes an intelligible form in and of the cultural artifacts that surround all of us.

Notes

1. This essay is a modified version of a chapter being prepared for the volume, *Emerging Selves: Identities in and Against Cultural Worlds*. My

coauthors on that volume have all made important contributions to the ideas expressed here. Debra Skinner's and Bill Lachicotte's help was especially integral. Other valuable comments were given by Richard Ashmore, Ken Gergen, Lee Jussim, Dan Linger, Catherine Lutz, Ana Smolka, and Geoffrey White.

2. Ito (1987), Skinner (1990), White (1992), Harris (1989), and Fogelson (1982) review the anthropological uses of "self," "identity," "person," and "individual."

3. "Identity" has been used in diverse conceptual models in anthropology. They include those inspired by Erikson (1968), role theory, and related ideas developed in the symbolic-interactionist literature (see Robbins, 1973). More recently, "identity" has been extensively used to refer to "cultural identity," or collective self-representations.

4. For reviews, see Geertz (1973), Harris (1989), LeVine (1982, pp. 291–304), Marsella, DeVos, and Hsu (1985), Shweder and Bourne (1984), and White (1992).

5. For a more hopeful vision, see Haraway (1988). Critical of classical views of objectivity but disavowing radical forms of the social-constructivist criticism of science, she opts for a "successor science project that offers a more adequate, richer, better account of a world in order to live in it well," and that has "*simultaneously* an account of radical historical contingency for all knowledge claims and knowing subjects, a critical practice for recognizing our own "'semiotic technologies'" for making meanings, *and* a no-nonsense commitment to faithful accounts of a 'real' world" (p. 579).

6. Especially relevant here, the construction of the psychological in modernization theory—as in theories of achievement motivation, "modernizing personalities" and the like—was complicit in rationalizing and depoliticizing processes of colonization.

7. In earlier decades, American anthropology did consider the culture/self relationship problematic (e.g., Honigmann, 1954).

8. Early efforts to study members of the same social position simply defined as women, for example, have proven to be problematic. Social positions are multidimensional and context is important. The solution has been to focus on historically and socially constituted groups relevant to the context in question and to avoid assumptions that any group is completely homogeneous.

9. Abu-Lughod (1986) and White (1991) are additional excellent examples.

10. Thanks to Ken Gergen and Ana Smolka who pushed me to think more about the limitations of the tool metaphor.

References

Abu-Lughod, L. (1986). *Veiled sentiments: Honor and poetry in a Bedouin society.* Berkeley and Los Angeles: University of California Press.

Asad, T. (Ed.) (1973). *Anthropology and the colonial encounter.* London: Ithaca Press.

Bakhtin, M. M. (1981). *The dialogic imagination: Four essays by M. M. Bakhtin* (M. E. Holmquist, Ed., Caryl Emerson and Michael Holmquist, Trans.). Austin, TX: University of Texas Press.

Bloch, M. (1985). From cognition to ideology. In R. Fardon (Ed.), *Power and knowledge: Anthropological and social approaches* (pp. 21–48). Edinburgh: Scottish Academic Press.

Cain, W. C. (1991). Personal stories: Identity acquisition and self-understanding in Alcoholics Anonymous. *Ethos, 19,* 210–253.

Clement, D. C. (1982). Samoan cultural knowledge of mental disorders. In A. J. Marsella & G. M. White (Eds.), *Cultural conceptions of mental health and therapy* (pp. 193–215). Dordrecht, Holland: D. Reidel.

Clifford, J. (1988). *The predicament of culture: Twentieth-century ethnography, literature and art.* Cambridge, MA: Harvard University Press.

Crapanzano, V. (1980a). Rite of return: Circumcision in Morocco. *Psychoanalytic Study of Society, 9,* 15–36.

Crapanzano, V. (1980b). *Tuhami: Portrait of a Moroccan.* Chicago: University of Chicago Press.

Csordas, T. J. (1994). *The sacred self: A cultural phenomenology of charismatic healing.* Berkeley: University of California Press.

Davies, B., & Harré, R. (1990). Positioning: The discursive production of selves. *Journal for the Theory of Social Behavior, 20,* 43–63.

Dumont, L. (1966/1980). *Homo hierarchicus: The caste system and its implications.* Chicago: University of Chicago Press.

Duranti, A. (1992). Intentions, self, and responsibility: An essay in Samoan ethnopragmatics. In J. H. Hill and J. T. Irvine (Eds.), *Responsibility and evidence in oral discourse* (pp. 24–47). Cambridge: Cambridge University Press.

Eggan, D. (1974). Instruction and affect in Hopi cultural continuity. In G. D. Spindler (Ed.), *Education and cultural process: Toward an anthropology of education* (pp. 311–332). New York: Holt, Rinehart & Winston.

Erikson, E. (1968). *Identity: Youth and crisis.* New York: W. W. Norton.

Ewing, K. P. (1990). The illusion of wholeness: Culture, self, and the experience of inconsistency. *Ethos, 18,* 251–278.

Fabian, J. (1983). *Time and the other: How anthropology makes its objects.* New York: Columbia University Press.

Favret-Saada, J. (1980). *Deadly words: Witchcraft in the Bocage* (C. Cullen, Trans.). Cambridge: Cambridge University Press.

Fogelson, R. D. (1979). Person, self, and identity: Some anthropological retrospects, circumspects, and prospects. In B. Lee (Ed.), *Psychosocial theories of the self* (pp. 67–109). New York: Plenum.

Geertz, C. (1973). Deep play: Notes on the Balinese cockfight. In *The interpretation of cultures* (pp. 412–453). New York: Basic Books.

Gregor, T. (1977). *Mehinaku: The drama of daily life in a Brazilian Indian village.* Chicago: University of Chicago Press.

Hallowell, A. I. (1955a). The Ojibwa self and its behavioral environment. In *Culture and experience* (pp. 172–182). Philadelphia: University of Pennsylvania Press.

Hallowell, A. I. (1955b). The self and its behavioral environment. In *Culture and experience* (pp. 75–110). Philadelphia: University of Pennsylvania Press.

Haraway, D. (1988). Situated knowledges: The science question in feminism and the privilege of the partial perspective. *Feminist Studies, 14,* 575–600.

Harré, R., & Van Langenhove, L. (1991). Varieties of positioning. *Journal for the Theory of Social Behavior, 21*, 391–407.

Harris, G. G. (1989). Concepts of individual, self, and person in description and analysis. *American Anthropologist, 91*, 599–612.

Henriques, J., Hollway, W., Urwin, C., Venn, C., & Walkerdine, V. (1984). *Changing the subject: Psychology, social regulation and subjectivity.* London: Methuen.

Henry, J. (1963). *Culture against man.* New York: Random House.

Hill, J. (1985). The grammar of consciousness and the consciousness of grammar. *American Ethnologist, 12*, 725–737.

Hollan, D. (1992). Cross-cultural differences in the self. *Journal of Anthropological Research, 48*, 282–300.

Holland, D., Skinner, D., Lachicotte, W., & Cain, C., (forthcoming). *Emerging selves: Identities forming in and against cultural worlds.* Cambridge, MA: Harvard University Press.

Holland, D., & Cole, M. (1995). Between discourse and schema: Reformulating a cultural-historical approach to culture and mind. *Anthropology and Education Quarterly, 26*(4), 475–489.

Holland, D., & Kipnis, A. (1994). Metaphors for embarrassment and stories of exposure: The not-so-egocentric self in American culture. *Ethos, 22*, 316–342.

Holland, D., & Skinner, D. (1995). Contested ritual, contested femininities: (Re)forming self and society in a Nepali women's festival. *American Ethnologist, 22*, 279–305.

Hollway, W. (1984). Gender difference and the production of subjectivity. In J. Henriques, W. Hollway, C. Urwin, C. Venn, & V. Walkerdine, *Changing the subject: Psychology, social regulation and subjectivity* (pp. 227–263). London: Methuen.

Honigmann, J. J. (1954). *Culture and personality.* New York: Harper.

Ito, K. L. (1987). Emotions, proper behavior (*hana pono*) and Hawaiian concepts of self, person, and individual. In A. B. Robillard & A. J. Marsella (Eds.), *Contemporary issues in mental health research in the Pacific Islands* (pp. 45–71). Honolulu: University of Hawaii, Social Science Research Institute.

Kipnis, A. (1995). Within and against peasantness: Backwardness and filiality in rural China. *Comparative Studies in Society and History, 37*, 110–135.

Kitayama, S., Markus, H., & Lieberman, C. (1995). The collective construction of self esteem: Implications for culture, self, and emotion. In J. A. Russell, J.-M. Fernández-Dols, A. S. R. Manstead, & J. C. Wellenkamp (Eds.), *Everyday conceptions of emotion: An introduction to the psychology, anthropology and linguistics of emotion* (pp. 523–570). Dordrecht, Holland: Kluwer Academic.

Kleinman, A. (1988). *Rethinking psychiatry: From cultural category to personal experience.* New York: Free Press/Collier Macmillan.

Kondo, D. K. (1990). *Crafting selves: Power, gender, and discourses of identity in a Japanese workplace.* Chicago: University of Chicago Press.

LeVine, R. A. (1982). *Culture, behavior, and personality: An introduction to the comparative study of psychosocial adaptation.* Chicago: Aldine.

Lutz, C. (1988). *Unnatural emotions: Everyday sentiments on a Micronesian atoll and their challenge to Western theory.* Chicago: University of Chicago Press.

Lutz, C. (in press). The psychological ethic and the spirit of permanent war: The military production of twentieth-century American subjects. In J. Pfister and N. Schnog (Eds.), *The invention of the psychological: The cultural history of emotions in America.* New Haven: Yale University Press.

Lutz, C., & Abu-Lughod, L. (1990). Introduction: Emotion, discourse, and the politics of everyday life. In C. Lutz & L. Abu-Lughod (Eds.), *Language and the politics of emotion* (pp. 1–23). Cambridge: Cambridge University Press.

Lutz, C., & Collins, J. (1993). *Reading National Geographic.* Chicago: University of Chicago Press.

Mageo, J. M. (1989). *Aga, amio* and *loto:* Perspectives on the structure of the self in Samoa. *Oceania, 59,* 181–199.

Marcus, G., & Fischer, M. (1986). *Anthropology as cultural critique: An experimental moment in the human sciences.* Chicago: University of Chicago Press.

Markus, H. R., & Kitayama, S. (1991). Culture and the self: Implications for cognition, emotion, and motivation. *Psychological Review, 98,* 224–253.

Marriott, M. (1976a). Hindu transactions: Diversity without dualism. In B. Kapferer (Ed.), *Transaction and meaning: Directions in the anthropology of exchange and symbolic behavior* (pp. 109–142). Philadelphia: Institute for the Study of Human Issues.

Marriott, M. (1976b). Interpreting Indian society: A monistic alternative to Dumont's dualism. *Journal of Asian Studies, 36,* 189–195.

Marsella, A., DeVos, G., & Hsu, F. L. (Eds.) (1985). *Culture and self: Asian and Western perspectives.* New York: Tavistock.

McHugh, E. (1989). Concepts of the person among the Gurungs of Nepal. *American Ethnologist, 16,* 75–86.

Miller, J. G. (1988). Bridging the content-structure dichotomy: Culture and the self. In M. H. Bond (Ed.), *The cross-cultural challenge to social psychology* (pp. 267–328). Newbury Park: Sage.

Mines, M. (1988). Conceptualizing the person: Hierarchical society and individual autonomy in India. *American Anthropologist, 90,* 568–579.

Murray, D. W. (1993). What is the Western concept of the self?: On forgetting David Hume. *Ethos, 21,* 3–23.

Obeyesekere, G. (1981). *Medusa's hair: An essay on personal symbols and religious experience.* Chicago: University of Chicago Press.

Parish, S. (1991). The sacred mind: Newar cultural representations of mental life and the production of moral consciousness. *Ethos, 19,* 313–351.

Parish, S. (1994). *Moral knowing in a Hindu sacred city.* New York: Columbia University Press.

Parker, I. (1992). *Discourse dynamics: Critical analysis for social and individual psychology.* New York: Routledge.

Peacock, J., & Holland, D. (1993). The narrated self. *Ethos, 21,* 367–383.

Reiter, R. R. (Ed.) (1975). *Toward an anthropology of women.* New York: Monthly Review Press.

Robbins, R. H. (1973). Identity, culture, and behavior. In J. J. Honigmann (Ed.), *Handbook of social and cultural anthropology* (pp. 1199–1222). Chicago: Rand McNally.

Rosaldo, M. (1980). *Knowledge and passion: Ilongot notions of self and social life.* Cambridge: Cambridge University Press.

Roseberry, W. (1982). Balinese cockfights and the seduction of anthropology. *Social Research, 49,* 1013–1028.

Sapir, E. (1949). Personality. In D. G. Mandelbaurm (Ed.), *Selected writings of Edward Sapir in language, culture and personality* (pp. 560–569). Berkeley: University of California Press. (Original work published 1934.)

Scheper-Hughes, N. (1992). Hungry bodies, medicine, and the state: Toward a critical psychological anthropology. In T. Schwartz, G. M. White, & C. A. Lutz (Eds.), *New directions in psychological anthropology* (pp. 221–247). Cambridge: Cambridge University Press.

Scheper-Hughes, N., & Lock, M. (1987). The mindful body: A prolegomenon to future work in medical anthropology. *Medical Anthropology Quarterly, 1,* 6–14.

Shore, B. (1982). *Sala'ilua: A Samoan mystery.* New York: Columbia University Press.

Shweder, R. (1991). *Thinking through cultures: Expeditions in cultural psychology.* Cambridge, MA: Harvard University Press.

Shweder, R. A., & Bourne, E. J. (1984). Does the concept of person vary cross-culturally? In R. A. Shweder & R. A. Levine (Eds.), *Culture theory: Essays on mind, self, and emotion* (pp. 158–199). Cambridge: Cambridge University Press.

Skinner, D. (1990). *Nepalese children's understanding of self and the social world.* Unpublished doctoral thesis, University of North Carolina, Chapel Hill.

Skinner, D., Holland, D., & Adhikari, G. B. (1994). The songs of *Tij:* A genre of critical commentary for women in Nepal. *Asian Folklore Studies 53,* 259–305.

Smith, P. (1988). *Discerning the subject.* Minneapolis: University of Minnesota Press.

Smolka, A. L. B., de Góes, A. C. R., & Pino, A. (in press). (In)determinacy and semiotic constitution of subjectivity. In A. Fogel, M. C. Lyra, & J. Valsiner (Eds.), *Dynamics and indeterminism in developmental and social processes.* Hillsdale, NJ: Erlbaum.

Spiro, M. E. (1993). Is the Western conception of the self "peculiar" within the context of the world cultures? *Ethos, 21,* 107–153.

Tolman, C. W., & Maiers, W. (Eds.) (1991). *Critical psychology: Contributions to an historical science of the subject.* Cambridge: Cambridge University Press.

Weiner, A. B. (1976). *Women of value, men of renown: New perspectives in Trobriand exchange.* Austin, TX: University of Texas Press.

Wexler, P. (1983). *Critical social psychology.* Washington, D.C.: Falmer.

White, G. M. (1991). *Identity through history: Living stories in a Solomon Islands society.* Cambridge: Cambridge University Press.

White, G. M. (1992). Ethnopsychology. In *New directions in psychological anthropology* (pp. 21–46). Cambridge: Cambridge University Press.

White, G. M. (1993). Emotions inside out: The anthropology of affect. In M. Lewis & J. Haviland (Eds.), *Handbook of emotion* (pp. 29–39). New York: Guilford.

Whittaker, E. (1992). The birth of the anthropological self and its career. *Ethos, 20,* 191–219.

The Self and Society

Changes, Problems, and Opportunities

Personal identity is a crucial interface between the private organism and society. The identity represents an important means by which the physical being takes its place in society so as to communicate and interact with other people. Meanwhile, the broader society assigns roles to the individual and shapes the values the person holds, so that identity is also an important means by which society can influence and control his or her behavior. It is no more correct to say that the individual is passively created by society than it is to regard society as a mere outcome of the choices and actions of autonomous, self-determined individuals; self and society shape each other.

The purpose of this chapter is to understand the special problems that attend the nature of selfhood in modern Western society. I begin by considering the universal roots of selfhood and then examine the historical and social processes that shaped the modern Western version of self. This will permit a consideration of both the distinctive features of the modern Western self and the special problems and burdens that it entails. My approach will focus on explaining the key points in simple terms rather than elaborating the many subtle implications of the research findings. Readers interested in an overview of empirical studies of self and identity in social psychology may prefer to consult other recent works (Baumeister, 1995, in press), in which hundreds of research findings are presented and integrated.

Roots of Selfhood

It is undeniably true that self begins with body. The number of selves in a given room is equal to the count of bodies. Understanding of selfhood begins with awareness of one's body, and the body continues to be an important basis of selfhood throughout life. Yet clearly there is more to self than the body. There are several basic kinds of experience that create a more elaborate and complex basis for selfhood than the mere fact of having a physical form. (Indeed, these adapt and transform the experience of having a body, too.) These have been of greatest interest to psychologists, and these will be the main focus of the psychology of self.

I propose three main, universal experiences by which bodies become selves and that thus form the basis of the psychological self. Society and culture can use, alter, shape, and adapt these experiences, but they constitute the essential nature of selfhood. Moreover, they seem sufficient to encompass the immense variety of research that social and personality psychologists have conducted to investigate the self (see Baumeister, in press).

The first of these is the experience of reflexive consciousness. Human consciousness can turn around in a circle, so to speak, and become aware of its source. Reflexive consciousness is what is involved when a man is ruminating about his triumphs or failures, when a woman wonders whether she could ever perform the sort of heroic sacrifice or cruel betrayal she has heard on the news, when the spiritual novice meditates on his breathing or spiritual center, when the dieter debates whether she needs to lose more pounds, and when the survey respondent tries to answer a series of questions about personal opinions, attributes, and values. Without reflexive consciousness, the very notion of self would be incomprehensible.

The second root of selfhood is the interpersonal being. People everywhere exist as members of groups and as partners in interpersonal relationships. The interpersonal aspect of self is the focal one in love and hate, in rivalry and competition, in trying to live up to someone's expectations or worrying about what impression one is making, in feeling pride in one's spouse or college team or ethnic group, and in taking people's praise or blame for what one has done. Selves do not and probably cannot develop in social isolation, and it is misleading to regard interpersonal patterns as mere accidental products of self-contained, wholly independent selves.

The third root of selfhood is the executive function. This is the active decision-making entity that initiates action, exerts control, and regulates the self. Making a promise or resolution, signing a mortgage or contract, resisting temptation, stifling one's feelings, choosing a car to buy, or forcing oneself to concentrate all involve the executive function.

The moral responsibilities of one's acts and choices are also an important basis for creating the unity and continuity of the self. The terms "agency" and "agent" are sometimes used to describe this aspect of the self, but they seem misleading in a fundamental way: to be an agent is to act on behalf of someone else, whereas the executive function essentially involves acting on one's own behalf. The self is a capacity for making choices, taking responsibility, and exerting self-control. Without the executive function, the self could still be self-aware and belong to groups, but it would be a mere helpless, passive spectator of events.

Culture Constructs the Individual

There is fair evidence that Westerners have not always had the strong sense of individuality that reigns now. Notions of selfhood in the Middle Ages in the West may have been far more collective than they are now. Some of the evidence behind this conclusion includes the lack of autobiographical writing, the indifference to factual accuracy in the writing of biographies, the indifference to privacy in architecture and social life, religious attitudes and practices (e.g., burial patterns), and the neglect of individuality and perspective in literature (Baumeister, 1986, 1987).

One of the best works on individuality is that by historian Karl Weintraub (1978). His definition of individuality has two criteria. First, individuality involves the appreciation, even the celebration, of ways in which each individual person is special or unique or different. Second, it involves a sense of unique destiny for each person. Weintraub concludes that the early modern period, roughly 1500 to 1800, saw a decisive shift, to this new, individualistic view of the human being. The first criterion was satisfied around the beginning of that era, and the second around the end. The early modern period saw extensive changes in the society and culture, and some of these altered the basic way in which human selfhood was shaped, used, and understood. For example, politically in Europe the feudal system broke down and had mostly disappeared by the end of the early modern era (except perhaps in Russia). People gained the right to move, to make their own decisions, to decide their own marriages and occupations.

Obviously, these new rights and opportunities were not simply given because someone thought they would be nice. The actual political struggles of the time involved the emergence of national states as major centers of power (except in Germany). These replaced the previous organization, in which most power was concentrated locally. The shift in power was not easily accomplished. Local power was held by small nobles and aristocrats in connection with extended families who controlled wealth and other resources. In that system, the extended family or clan was of decisive importance because it formed the power base of the local nobles and officials. To thwart that axis and concentrate political power at the national level, the central governments needed a different power base, and they found this by using individual citizens. Concepts of justice, wealth, duty, and rights were refocused on the individual instead of the kinship network.

Also underlying the social reorganization was a series of economic changes. The feudal system, after all, was economic even more than it was a political arrangement: it kept people locked in place and manipulated their labor so that the wealth it created supported the status quo. Most people worked as serf farmers, toiling without ever accumulating much wealth or having the opportunity to do anything else.

Some historians think that the Black Death dealt a fatal blow to the feudal system. In large parts of Europe, a third of the population died. Two economic consequences were a shortage of labor and a surplus of available land. Despite the effort to restrict movement and pass laws regulating wages, it almost inevitably resulted that poor people could begin to move around, get different jobs and homes, and in essence find a new position in society if they disliked their old one. The Black Death also gave people more money; after all, if the amount of wealth is constant but one third of the population dies, then on average each survivor becomes richer by half. The greater wealth offered more scope for the middle class to gain money and influence, and hence power. This, too, was something that fed into the emergence of national governments, because the middle classes were not so dependent on the local barons as the serfs had been and their cash made them a desirable ally for the emerging national governments against the local barons (who were after all a common enemy).

These social changes centrally affect two of the most important aspects of the self—namely, the interpersonal one and the executive function. The part of the self that takes initiative and makes decisions is a trivial one when there are relatively few major choices to be made, such as in the rigid and restrictive society of medieval Europe. In contrast, the new opportunities gave vastly expanded scope for making choices. By 1800, in fact, people could, to a substantial extent, choose their own occupations, their spouses, and where they wanted to live. And city dwellers mostly had some choice among food, housing, and other elements of their lifestyles. The executive function suddenly had a significant role to play in both the consequential and the mundane.

The change should not be overstated, of course. Undoubtedly there have always been choices and decisions to make. Yet it seems hard to deny that the range and variety of such choices is much greater in modern Western society than it has been in many other times and places. Simply deciding what to have for supper and what form of entertainment to pursue afterward presents the modern Western individual with an immense array of options and requires the self to have a reasonably well articulated set of preferences, priorities, and criteria. The range of possible supper entrées and evening entertainments available to a 16-century farmer in a small European or African village was undoubtedly much narrower, and so his self did not require such an elaborate structure.

Meanwhile, the interpersonal aspect of self has been severely altered in the modern world. The self is no longer immersed in the local clan and small society where it lived for centuries. Instead, it is relatively free to choose and change its relationships. A particular self is not necessarily or permanently a part of a particular neighborhood; one can move away and become part of a different one.

The upshot is not merely the abilitiy to change one's interpersonal connections, though: it is to separate selfhood from its immersion in these connections. As Alasdair MacIntyre (1981) has argued, the new view of selfhood involved thinking of it as existing prior to and apart from its roles in society. Thus was created the paradox or tension that continues to define (and plague) modern selfhood: the self exists as something outside of its particular connections, yet everywhere it seeks such connections.

Emergence of Inner Selfhood

I turn now to a second development in how cultural changes have fundamentally altered the nature of selfhood: the rise in Western societies of a strong belief in the self as a hidden entity that exists inside the person. The inner self refers to a self that is not directly visible in one's actions and physical appearance, not the same as one's social roles. These appearances are regarded as expressions of the inner reality of selfhood. In some cases, according to the new belief, these appearances may be misleading or may contradict the true self. Another corollary of the belief in an inner self is that often it becomes necessary for a person to exert him- or herself to discover the nature of this inner self. People generally assume that each individual self contains many hidden depths that are essential to its individual nature but that must be searched for and then cultivated.

Clearly, the notion of an inner or hidden self is not one that was invented overnight or even in one single development. The Christian concept of soul, which has been widely influential in our culture, is an important precursor of the idea of an inner self, though even the concept of soul has evolved and changed. The theological changes around the 11th and 12th centuries led to the consideration of souls as much more individually different from each other than in the prior views. In the new Christian thought emerging at that time, the concept spread that people would be judged as individuals, based on the morality and piety of their personal actions during life. The soul came to be seen as carrying around a record of one's acts, both virtuous and sinful.

Still, many scholars believe that it was in the 16th century that the culture most decisively expanded its conception of an inner selfhood. Many significant developments reflected this change. Theater began to feature plots based on the idea that many characters pretended to be someone or something other than who they actually were. This in particular included the standard character of the villain, who is evil but deceives the other characters about his (or, less often, her) evil intentions. In contrast, in medieval morality plays, the evil characters came clearly and overtly named as evil (Trilling, 1971).

Other signs of the emergence of an inner self included social practices in which people might adopt the dress and mannerisms appropriate to a different, especially a better, class of people. There had always been fairly rigid dress codes, and one's rank in society dictated what one was permitted to wear, with the result that one could tell someone's position in society from a distance simply by seeing his or her clothes. In the modern period, however, some people began to break those rules and "dress up." The relative anonymity of city life made it harder for the collectivity to recognize and punish people who were dressing better than they should have been allowed, and the increasing wealth of many middle-class people gave them the means to buy finer clothes. In many cases, the motives for such deceptions went beyond mere short-term narcissism. The political and economic changes of the times meant that many aristocrats began to have money problems. Marriages between upwardly mobile, well-heeled bourgeoisie and cash-poor blue bloods became increasingly frequent because both parties got something they coveted. Still, the aristocrats would not marry just any common person who happened to have money; to be eligible, the middle-class person and to some extent the whole family had to have at least the veneer of social acceptability to the upper classes. The eighteenth century saw the spread of "finishing schools" and other institutions designed to teach the children of the ambitious middle class how to pass for ladies and gentlemen, so that they might become eligible to intermarry with people of quality (e.g., Sennett, 1974; Stone, 1977).

The increased recognition that inner and outer selves might differ was also reflected in the new 16th-century virtue of sincerity (Trilling, 1971). Sincerity came to mean that one's visible actions and statements were in agreement with one's inner thoughts, feelings, and intentions. To elevate sincerity to the status of an important virtue indicates that the society has developed some pervasive concerns about people who present a face that does not express their true sentiments.

As a related trend, self-deception also became much more commonly recognized. The concept of self-deception implies that there is an inner, hidden reality to the self that even the person's own conscious self fails to see. Many historians have argued that the Puritans provided a great stimulus to the acknowledgment of self-deception. Puritan doctrine believed in one particularly crucial inner reality—namely, the predestined eternal fate of the individual soul. Calvin thought that one could tell during life whether a particular individual was fated to spend eternity in heaven or hell, and perhaps unfortunately this stimulated many ordinary Puritans to spend much of their time examining their own thoughts, feelings, and actions for signs of exceptional piety or sinful depravity. Inevitably, they began to notice that everyone wanted to believe himself or herself among the elect and that people often tried to put an optimistic interpretation on their own responses. Self-deception was widely discovered. Self-knowledge would never enjoy that same total easy confidence again.

Once the notion of an inner self was established, successive generations elaborated on it. The Romantics expanded the notion of an individual destiny and therefore gave us the by now quite familiar notion that a person must look inside oneself to discover one's calling and then pursue that throughout life in order to reach fulfillment. In tandem, they expanded the view of art and creativity as a process of reaching inside oneself to find the makings of major artistic achievements. Later yet, the Victorians came to regard the visible actions and appearances as merely being small clues about the vast and inner realms of selfhood. The quintessential Victorian hero Sherlock Holmes, for example, would frequently solve crimes simply by noticing some detail of appearance or some seemingly trivial act and appreciating its broad significance for revealing crucial facts about an individual. Likewise, Sigmund Freud succeeded by explaining what vast hidden forces of desire, violence, and trauma lay hidden beneath the seemingly ordinary and mundane surfaces of well-to-do bourgeois citizens, sometimes glimpsed through such easily overlooked signs as slips of the tongue and dreams.

There are two further points to make about the evolution of the hidden, inner self as a standard way of thinking about selfhood. First, it increases the problematic nature of selfhood. If the self is a secret entity, indeed in important respects concealed even from the very person whose self it is, then self-knowledge is a difficult and elusive matter. Indeed, if all a person's actions and statements fail to reveal some inner truth, then it is unclear how one can ever be certain that one has understood the true inner self. And if self-deception is always a possibility, it is unclear how one can ever surely know oneself. The modern concept of self-actualization takes the problem even a step further because it requires first a process of discovering the hidden inner realities and then a process of working to cultivate and develop these inner traits to reach their full potential. The version of selfhood implicit in all these modern concepts is one that carries a significant burden and a recipe for uncertainty, difficulty, and dissonance.

Second, the evolution of the inner self is in many respects a cultural elaboration of the reflexive consciousness aspect of the self. To be sure, it invokes a couple of the other aspects as well. Some of the early factors that gave rise to the concept of the inner self were interpersonal, such as the concern with sincerity of other people. Our culture has come to regard the process of choice as often involving looking inside oneself to discover the correct attitude or nature of one's inner self, which is then presumed to be a basis for making correct choices (see Bellah, Madsen, Sullivan, Swidler, and Tipton, 1985). Thus, the interpersonal partner and the executive function aspects of self are involved.

Still, though, the most centrally involved is the reflexive consciousness of the self. One becomes aware of oneself as trying to discover what one is really like inside. One knows that such self-discovery is often difficult and one may even become aware of tendencies toward self-deception. Although many influential experiments have manipulated self-awareness by having students look at a mirror, this is of course regarded as a stimulating cue rather than the essence of the process. One does not see everything in the mirror. Self-awareness is a matter of examining inner realms to learn the elusive truths about a presumably extensive and fixed nature. Thus, the culture transformed reflexive consciousness from a mere act of attending to one's own sensations or states into a challenging journey of exploration: a treasure hunt.

The New Moral Role of Selfhood

To achieve a full understanding of the modern problems associated with Western selfhood, it is necessary to examine social and cultural shifts in yet another context. Some social changes unrelated to the self created a new psychological need in the culture, and the self was mobilized to provide it. A new kind of demand has been placed on selfhood recently, and this is altering the role of selfhood in Western society, as well as increasing the concern and fascination with it.

One important shift in the modern era is a gradual loss of moral consensus. This does not mean that modern Western citizens are necessarily any less honest or decent or virtuous than their ancestors. It does mean, however, that the difficulty of being a virtuous or decent person has increased insofar as firm rules of right and wrong have been lost and tolerance for personal values, situational ethics, and differing moral outlooks has been promoted. The separation of church and state has in many cases been accompained by a reluctance to impose one set of moral values on everyone. As a result, many citizens of today's Western countries believe that they must look inside themselves to find some basis for making moral decisions. As Bellah et al. (1985) have described in their insightful analysis of this moral vacuum, today's Americans tend to ask themselves whether something "feels right" as their primary basis for making moral judgments.

The loss of consensus about moral principles is only part of a broader development. The essence of this development is that Western society has gradually weakened or lost its *value bases*, which are defined as firm, recognized sources of justification and moral worth (see also Habermas, 1973). Most justifications of specific actions operate by citing some other source, authority, or principle from which they derive their goodness. These in turn can be challenged and defended by citing yet more basic values or principles. Ultimately, however, moral discourse requires that there must be some things whose moral goodness is not derivative but that rather are accepted as good in and of themselves. God's will is a traditional example: if something is consistent with God's will, then it is good, but God's will does not require further justification. No believer challenges this justification by asking, "So what?"

Clearly, however, the scope of everyday actions that ordinary citizens base on God's will has dwindled over the centuries with the shift toward modern, secular society. Other value bases, such as tradition, have also been weakened or undermined (see Shils, 1981), and as Habermas (1973) has explained, they are difficult to replace. For example, instituting a bureaucracy based on rational systems may easily replace tradition as a means of making decisions and solving problems, but it does not effectively supply the sense of goodness and value that tradition also furnished.

In my own analysis of the evolution of meaning of life (Baumeister, 1991b), I referred to this same loss of moral sense as the *value gap*. The value gap appears to have become acute with the Enlightenment's critique and partial rejection of Christianity because no secular humanism can muster the potent value bases that a religion usually has. As a source of moral authority, utilitarian analysis lacks the emotional force of God's will, even if it may be more adaptable to new social conditions.

It does appear that Western culture struggled to find new value bases to replace the lost ones. The work ethic was an attempt to consider work as a source of positive value in and of itself, although social attitudes and the changing nature of work may have doomed it, and in any case it no longer commands a consensus or guides the actual moral choices of most workers (Rodgers, 1978). Likewise, an enhanced value placed on the nuclear family, including elevating the perceived moral importance of love and motherhood, can also be understood as an attempt by the culture to endow a new value base that would help people know what was right and wrong without appealing to the fading authorities of religion and tradition (e.g., Lasch, 1977; Margolis, 1984). Today, clearly, family is a far more important and potent moral authority (e.g., what is right is whatever is best "for the sake of the children") than the work ethic.

For present purposes, however, the most important cultural response to the value gap is the attempt to transform the self into a major value base. Today's Americans believe that they have a right and even a duty to do what is best for their individual, unique, esteemed selves. They believe that every person should try to know him- or herself, which includes working to learn about his or her inner traits. They also believe that a person should try to fulfill his or her potential, which means identifying one's capabilities and unique talents, finding a suitable environment in which one can grow and flourish, and working to cultivate these capacities so as to "be all that you can be," in the phrase that ironically is used by the military services to recruit gullible young seekers after selfhood into combat training (Baumeister, 1991b; see also Bellah et al., 1985).

The new power of selfhood as an important value base can be seen in how people face moral conflicts between the self and other value bases. A well-known article by Zube (1972) documented how women's magazines showed a meaningful shift in moral attitudes from the 1940s to the 1960s in how they treated conflicts between marriage and self. In the years after World War II, whenever the self was unable to grow or thrive or reach its potential because of the press of marital obligations, the value judgment expressed in these magazine stories indicated that the morally right line of action was to maintain the marriage, even at the expense of the self. By the late 1960s, however, this had reversed: it became right and even obligatory for a woman to leave an oppressive, stultifying marriage in order to purse her own identity and self-fulfillment. Thus, between two of the most potent values of 20th-century America—selfhood and family—selfhood evolved from the lesser to the stronger value.

Recent analyses of religious movements suggest a similar theme. Although I have indicated that Christian religion lost the grip it once had on the collective workings of society, this should not be overstated. Most Americans continue to believe in God and to participate in some church. Religion thus remains an important force in their lives and presumably a welcome source of moral authority. The most successful churches today, however, appear to have shifted their attitude toward the self. The traditional emphasis on sin, damnation, weakness, and hellfire is largely gone. Instead, churches try to attract worshipers by invoking the value of selfhood. Churches offer multiple self-help programs, and sermons present a modernized view of spirituality that can seem little more than a form of self-esteem therapy with metaphysical overtones. Delbanco (1995) noted that the pursuit of self-interest could no longer be equated with the devil, as earlier eras had done, because in modern American everyone is permitted and even expected to pursue self-interest.

The functioning of the self as an important value base can also be seen in its influence over work. Each society must find one way or another to motivate people to work in order that the necessary goods and services will be provided. In early civilizations, peasant farmers work because they know they will starve otherwise, but in modern societies the unemployed do not typically starve to death. Christianity motivated people to work because that was their sacred duty, but few of today's workers believe that their daily activities on the job are directly required by divine mandate. The work ethic insisted that people should work as a good end in and of itself, or as a means toward building their character, but these attitudes, too, have lost most of their force.

Modern society, then, must motivate people to work by mobilizing the self as a relevant, potent value base. The modern concept of work as career treats work as a vital means of glorifying and fulfilling the self. The true careerist is motivated neither by shallow extrinsic goals such as making a living nor by deep intrinsic factors such as love of the work itself. Rather, the careerist aims to accumulate a record of promotions, achievements, and honors that will reflect favorably on the self. Hence people work very hard at things they personally may care rather little about in order to gain respect and esteem through their achievements. The value that drives them is the value placed on the self.

It is important to appreciate that the new moral value of selfhood is a radical departure from traditional attitudes. For most of history, morality and self-interest were opposites. Indeed, one of the crucial functions of morality has always been to oppose and prevent people from acting in selfish ways; pride, greed, and other sins essentially involved pursuing the best interests of the self at the expense of others. In the 1680 edition of the *Oxford English Dictionary*, the sample use of "self" supplied with the definiton was, "Self is the great Anti-Christ and Anti-God in the world" (Rosenthal, 1984). In contrast, modern thought now usually puts self and morality on the same side. Moral duties and obligations do not all involve restraining or opposing the self—and sometimes they require promoting the self.

In an important manner, this emphasis on self as a value base constitutes an extension of the agent aspect of the self. The self becomes more than just the agent who decides how to implement moral principles and other obligations and who carries out those decisions; it is now the source of those moral principles and obligations. Selfhood has become the root of moral authority. In the words of Bellah, et al. (1985), "In the absence of any objectifiable criteria of right and wrong, good and evil, the self and its feelings become our only moral guide" (p. 76). Thus, this cultural shift has greatly extended the agent aspect of the self.

Modern Western society has devised a new role for the self, which involves supplying important meaning to life. Hence many individuals' problems with finding a meaningful life will be expressed as selfhood problems and identity crises. Moreover, it is arguably unfair and unrealistic to expect the self to provide a firm basis for making moral decisions and supplying life with value, and so this modern use of the self seems likely to lead to serious problems and difficulties of selfhood.

The Vicissitudes of Self-Control

As a corollary of the rising reliance on self as a major value base, many people have in practice become skeptical or even negative toward self-control. This is difficult to document, if only because it is hard to measure self-control as a personality trait or capacity, and indeed at present the lack of useful questionnaire measures has been an obstacle to researchers. These difficulties naturally are compounded when one seeks to compare across different historical periods or eras. Still, there seems to be some validity to the stereotypes of Victorian self-control and modern self-indulgence.

One common explanation for such shifts focuses on the change in emphasis in the economy (e.g., Potter, 1954). As a general rule, economic changes do have strong effects on people's behaviors and attitudes (e.g., Harris, 1978, 1979). Prior to 1900, the limiting factor on sales was manufacturing. If the product was good, one could sell as many as one could make. In the 20th century, manufacturing technology advanced so rapidly that in many cases one could make almost unlimited quantites of goods. The limiting factor therefore became consumer demand. One can sell as much as people want to buy. In response to this new economic reality, advertising emerged as a vital means of stimulating consumer demand. The modern individual is almost constantly subjected to a barrage of messages exhorting him or her to buy and consume. The Protestant ethic was one of saving money, but that became obsolete in the modern world. Instead, 20th-century citizens are urged to spend their money as fast as—and now even faster than—they earn it. Many people consume so much that they remain chronically in debt.

Thus, the self-restraint urged by past eras fit the economic realities of the time, but these have changed, and self-restraint has become the enemy rather than the ally of the main economic forces. Self-control can be understood as the resisting of one's impulses, or other responses, so as to alter them. Today's economy does not want people to resist their impulses: it wants them to act on them and indeed to have more of them.

Other societal factors may have contributed to the erosion in the popularity of self-control. The 20th century tends to view the Victorian era as marked by neurosis, frustration, and unhappiness deriving from excessive control. Freud's famous insights are widely understood to suggest that repression is unhealthy and that to stifle any impulse is damaging. (I suspect that Freud would be horrified to see self-indulgence justified on the basis of his theories.) People are reluctant to force their children to conform to external controls and standards, fearing that imposing such authoritarian controls will stifle their creativity and create low self-esteem.

The current problems with violence in society probably have roots in this same issue of self-control. Of course, the idea that social and cultural factors contribute to violence is hardly a new idea. In the 1960s, the hypothesis of "subcultures of violence" was put forward to explain the high rates of crime in poor urban centers. This hypothesis said that certain subcultures placed a positive value on violent action and so young men would commit crimes as a way of gaining prestige and respect. This hypothesis was largely discredited in the 1970s because researchers persistently failed to find any evidence of subcultures that placed a positive value on violence (see Tedeschi & Felson, 1994, for review) or that people behaved violently in the expectation of gaining prestige (e.g., Berkowitz, 1978).

Yet the subculture-of-violence hypothesis may be worth reviving, with one crucial change. Criminologists have increasingly come to recognize that crimes are committed impulsively and by people who show a pervasive lack of self-control in all spheres of life (Gottfredson & Hirschi, 1990). This means that it is not necessary for a society to advocate violence in order to promote it; all one has to do is remove the inner blocks. A subculture (or indeed a culture) of violence may emerge simply because the society lowers its standards for self-control. The point at which people abandon self-control is highly negotiable and flexible (see Baumeister, Heatherton, & Tice, 1994). Cultural prescriptions can exert considerable influence by telling people at what point it is appropriate to turn violent, ranging from "only when someone is attacking you in a life-threatening fashion" to "when the person implies disrespect toward you by making eye contact."

Creating the Burden of Selfhood

By all accounts, modern Western society has surrounded individual selfhood with much greater demands and expectations than have most other cultures in the history of the world. To be sure, most societies have expected individuals to live up to various standards, and sometimes these have been high. But only the modern West has expected its citizens to generate and validate their own standards, as well as constructing and maintaining a unique and autonomous self that can be socially validated through a constantly changing series of interpersonal relationships and transactions. The task is a daunting one, and indeed the transformation of adolescence into an age of identity crisis and self-exploration is one sign of how difficult people often find it to satisfy the paradoxical modern demand that the self must create and discover itself (e.g., Baumeister & Tice, 1986; see also Demos & Demos, 1969; Kett, 1977).

Some problems of selfhood are age-old. Undoubtedly, when a person falls far short of an important standard, such as when a man does something that brings ruin or disgrace on himself and his family, then the person will feel bad and suffer over the tarnished image of self. Possibly the distress is magnified in modern life because of the value-base aspect: not only has the person damaged a self-image, but he or she has also damaged an important source of value in life. Still, the problem of coping with a temporarily damaged self-image is an ancient one.

Other problems of selfhood are new, however. The new cultural demands on selfhood make it into a burdensome concern that can produce frequent stress (Baumeister, 1991a). People feel they must maintain a highly positive image of self that requires constant vigilance against dangers and threats. Even if they do not encounter major experiences of humiliation or disgrace, the ongoing threat and the resulting demand for vigilance may become tiresome and draining. Awareness of self may often be tinged with worry or stress and hence may take on an aversive aspect.

The Shape of Modern Selfhood

Before turning to consider how the special nature of modern Western selfhood creates specific problems and difficulties, it is useful to reexamine that distinctive form of selfhood as social history has shaped it. Selves do of course remain tied to physical bodies, but the three other aspects of selfhood have been fundamentally altered by the historical changes.

Reflexive Consciousness

First, the basic degree of self-consciousness appears to have intensified. Although various ancient thinkers such as St. Augustine engaged in lengthy, thoughtful exercises of introspective self-examination, there has been a substantial increase in the frequency with which ordinary people examine and question themselves. The pursuit of self-knowledge has come to be regarded as an important, large, and difficult task.

The escalating belief in the hidden, inner nature of essential selfhood has undoubtedly shaped modern reflexive consciousness and contributed to the perceived difficulty of self-knowlege. Exploring the vast hidden realm of the self takes considerable time and effort, especially because pervasive trends toward self-deception are seen as ever ready to thwart the diligent efforts of the self-seeker. In some ways psychoanalysis furnishes a prototype of the modern difficulty of self-knowledge: self-knowledge can only be achieved by means of years of work with an expert and expensive professional, and even then it remains incomplete.

Psychoanalysis may have been too pessimistic to retain its appeal to the modern Western imagination, but the unappealing pessimism pertains to the ugliness of what is supposedly locked inside the self rather than the difficulty of finding it. If people are to go digging for self-knowledge deep in their own psyches, they want to find some beautiful treasures reflecting a gifted and wondrous self, as opposed to merely discovering perverse sexual desires and bloodthirsty rages. In recent decades, a fascination with self-esteem has come to dominate American notions of self-understanding. The public is eager to learn how people can love themselves better and raise ever more confident, egotistical children. It is widely hoped that most of the societal and personal problems that plague American society can be blamed on low self-esteem, so that if only people can be taught to forgive themselves and admire themselves everything will be much better. The new moral value of selfhood has created a broad sense of moral obligation for people to explore their inner nature. It is presumed that improved self-knowledge will make the person feel and perform better and permit a gradual actualization of the self.

Interpersonal Being

The transience of social bonds is a pervasive and overdetermined feature of modern Western society, and its implications for interpersonal selfhood are difficult to overstate. It is not just marriages that break up: work collaborations, friendships, neighborhood acquaintanceships, filial ties, and all other social bonds are vulnerable to being disrupted or even terminated when one person moves far away or simply abandons the relationship to pursue new ones. If a close relationship does manage to endure for several decades, this is often surprising and exceptional.

The modern self must therefore function as a tool to attract and retain social ties to other people. It is common among historians and others to remark on how 20th-century parenting and self-help literature focuses on building charm and social appeal whereas 19th-century works emphasized building moral character. To some extent the shift can be understood as an almost inevitable response to the transience of social relationships. A reputation for honesty, trustworthiness, and other moral character traits depends on long-term social bonds, partly because people know that if they behave immorally they will have to continue to live among others who know their misdeeds. Such stable small communities have diminished in power and frequency in the 20th century, and indeed if a person is caught in minor dishonest behavior he or she can often simply move to a new home and start over. In contrast, sociable traits such as charm, attractiveness, and likability are chiefly useful for inducing other people to want to interact with oneself, and they become increasingly important as social relationships become temporary and unstable.

Indeed, the modern preoccupation with self-esteem may itself reflect the changed interpersonal world. Although theorists differ as to the basis of self-esteem, it is apparent that self-esteem is generally based on the main criteria by which groups include and exclude individuals: physical attractiveness, competence, and likability. Moral traits such as reliability and honesty are also sometimes used to include or exclude individuals, such as when a group expels someone who betrays it or breaks its rules, and these traits are also sometimes relevant to self-esteem. Self-esteem can thus be understood as a private measure of one's suitability for interpersonal relationships (see Leary, Tambor, Terdal, & Downs, 1995). That is, high self-esteem means that the individual regards him- or herself as the sort of person with whom others would like to form relationships or groups. Low self-esteem entails a lack of social desirability and hence carries the implicit threat of potential social rejection, which explains the very high negative correlation between self-esteem and social anxiety (see Leary & Kowalski, 1995, for review).

Executive Function

The executive function has also been shaped in distinctive ways by modern Western society and culture. People have many more potential choices to make, every day, than their ancestors did, and so the executive function of the self is needed on a relatively frequent basis. The faith in the rightness of self-interest provides one welcome means of making choices, though it can serve as a rationalization for selfish and self-indulgent behaviors; indeed, modern moral discourse cannot easily maintain an operational distinction between self-actualization and self-indulgence. The problem is exacerbated by society's growing skepticism toward self-control.

Ultimately, the modern self is seen as having the license and obligation to create itself (see also Bellah et al., 1985). Acting on anything found inside the self is given a positive value unless it is directly harmful to others. People are expected to make whatever they want out of themselves. Although the reality is usually much more limited, the reigning ideology allows almost unlimited scope to the executive function.

Problems of Selfhood

I now consider the particular problems and difficulties that accompany the modern Western self. The focus on problems should not however be taken to indicate that this self is wholly bad, unhealthy, or otherwise catastrophic: it should be understood as an adaptation to certain patterns, pressures, and opportunities in society, and as such it is probably a reasonably effective if not fully optimal version. Some of the much decried features of modern Western culture, such as its problematic emphasis on individualism, likewise carry significant advantages. A recent cross-cultural investigation of happiness found that individualism was strongly and positively correlated with subjective well-being across a variety of different cultures (Diener, Diener, & Diener, 1995). Thus, there may be costs to living in a highly individualist society, but the net effect is to make people happier.

The Elusive Self

The first and most obvious problem in the modern Western version of selfhood is that simply creating it is a difficult and daunting task. Western society has developed a conception of selfhood as vast, complex, and in many key respects hidden from view. The problem is that much further complicated if the self does not in fact come fully supplied with all the buried contents that the culture promises. The inner search may therefore sometimes become a quixotic quest for nonexistent realities, and the sometimes arbitrary creation of the self's attributes must masquerade as discovery. Thus, for example, the notion that one can use reflexive consciousness to introspect in order to discover what one's true interpersonal traits are—traits that may moreover be contrary to one's overt interpersonal behavior—seems ironic to the point of absurdity, though it is nonetheless popular.

The difficulty of self-discovery falls most heavily on adolescents, because in the present society that is the age at which identity must appear. Historical changes have enabled young people to postpone the choices that will define adult identity until adolescence, and increased freedom has allowed young people to make such choices themselves instead of having family and other connections make them. To be sure, such freedom is a continuum, not a dichotomy. Even in the era of arranged marriages, young people often had some say in the matter, and family pressures are not irrelevant to career choices today. Still, the modern Western adolescent has a remarkable range of options for defining identity, combined with an equally remarkable lack of compelling bases for making the choices.

Hence, adolescence has taken on the nature of being a time of struggle to create identity. This is not to say that adolescence has only recently become problematic, but rather only to say that the nature of the problem has changed. Kett (1977) and others have observed that adolescence is a problematic phase of life in most cultures, but usually the main complaints are unruliness, disobedience, and proneness to get into trouble through minor sexual or aggressive transgressions. Those complaints have hardly disappeared from modern adolescence, but the vulnerable and difficult problem of self-discovery has been added. In plain terms, teenagers have always been rambunctious and prone to mischief, but only recently have they started to have identity crises.

Escaping the Burden of Self

A second problem of modern Western selfhood involves the stress of living up to the exalted expectations about the nature of selves. Modern Western society presents people with a remarkable opportunity to become autonomous, self-determined, unique, and fulfilled, but the pressure to be all those things can be daunting. Moreover, the need to have an attractive, likeable, competent self to serve as an interpersonal tool for attracting and retaining relationship partners is also burdensome. Trying to appear brilliant, charming, successful, and thin often requires considerable and sustained exertion. When something happens to cast the self in a less desirable light, the person may experience a crisis.

If the burden of selfhood is indeed stressful, then one could predict that members of this society would show some behavioral signs that reflect their responses to that stress. These would most likely involve efforts to escape, at least temporarily, from the burdensome self-awareness (in the same way that small safe periods greatly diminish the stressfulness of various anticipatory threats). Moreover, if these responses are indeed a product of modern Western culture, then they should be culturally and historically relative. At least, they should be more common and more centered on selfhood issues than elsewhere.

One might well ask what would be involved in escaping from self-awareness, because people cannot simply force themselves not to think about themselves. The effort to avoid thinking abut oneself has a paradoxical aspect, because any attempt to monitor the success of one's efforts will direct attention to the self—precisely where it is not supposed to be. As a result of this problem, it appears that efforts to escape self-awareness generally involve narrowing the scope of selfhood. Vallacher and Wegner (1985, 1987) showed how the same action can be understood at different levels of meaning, and the same applies to the self. Hence, one can be aware of oneself in minimalist terms, such as being merely a body standing in a room, as opposed to understanding the self in a complex and elaborate fashion.

The difference between those two forms of self-awareness may be decisive for escaping from the burden of selfhood. After all, it is the complex and elaborately defined self that is the source of stress. In contrast, if one could be aware of oneself as merely a physical entity existing in the immediate present, there would be far less to worry about, and stress would be minimized. Accordingly, if people cannot turn self-awareness off, they can accomplish many of the same results by merely becoming aware of themselves in minimal, here-and-now terms.

One prototype of such an escapist response is furnished by sexual masochism (Baumeister, 1988, 1989). Masochism involves a set of techniques that seem designed to render complex, symbolic self-awareness impossible, because the masochist is seemingly forced to do things that would be incompatible with his or her normal identity. The masochist sacrifices esteem and control by, for example, submitting to being tied up, being given commands by others, or being subjected to embarrassing or humiliating experiences (e.g., being required to kiss someone's feet). Masochism does not, however, prevent awareness of the self as a physical entity existing in the immediate present; indeed, it seems to increase self-awareness at that level, such as by inducing pain, which forcibly seizes attention and directs it to the part of the body that is hurting. Pain is in fact a potent means of thwarting meaningful, elaborate thought and focusing attention narrowly on the immediate bodily sensations (Scarry, 1985).

Moreover, the historical and cross-cultural evidence seems to indicate that masochism is largely confined to the modern West (Baumeister, 1988, 1989). Unlike most sexual variations, it is absent from the sex manuals, theological debates, and other (extensive) writings about sex that existed before the Renaissance. Indeed, the spread of masochistic practices and literature in Western culture coincided very neatly with the emergence of individualist conceptions of identity: the first clear references to masochistic sexuality appeared around 1500, and by 1800 it was a familiar and well-documented feature of the sexual landscape.With the possible exception of Japan, it seems to have been confined to Europe and America until quite recently.

Another interesting pattern of escape from self-awareness is binge eating (see Heatherton & Baumeister, 1991). The binge eater is typically a late adolescent or young adult female whose self-concept is heavily bound up with severe, possibly unrealistic standards of physical thinness, and often other standards (unrelated to thinness and eating) are also relevant. During an eating binge, she tends to lose track of abstract, meaningful, and long-range awareness of the self, narrowing her awareness instead to the physical sensations of chewing and swallowing food.

Although episodes of heavy eating have marked festivals and other rituals for centuries in many parts of the world, the psychological problem of binge eating appears to be a fairly recent and Western one. Most experts agree that pathological patterns of binge eating have been on the rise for much of the 20th century. It is not clear whether they began to flourish during the early modern period to coincide with the emergence of modern selfhood, although there is an approximate match. One might suggest, however, that the burden of selfhood has only really fallen heavily on women in the 20th century because gender discrimination prevented women from participating fully in Western societies during the last few centuries. Insofar as eating binges tend to be found among women, then, some delay in the historical emergence of escapist patterns may be unsurprising.

Thus, there do seem to be some patterns of escapism that seem linked to the burdensome and stressful nature of modern selfhood and that have indeed emerged or increased in step (approximately) with that burden. Several other patterns of escaping the self have been identified, such as suicide and alcohol abuse (Baumeister, 1991a; Baumeister, 1990; Hull, 1981). These seem more widely spread across cultural and historical boundaries. It may be, however, that the patterns of suicide and alcohol abuse have changed to accommodate the stress of self in modern Western cultures, even though non-Westerners and our Western ancestors drank alcohol and occasionally killed themselves for other reasons. A more recent form of escape involves spurious beliefs in being abducted by extraterrestrial aliens in spaceships, and it is well documented that reports of such experiences are quite recent in origin and have been escalating dramatically over the past few decades (Newman & Baumeister, 1996).

Of course, many ordinary behaviors can be understood as providing some escape from self-awareness. Watching television or a movie allows people to forget themselves while becoming immersed in someone else's life and problems. Becoming a sports fan allows someone to experience the emotional highs and lows of a team's performance outcomes without suffering any practical consequences. Exercise provides a low-level focus of attention on bodily processes and actions, thereby taking one's mind off broad, more worrisome or threatening events and their implications for the self. Other hobbies and pastimes presumably serve the same function.

In general, then, there is ample evidence that fits the view that Western culture has created a problematic form of selfhood. The demands and expectations that accompany the highly individualist, autonomous modern form of selfhood may create a stressful burden on those who embrace it and seek to live up to it. Escapist and possibly pathological patterns attend some of the ways in which modern Western citizens seek to cope with this burden.

The Narcissistic Imperative

A large part of the burden of self derives from the societal pressure to construct and maintain a highly attractive, competent, successful self that is worthy of admiration by self and others. A popular corollary of this belief is that people ought to end up with high self-esteem. It is somewhat misleading to say that Americans are simply in love with themselves; instead, they are in love with self-esteem (e.g., California Task Force, 1990).

There are relatively few unmixed blessings in psychology, and self-esteem is not among those few. It is chiefly useful in making the individual feel better and possibly in increasing persistence and initiative and the other few performance aspects that benefit from confidence. Meanwhile, it can have a variety of costly consequences, such as if people overcommit themselves (Baumeister, Heatherton, & Tice, 1993), disregard valid advice against fruitless persistence (McFarlin, Baumeister, & Blascovich, 1984), or offend others by arrogant, insensitive styles (Colvin, Block, & Funder, 1995).

A recent investigation into the causes of violence revealed both the social costs of high self-esteem and the reluctance of American society to acknowledge them (Baumeister, Smart, & Boden, 1996). We were able to list a long series of writers and psychological researchers who have expressed the belief that low self-esteem causes violence. Yet a review of empirical findings across a broad array of spheres (e.g., murder, assault, rape, war, terrorism, torture, prejudice, oppression) repeatedly contradicted that view. The actual cause of violence appears to be some highly favorable view of self that encounters an external, unfavorable evaluation—that is, threatened egotism is the main cause of violence. Persuading people simply to hold more favorable views of themselves is therefore likely to increase rather that decrease violence. (This appears to have been the societal trend during the recent decades, in which rising cultivation of self-esteem for everyone has accompanied rising violence, although such broad trends may be coincidental or multiply determined.)

One way to integrate these disparate views and findings into a broad picture is to conclude that self-esteem is generally a benefit to the individual but a cost or risk to those around him or her. Thus, high self-esteem does improve one's affect balance and subjective well-being (e.g., Campbell, 1981), but it increases violent tendencies that may victimize other people. It would thus be the opposite of guilt, which is costly and unpleasant to the person feeling guilty but often ends up benefiting relationship partners and others who may interact with him or her (Baumeister, Stillwell, & Heatherton, 1994).

Recent work on self-presentation provides evidence that converges in an interesting way with this view of self-esteem. For years, self-presentation researchers have documented how people typically seek to make a very positive impression and present their good points (e.g., Schlenker, 1980). Most of that research has however been focused on first-time interactions with strangers. Tice, Butler, Muraven, and Still-well (1995) showed that people do indeed present very positive views of themselves when interacting with strangers, but they become modest and self-effacing when interacting with friends. These patterns more-over were shown to be automatic, habitual-response patterns that could only be overcome with difficulty and exertion.

Why would people behave modestly with friends while acting confident and boastful with strangers? The function of the self as an interpersonal tool is relevant here. With a stranger, presumably, the question is whether a friendship will form or not, and so it may be necessary to present a positive view of self in order to make oneself appear a desirable friend (or employee or relationship partner). Once a friendship or other social bond exists, however, there is less need to present one's good points, because the friend presumably knows about them. Meanwhile, if my suggestion of the social costs of egotism is correct, then boasting would be unwelcome to friends. They might begin to dislike or reject someone who persistently behaved in an egotistical fashion, even though that very self-confidence was instrumental in creating the initial attraction.

More than affect is at stake. Social groups (including dyads such as marriages) generally have tasks to do, and some notions of equity typically prevail (e.g., Lerner & Mikula, 1994). People who regard themselves as superior beings may feel entitled to contribute less and consume more. For example, a more egotistical man may expect his wife to cook and clean for him, while a more modest one may feel an obligation to share such tasks or balance them with other contributions. Each person's egotism is therefore a potential threat to group stability and equity, which is why group norms may oppose and constrain egotism.

Meanwhile, the cultural pressure to love oneself above all has probably worked to the detriment of self-control. Self-control entails overriding one's wishes and inclinations, whereas the narcissistic impulse is presumably to cherish them. Ironically, evidence suggests that the long-range benefits of self-control to the self are immense, such as indicated by findings that link capacity to delay gratification in early childhood with success in high school and college (Mischel, Shoda, & Peake, 1988; Shoda, Mischel, & Peake, 1990). But it is hard to argue that self-love can readily be reconciled to self-denial. The majority of America's current social problems and individual pathologies reflect failures of self-control (see Baumeister, Heatherton, & Tice, 1994, for review), and this is unlikely to change during the reign of the narcissistic imperative.

Self as Value Base

A final set of problems is linked to the cultural transformation that has come to regard the self as a major source of value. People feel they have a moral right and even a duty to do what is best for themselves, and people pursue self-knowledge and self-actualization with faith that what they are doing is right. The high value placed on the family was another response of modern Western society and culture to the value gap (along with the elevation of the self), and it moreover appears that the self has become for many people a higher value than the marriage, which has undoubtedly contributed to marital instability. Marital instability is not necessarily a social problem, however, particularly when there are no children involved: people can dissolve their marriages and pursue other possibilities without causing substantial costs to society.

The same does not apply, however, to filial bonds. If parents were to begin placing self-interest above the obligations of parenthood—in other words, if the self became a stronger value base than the good of one's children, so that people would with minimal guilt abandon their children in order to cultivate and fulfill themselves—society would suffer a considerable increase in a broad variety of problems because children cannot care for themselves effectively. Whether recent social trends such as delinquent child-support payments and involuntary institutionalization of troublesome children reflect the beginnings of this trend is difficult to say. One can, however, confidently predict that the rise of the self as a major value base poses a potentially enormous danger to the family and indeed the entire capacity of society to take care of its children.

A more complex and troubled consequence of the elevation of selfhood to a major value base is the effect on death. The authoritative historical overview of Western attitudes toward death by Aries (1981) characterized the 20th century as the era in which the concept of death became so threatening and fearsome that it had to be banished from daily life. Hence death is kept secret and hidden, and dying people are cheerfully enjoined by family members from even saying that they might die. The threat of death apparently has become more upsetting than in the past.

One explanation is that death now constitutes a threat to the meaning of one's life in a way that it never did previously. To the extent that selfhood was one's main value base, then the value of all one's actions during life is nullified by death. For example, if one's life's work was meant to serve God, then its value is retained after one's death, because the project of serving God continues and is carried on by others. But if one's work was devoted to serving the self (e.g., building an impressive résumé of honors and promotions), then when the self ceases to exist, all those actions become trivial. No one reads your résumé after you are dead. To put this another way, the self is a far more temporary and hence fragile value base than its rivals (religion, family, tradition, and so forth). Making the self into a value base entails that death is not just the end of life: it signifies the nullification, the stripping away of meaning, of life.

The elevation of selfhood into a great value base is in many ways one of the most intriguing experiments of modern Western society. It is difficult to remain highly optimistic about this experiment: one is asking the self to do too much, it seems. The self may not really contain sufficient basis for moral decisions, and inevitably the capacity of morality to restrain self-interest will be impaired. Then again, the notion of a spark of divinity existing inside each person is an ancient religious doctrine, and perhaps there is some way to reconcile the moral glorification of self with the need to accommodate oneself so as to participate effectively in society. This will be one of the great social questions of the 21st century.

Conclusion

The interaction between self and society is one of mutual influence and mutual adaptation. The basic facts of selfhood (reflexive consciousness, interpersonal being, and executive function) may be universal, but the particular features of modern Western selfhood can be understood as adaptations to the special historical and social forces that have led to the current social situation. Although selfhood has flourished in almost unprecedented fashion in this society, its current form has also brought a host of problems and difficulties. Strong self-love, the enjoyment of unique individuality, belief in inner realities, and the belief in self as a major value base are strongly entrenched in both the preferences of individuals and the structures and realities of society.

References

Aries, P. (1981). *The hour of our death*. (H. Weaver, Trans.). New York: Knopf.

Baumeister, R. F. (1986). *Identity: Cultural change and the struggle for self*. New York: Oxford University Press.

Baumeister, R. F. (1987). How the self became a problem: A psychological review of historical research. *Journal of Personality and Social Psychology, 52*, 163–176.

Baumeister, R. F. (1988). Masochism as escape from self. *Journal of Sex Research*, *25*, 28–59.

Baumeister, R. F. (1989). *Masochism and the self*. Hillsdale, NJ: Erlbaum.

Baumeister, R. F. (1990). Suicide as escape from self. *Psychological Review*, *91*, 90–113.

Baumeister, R. F. (1991a). *Escaping the self: Alcoholism, spirituality, masochism, and other flights from the burden of selfhood*. New York: Basic Books.

Baumeister, R. F. (1991b). *Meanings of life*. New York: Guilford.

Baumeister, R. F. (1995). Self and identity: An introduction. In A. Tesser (Ed.), *Advanced social psychology* (pp. 51–97). New York: McGraw-Hill.

Baumeister, R. F. (in press). The self. In G. Lindzey, S. Fiske, & D. Gilbert (Eds.), *Handbook of social psychology* (4th ed.). New York: McGraw-Hill.

Baumeister, R. F., Heatherton, T. F., & Tice, D. M. (1993). When ego threats lead to self-regulation failure: Negative consequences of high self-esteem. Journal of Personality and Social Psychology, 64, 141–156.

Baumeister, R. F., Heatherton, T. F., & Tice, D. M. (1994). *Losing control: How and why people fail at self-regulation*. San Diego, CA: Academic Press.

Baumeister, R. F., Smart, L., & Boden, J. M. (1996). Relation of threatened egotism to violence and aggression: The dark side of high self-esteem. *Psychological Review*, *103*, 5–33.

Baumeister, R. F., Stillwell, A. M., & Heatherton, T. F. (1994). Guilt: An interpersonal approach. *Psychological Bulletin*, *115*, 243–267.

Baumeister, R. F., & Tice, D. M. (1986). How adolescence became the struggle for self: A historical transformation of psychological development. In J. Suls & A. G. Greenwald (Eds.), *Psychological perspectives on the self* (Vol. 3, pp. 183–201). Hillsdale, NJ: Erlbaum.

Bellah, R. N., Madsen, R., Sullivan, W. M., Swidler, A., & Tipton, S. M. (1985). *Habits of the heart: Individualism and commitment in American life*. Berkeley and Los Angeles: University of California Press.

Berkowitz, L. (1978). Is criminal violence normative behavior? Hostile and instrumental aggression in violent incidents. *Journal of Research in Crime and Delinquency*, *15*, 148–161.

California Task Force to Promote Self-esteem and Personal and Social Responsibility (1990). *Toward a state of self-esteem*. Sacramento, CA: California State Department of Education.

Campbell, A. (1981). *The sense of well-being in America*. New York: McGraw-Hill.

Colvin, C. R., Block, J., & Funder, D. C. (1995). Overly positive evaluations and personality: Negative implications for mental health. *Journal of Personality and Social Psychology*, *68*, 1152–1162.

Delbanco, A. (1995). *The death of Satan: How Americans have lost the sense of evil*. New York: Farrar, Straus, & Giroux.

Demos, J., & Demos, V. (1969). Adolescence in historical perspective. *Journal of Marriage and the Family*, *31*, 632–638.

Diener, E., Diener, M., & Diener, C. (1995). Factors predicting the subjective well-being of nations. *Journal of Personality and Social Psychology*, *69*, 851–864.

Gottfredson, M. R., & Hirschi, T. (1990). *A general theory of crime*. Stanford, CA: Stanford University Press.

Habermas, J. (1973). *Legitimation crisis*. (T. McCarthy, Trans.). Boston: Beacon.

Harris, M. (1978). *Cannibals and kings: The origins of cultures*. New York: Random House.

Harris, M. (1979). *Cultural materialism: The struggle for a science of culture*. New York: Random House.

Heatherton, T. F., & Baumeister, R. F. (1991). Binge eating as escape from self-awareness. *Psychological Bulletin, 110,* 86–108.

Hull, J. G. (1981). A self-awareness model of the causes and effects of alcohol consumption. *Journal of Abnormal Psychology, 90,* 586–600.

Kett, J. F. (1977). *Rites of passage: Adolescence in America 1790 to the present*. New York: Basic Books.

Lasch, C. (1977). *Haven in a heartless world: The family besieged*. New York: Basic Books.

Lasch, C. (1978). *The culture of narcissism: American life in an age of diminishing expectations*. New York: Norton.

Lawson, A. (1988). *Adultery: An analysis of love and betrayal*. New York: Basic Books.

Leary, M. R., & Kowalski, R. (1995). *Social anxiety*. New York: Guilford.

Leary, M. R., Tambor, E. S., Terdal, S. K., & Downs, D. L. (1995). Self-esteem as an interpersonal monitor: The sociometer hypothesis. *Journal of Personality and Social Psychology, 68,* 518–530.

Lerner, M. J. & Mikula, G. (Eds.) (1994). *Entitlement and the affectional bond: Justice in close relationships*. New York: Plenum.

MacIntyre, A. (1981). *After virtue*. Notre Dame, IN: University of Notre Dame Press.

Margolis, M. L. (1984). *Mothers and such: Views of American women and why they changed*. Berkeley and Los Angeles: University of California Press.

McFarlin, D. B., Baumeister, R. F., & Blascovich, J. (1984). On knowing when to quit: Task failure, self-esteem, advice, and nonproductive persistence. *Journal of Personality, 52,* 138–155.

Mischel, W., Shoda, Y., & Peake, P. K. (1988). The nature of adolescent competencies predicted by preschool delay of gratification. *Journal of Personality and Social Psychology, 54,* 687–696.

Newman, L. S., & Baumeister, R. F. (1996). Toward an elaboration of the UFO abduction phenomenon: Hypnotic elaboration, extraterrestrial sadomasochism, and spurious memories. *Psychological Inquiry, 7,* 99–126.

Potter, D. M. (1954). *People of plenty*. Chicago: University of Chicago Press.

Rodgers, D. T. (1978). *The work ethic in industrial America 1850–1920*. Chicago: University of Chicago Press.

Rosenthal, P. (1984). *Words and values: Some leading words and where they lead us*. New York: Oxford University Press.

Scarry, E. (1985). *The body in pain: The making and unmaking of the world*. New York: Oxford University Press.

Schlenker, B. R. (1980). *Impression management: The self-concept, social identity, and interpersonal relations*. Monterey, CA: Brooks/Cole.

Sennett, R. (1974). *The fall of public man*. New York: Random House.

Shils, E. (1981). *Tradition*. Chicago: University of Chicago Press.

Shoda, Y., Mischel, W., & Peake, P. K. (1990). Predicting adolescent cognitive and self-regulatory competencies from preschool delay of gratification: Identifying diagnostic conditions. *Developmental Psychology, 26*, 978–986.

Stone, L. (1977). *The family, sex and marriage in England 1500–1800*. New York: Harper & Row.

Tedeschi, J. T., & Felson, R. B. (1994). *Violence, aggression, and coercive action*. Washington, DC: American Psychological Association.

Tice, D. M., Butler, J. L., Muraven, M. B., & Stillwell, A. M. (1995). When modesty prevails: Differential favorability of self-presentation to friends and strangers. *Journal of Personality and Social Psychology, 69*, 1120–1138.

Trilling, L. (1971). *Sincerity and authenticity*. Cambridge, MA: Harvard University Press.

Vallacher, R. R., & Wegner, D. M. (1985). *A theory of action identification*. Hillsdale, NJ: Erlbaum.

Vallacher, R. R., & Wegner, D. M. (1987). What do people think they're doing? Action identification and human behavior. *Psychological Review, 94*, 3–15.

Vaughan, D. (1986). *Uncoupling*. New York: Oxford University Press.

Weintraub, K. J. (1978). *The value of the individual: Self and circumstance in autobiography*. Chicago: University of Chicago Press.

Zube, M. J. (1972). Changing concepts of morality: 1948–1969. *Social Forces, 50*, 385–393.

Zweig, P. (1980). *The heresy of self-love*. Princeton, NJ: Princeton University Press. (Original work published 1968.)

Lee Jussim
Richard D. Ashmore

9

Conclusion

*Fundamental Issues in the Study of Self and
Identity—Contrasts, Contexts, and Conflicts*

This volume has identified some of the conceptual contrasts and historical and sociocultural contexts with which social scientists are grappling
as we begin a second century of exploration of self and identity. The
chapters in this book have highlighted two contrasts: self as multiplicity
versus unity of identity, and self as personal versus self as social. They
have also addressed three contexts: history, culture, and American society at the end of the twentieth century. In doing so, several important
metatheoretical conflicts have emerged regarding how the self should be
construed and studied and regarding which aspects of the self are most
important to study.

Conflict can be valuable in scientific inquiry (and the contributors'
chapters, even when arguing for opposing viewpoints, are models of
how to engage in open inquiry). Some conflicts occur because of differences in perspective or emphasis, and these are extremely useful in
making salient to each of us aspects of self and identity that we had not
previously considered. Other conflicts are more basic, involving metatheoretical and even epistemological issues. By explicitly reconsidering
our underlying assumptions, however, we may deepen and strengthen
our insights into phenomena as potentially difficult and complex as self
and identity.

This concluding chapter is divided into two main sections. First, we
address the seemingly more readily resolvable contrasts in perspective
and emphasis in the study of self and identity. Second, we discuss the
authors' differing views regarding the extent to which the self is con-

textualized, an issue which brings to the fore some of the more basic and perhaps less easily resolvable conflicts.

Contrasts in Perspective and Emphasis

Four of the chapters addressed two classic contrasts in the study of self and identity. First, we discuss differences between the conceptual frameworks presented by Rosenberg and McAdams on the multiplicity versus unity contrast; and then we suggest that those perspectives might be more compatible than they first appear. The second contrast, the personal versus social aspects of identity, was addressed by Harter and by Thoits and Virshup. Again, after highlighting their differences, we note points of connection between the two perspectives.

Multiplicity versus Unity of Self

Rosenberg's chapter and research clearly emphasized the multifaceted nature of identity. His work has revived Baldwin's (1897) concept of the socius, which was conceptualized and operationalized as "a *multiplicity* [italics added] of ego and alter elements and their interrelationships." He has also helped develop the powerful hierarchical classes algorithm and associated methodology for assessing the perception of self and important others—how people view their multiple selves and multiple significant people in their lives.

Thus, Rosenberg utilized a 21st-century methodology to examine the socius, a 19th-century construct put forth at the very beginning of the modern scientific analysis of self and identity. A particularly unique contribution of Rosenberg's theoretical approach to the socius is that it includes autobiographical accounts of both self-beliefs (ego elements) and beliefs about important others (alter elements). Furthermore, he described three studies demonstrating the fruitfulness of this multiplicity perspective. Rosenberg illustrated the importance of including alter elements in a study of teen mothers who were abused as children. The more the teen mother ascribed a variety of positive attributes to important others, the more secure was the attachment of her child.

McAdams, in contrast, emphasized the unity of personal identity. Drawing on and extending James's notion of the I, McAdams created the term "selfing," which refers to the act of knowing about self, to self-consciousness, and to the process of appropriating experiences as one's own. As he aptly pointed out, there is a strong, if implicit, unity in my sense of self simply by virtue of knowing that my experiences are mine and not yours (and if I have difficulty with this distinction, I probably am suffering from a serious psychosis). Second, McAdams suggests that, beginning in adolescence, most people have a need to (and do successfully) construct a coherent and unifying life story that binds together the important events, relationships, and people in their lives.

McAdams exploited the story metaphor as the vehicle for unity of self by identifying seven features of stories (including life stories) and explaining how each of these features can contribute to unity through narrative. For example, all stories have characters, and in life stories the main character is the self. The self may appear in many different roles and relationships. "Imagoes are . . . one-dimensional, stock characters" who, because of their simplicity, can crystallize unity of self-conception. McAdams noted several examples of imagoes, including "the loyal friend" and "the clown" that people use to give unity to their personal identity.

Although Rosenberg and McAdams differed most dramatically in emphasizing multiplicity versus unity, another important difference in their perspectives concerns whether unity is primarily phenomenological. Is my identity a unified coherent whole simply because it feels that way to me? Rosenberg and McAdams provided very different answers to this question. Rosenberg's answer was a clear no: "I think it would be a mistake to use a phenomenological sense of unity as a way to define unity of self." Instead, Rosenberg opted for a structural definition of unity—unity exists in the structual organization, relating elements of the socius to one another.

Rosenberg, however, did not provide much detail about the general nature of such a structural and organizational view of unity. This is because Rosenberg's approach is largely idiographic—HICLAS provides a very clear depiction of the structure and organization of a particular individual's socius. Still, reaching broadly generalizable conclusions regarding the structure and organization of the self and socius would seem to be a potentially valuable area for theory development and empirical research in set-theoretical approaches to the self. For example, the "equivalence" relationship in set theory, empirically identifiable by HICLAS, can be used to assess identification with an important other. Since Freud, a variety of theories have suggested that such identification can provide an important source of unity in self-conceptions. In contrast, however, McAdams virtually defined unity as the phenomenological experience of unity, which is implicit in the themes and other features of people's life stories. For him, if a person creates a unified story in a conscious and phenomenological manner, their self is unified.

Although McAdams's and Rosenberg's chapters presented differing perspectives and emphasize different phenomena, we do not see their views as incompatible. In fact, neither do they—McAdams acknowledged a great deal of value in viewing the self as a multiplicity, and

Rosenberg agreed that the multiple selves are organized into a unifying or unity-creating personal-identity structure.

Furthermore, both perspectives can readily incorporate seemingly opposing ideas. If, as McAdams suggests, the unifying aspects of self are captured in one's life story, there is ample room for multiple selves. Many long stories and novels have chapters and scenes within chapters and numerous and rich subplots. Taking the story metaphor seriously seems to call for theory and research that examines just how people integrate their multiple selves into unifying stories. McAdams and others (e.g., Gergen & Gergen, 1988) have taken on this challenge. McAdams sets the stage for future work by using the story metaphor to indicate seven features of stories, including life stories. Furthermore, he described how individuals use these features to create a personal narrative that confers unity and purpose upon their identity. In most instances, this involves putting together multiple, often disparate, self-views into a coherent whole.

Rosenberg's approach explicitly incorporated some unifying principles. For Rosenberg, the self is not just a grab-bag collection of self-perceptions and beliefs about important others. The structure among the multiple elements of ego and alter are extremely important and brings a degree of unity to the system. The nature and meaning of unity in approaches emphasizing multiplicity (see also Marsh, 1993) is a potentially rich area for theoretical development. Empirically, it would be valuable to discover whether there are commonalities across individuals in their unifying self-structures. For example, is identification with parents a unifying principle for some people? Do other people explicitly disidentify with or reject (what they perceive to be) their parents' attributes? The HICLAS methodology would be especially well-suited for addressing questions such as these to discover structual unity themes within a multiplicity of selves.

Their differences regarding whether unity is primarily phenomenological may be less easily resolved. At best, perhaps McAdams and Rosenberg are discussing different aspects of the self. McAdams is clearly discussing unity in the phenomenological self. In contrast, unity for Rosenberg has more to do with relations among self-components, and he argues that this type of unity may indeed be independent of phenomenological unity.

Research that used both Rosenberg's HICLAS procedure and McAdams's life-story methods might help reconcile their differing perspectives on the relation between phenomenological unity and structure, and help identify empirical convergences in types and forms of self-unity. For example, what types of self-narratives go with personal identity structured around identification with same-sex parents? Are stories more coherent and unified when the structure of ego and alter elements are arranged in a tight hierarchy?

Personal versus Social Identity

Although Harter regards self and identity phenomena as inherently both personal and social, her research focuses on a very personal self (the "real" me) that has been distorted by perceived social forces. She has shown that people who feel that their self-esteem depends on approval from others often come to present themselves in ways that do not fit with their own sense of who they are. Such false self-behavior distances people from their own authentic selves.

The concepts of "authenticity" and "false self-behavior" emphasize the highly individualized and personal nature of the self. For Harter, each individual is the final and absolute arbiter of just what constitutes authentic behavior—i.e., behavior that reflects the "real me." Harter reviewed research and theory on the role of social relationships in creating obstacles to authenticity. Among infants, authenticity may be undermined through overinvolved parents or the acquisition of language itself. In childhood, authenticity may be damaged by parents whose love appears contingent on external standards or by physical or sexual abuse.

The major portion of Harter's chapter is devoted to her research on false self-behavior. A particularly important set of studies focused on loss of voice among adolescents. Voice is a form of authenticity in which a person feels free to express their "real" beliefs and feelings. Loss of voice occurs when people feel unable to express their real beliefs and feelings. In contrast to earlier perspectives (e.g., Gilligan, 1982), Harter presented empirical evidence showing that loss of voice is as much a problem for boys as for girls. She also found, contrary to Gilligan, no age differences in loss of voice. Furthermore, Harter identified many of the correlates of loss of voice (low levels of emotional support, conditionality of support, low self-esteem, and depression).

In contrast, Thoits and Virshup's chapter reviewed four major theoretical approaches, two by sociologists and two by psychologists, all of which emphasized the more social aspects of identity. They began with the sociological models. Both McCall and Simmons's (1966) role-identity theory and Stryker and Statham's (1985) identity theory focus on how identity is shaped by societally defined roles and positions (such as sociodemographic characteristics, family and occupational roles, and activities). In these perspectives, social structure largely determines and shapes self-definition. One person's set of identities may include "bus driver," "father," and "soccer player"; another person's may include "African-American," "female," and "librarian."

Despite their emphasis on social structural influences on self-conception, sociological role-identity theories imply that the self is primarily an individual-level phenomenon. People's answers to the question, "Who am I?" involve taking on specific roles (e.g., "I am a graphic artist, a girls' soccer coach, a mother, and a good friend") and these become part of their self-definition. Thus, Thoits and Virshup refer to role-identity selves as "me's."

Thoits and Virshup distinguish these me's, which are social identities based on roles and positions that the individual appropriates as self-defining, from "we's," which are collective identities that explicitly link the person to identifiable social groups. Two psychological theories emphasize we's more than me's. As suggested by Tajfelian theories (social-identity theory and self-categorization theory), the collective answers to the "Who are we?" question involve group memberships—e.g., "We are white, male, French Canadian supporters of the Party Quebecois" (political party pushing for independence of Quebec from Canada). Individual identity is determined, in large part, by who these various we's are and what we stand for.

As Thoits and Virshup aptly pointed out, both me's and we's are clearly social identities. Both sets of responses to the "Who am I/Who are we?" question involve locating the self in the social structure of the broader society—either one's roles or one's membership in collectivities. In contrast, Harter's concepts of authenticity and false self-behavior emphasized the self as a personal phenomenon (although one that can be affected by social forces). For Harter, in fact, societal norms and social pressures often operate as *barriers* to authenticity—i.e., as factors working against the person's expression of their true self.

So, is the self primarily social or largely personal? It is, obviously, a bit of both. The boundaries between personal and social identity seem to be highly fluid, as Thoits and Virshup note. Certainly, Harter has made a convincing case for a strong relationship between perceptions of social relationships and self-perceptions. Similarly, Rosenberg, although focusing primarily on self-as-multiplicity, has shown that other people and social relationships are a deeply embedded component of the self for most people. The two sociological theories (emphasizing roles and positions) are perhaps clearest in documenting how the social becomes personal. Social identities can become as much a part of the me as traits and habits. Traits can even be viewed as roles—seeing myself as extroverted could be viewed, for example, as taking on the role of an extrovert, according to role-identity theories (Stryker & Statham, 1985).

Clearly, as documented in both chapters, social factors influence the self-concept. For Harter, people's perceptions of others' views and their relationships with those others strongly relate to the expression of one's true self. For Thoits and Virshup, social roles and collectivities provide preexisting identities that people can try on to see how they fit, and, if they fit well, they may then become important aspects of personal identity.

Just as clearly, however, personal identity both reflects and influences that social structure. As Thoits and Virshup point out, role and collective identities are not simple statements describing one's social positions—to consider them "identities" at all requires that the person attaches importance to these social positions. Furthermore, each individual usually adds their own unique style and flourishes to societally prescribed roles and to their identifications with collectivities. When enough people change how they enact a role, the personal can change the social structure. For example, the dramatic increase in the number of working women over the last 30 years has fundamentally changed how many Americans think about women's roles, even though whether to work is primarily an individual-level, personal decision.

Are social factors primarily obstacles to, or supporters of, authentic expressions of self? This depends primarily upon how comfortable the individual feels enacting various roles and as a member of various collectives, and how much support others express for the individual's belief and behaviors. For example, we suspect that there would be considerably greater problems of authenticity at work among people who do not like their jobs but need the money than among people who love their jobs. Similarly, atheists may experience considerably more authenticity problems when attending a public school that has a daily minute of prayer than would true believers. And, even a devout nondenominational Christian might experience considerably more authenticity problems among a born-again fundamentalist group than would long-standing members of that group. In all these cases, social factors present an obstacle to authenticity for one person and an opportunity to express one's true self for another.

It seems likely, therefore, that much could be gained by integrating the perspectives and methods used in one approach with those favored by researchers using a contrasting approach. For example, perhaps an authenticity analysis could enhance our understanding of when people are more or less likely to be successful enacting various roles. Similarly, perhaps understanding the fit between adolescents' self-concepts and their societally prescribed roles and collective identities might enhance an understanding of when adolescents feel more or less authentic (and all the adjustment problems identified by Harter that seem to correspond with feelings of inauthenticity).

How Contextualized Is the Self?

Although there are differences in perspective between those emphasizing unity versus multiplicity and the social versus the personal, an even greater chasm exists between those emphasizing the highly contextualized versus the universal aspects of the self. In 1890, William James urged psychologists to make the self an object of empirical scientific analysis. In 1897, Baldwin argued that the development of the self was intricately intertwined with learning a sense of morality and ethics. Now, as we move toward the 21st century, these issues have returned to the forefront of the social sciences, although the debate surrounding these issues has become significantly more complex and sophisticated. Several of the authors, especially those addressing the central contexts of self and identity, have taken up this debate,[1] and in the remainder of this chapter we address two issues: (1) Can the self be studied objectively? (2) Is the self a moral issue?

Can the Self Be Studied Objectively?

There is a clear schism between authors in this volume regarding this topic. The two authors presenting social constructivist perspectives (Danziger in chapter 6 and Holland in chapter 7) express deep reservations about the possibility of objectivity. Baumeister and the authors of the four contrast chapters seem to implicitly assume that objective scientific analysis of self and identity is indeed possible.

At one level, Danziger's analysis documents differences in conceptualizations of the self across different historical epochs in Western society. He does not explicitly deny the possibility of studying the self objectively. However, Danziger has also done more than simply identify historical variations in the self—he has argued that the self emerges from specific historical conditions. As such, self and identity phenomena are highly context dependent. He goes even further and suggests that "the phenomena studied are not natural objects at all but historically constituted objects." Although Danziger did express some reservations about the applicability of this claim to all of psychology, he clearly believed it applicable to the study of the self, to which "we must surely assign a historical rather than a natural status."

Even this does not quite baldly deny the possibility of objectively studying the self. However, the difficulty of objectivism for Danziger becomes clearer: "The self may be an example of what some philosophers have called 'essentially contested concepts.' . . . [such concepts] are saddled with an inescapable ambiguity." Although Danziger acknowledges that even contested concepts can be studied empirically ("verified in experience" in his words), he ascribes to them an "inescapable ambiguity." This strongly implies that it is extremely difficult, if not impossible, to study such concepts (other examples Danziger cited were justice and democracy) objectively, because, our own values, status positions, and experience often influence our interpretations of ambiguous situations and phenomena (e.g., Bruner, 1957; Fiske & Taylor, 1991; Hastorf & Cantril, 1954).

Holland went even further. In her discussion of the "critical disruption" in anthropology created by social constructivism, she explicitly denied the possibility of objectivity. Consider the following: "No matter how scrupulous the attempts of individual scientists to be objective, social scientists, today as in the past, are, in effect, studying what their field of study has helped to create. In this Foucauldian vision, unreflexive claims to 'objectivity' become hollow, at best; at worst, they are a self-serving means by which science rhetorically claims authority." In fact, this section seems to deny the possibility of objectivity, not merely in the study of self, or even in the social sciences, but in the sciences more broadly. In Holland's presentation of social-constructivist perspectives, the main question is not so much "What is the nature of the self?" as "Whose view is being privileged in 'scientific' discourses about the self?" Inasmuch as we should not even pretend to study objective phenomena, we are left with the study of the social discourse regarding various phenomena.

This perspective is in sharp, but implicit, contrast, to the other perspectives presented in this book. None of the other authors, however, address the issue of objectivity head-on. We suspect that for them, as for most other researchers in psychology and sociology (and perhaps most social and behavioral sciences), this is because the issue of objectivity is not problematic. They implicitly assume that objectivity is both possible and desirable. Most of these chapters are written as if the authors believe that they are searching for relatively objective descriptions of nature, and that, even when they disagree, such disagreements will be resolvable through better theories, better methods, or simply more research.

What is objectivity? None of the authors quite tell us. It probably is a contested concept, much like justice, democracy, and perhaps the self (as Danziger suggested). Furthermore, a thorough analysis of objectivity is a major undertaking of the philosophy of science that is beyond our current scope. If objectivity refers to an ability to discover universal truths, then we agree that it is extremely difficult to be objective. However, this is not how we think about objectivity, and we doubt that this is how most scientists who consider themselves objective think about it. Rather, we suspect that most social scientists think of objectivity as more of a process, as an attempt to collect, evaluate, and consider information (data, experience, etc.) in as unbiased and unprejudiced manner as possible.

We agree with the social constructivists that one can often discover hidden assumptions about power and status relationships by analyzing social and scientific discourses. However, we disagree that discourse and "practice" are the only data worth considering. Even with all of our limitations, which are extremely important to acknowledge, we can attempt to make sense of social and psychological phenomena, such as the self, in ways that are relatively free of intentional and blatant social and political agendas.

For example, McAdams's chapter provided evidence that toward the end of the 20th century many Americans attempt to construct coherent stories about their lives. A social constructivist might ask, "Whose account is being privileged here?" but the question seems misplaced. For McAdams, the whole point is that each person privileges their own account—that is the phenomenon being studied. McAdams's approach to the phenomenon does not seem to privilege any particular group. Although McAdams did not explicitly acknowledge historical or cultural limitations to his analysis, he also did not claim that all people in all cultures across all time construct unified stories.

Even though the objectivity issue presents a major and substantial divide, there are several important points of contact between authors on different sides of this conflict. For example, we see a great deal of overlap between McAdams's perspective and those of Holland and Danziger. Just as the constructivists would predict, McAdams finds that social structure (e.g., socioeconomic status) influences and circumscribes the stories that people tell. Furthermore, Holland's theoretical and empirical emphasis on discourse, practice, and phenomenology is quite similar to McAdams's emphasis on the active personal construction of life stories. Both perspectives emphasize the subjectivity of personal experience.

It is clear that both social-constructivist and classic scientific approaches to self and identity have limitations and difficulties. At this time, it appears to us that the metatheoretical gap between the two perspectives will not be easily bridged. Perhaps the gap will simply fade away, or be superseded by some other, more powerful perspective. Regardless, it seems likely that the classic scientific approach to self and identity would be strengthened by a serious consideration of the critical issues raised by the social-constructivist challenge (and the chapters by Danziger and Holland present these issues in clear and compellingly elegant fashions); at the same time, constructivist approaches might be advanced through a more explicit consideration of some of their own limitations. Similarly, we feel it would be fruitful to bring into closer contact social-constructivist and classical scientific analyses of power and social perception (e.g., Fiske, 1993), because these are phenomena considered important on both sides of the objectivity chasm.

Is the Self a Moral Issue?

Baumeister's chapter has pointedly suggested that in at least one particular context—America in the 1990s—the self has become a moral issue. Baumeister points out that the 20th-century American self is laden with major moral baggage. Many of the traditional sources of morality in Western society—God, work, and family—have been severely, perhaps fatally, weakened over the last 500 years. The self, he argued, seems to be replacing those older sources of morality. As self-fulfillment has become the highest, or at least a very high, value, the self has simultaneously become a moral compass.

Baumeister's suggestion that there has been a slow but steady transfer of morality from cultural institutions to the self is a powerful insight. One of the few historical pieces that he did not explicitly discuss was Ayn Rand's (1964) *The Virtue of Selfishness*, which explicitly portrays self-advancement as a high moral value. This moral value placed on self-advancement may be seen in the disdain often expressed in late 20th-century America for the economically disadvantaged (the resurrection of the Victorian concept of the "undeserving poor"; popular opposition to many of the social programs that provide a safety net for the poor). "Me first" as a moral imperative may fuel support for lower taxes, even at the expense of eliminating social programs, and for policies over the last 15 years that have created an environment in which 2% of the people possess an increasingly large proportion of the nation's wealth, while the income of middle- and lower-class people has remained stagnant or declined (e.g., Hacker, 1995; Thurow, 1995). Clearly, modern perspectives on selfhood could be greatly enriched by more explicitly addressing the new moral emphasis placed on the self.

McAdams, too, argues for an important role of morals in self and identity, although in a somewhat different way than Baumeister. McAdams's research shows that most life stories are set in a context of morals and fundamental values. For some people, their story portrays a lifelong struggle to understand what is right and true whereas for others their story conveys their attempts to stay on the straight and narrow path to righteousness. Thus, McAdams does not argue that self-fulfillment is necessarily the highest form of morality; however, issues of morality are intricately interwoven into many people's life stories.

A similar view of the self as moral compass is present, albeit implicitly, in Harter's work on authenticity. It is not just psychologically distressing to be unauthentic—it is an injustice. The idea of injustice is also a powerful implicit thread running through Gilligan's (1982) initial work on loss of voice among early adolescent girls. It is unfair that society places a special burden on these girls: to be a good woman, they must suppress their ideas and wishes.

The role of morals is also strong in Holland's analysis of social-constructivist perspectives and research. Social constructivists, according to her analysis, are generally concerned with power and status relationships—often because they are interested in documenting the injustices suffered by those in lower power and status positions. They are also concerned with the moral stance of self researchers (e.g., the extent to which their perspectives privileged higher power and status individuals and groups and ignored lower-power or lower-status groups). Again, injustice is a moral and political issue, more than a psychological one, although *perceptions* of justice and injustice is indeed an important psychological issue for both social constructivists and other social scientists (e.g., Brigham, 1971; Lerner, 1980).

Conclusion

The notions of self and identity have been important parts of psychology from its formative years as a scientific discipline. Over the past 20 years, psychologists and other social scientists have begun to develop and refine the conceptual and empirical tools appropriate for understanding the complex nature of self and identity. The chapters in this volume have taken stock of the progress made to date by this recent wave of interest in the self; they have highlighted some of the most important contrasts in perspective and emphasis taken by different researchers and even by different social science disciplines; and they have identified important contextual influences on identity and on the relationship between self, behavior, and society.

At the turn of the last century, James (1890), Baldwin (1897), and Cooley (1902) provided a strong scientific foundation for the study of self and identity. As we enter the second century of scientific analysis of self and identity, we are highly optimistic. We hope that the analyses of fundamental issues described in this book will contribute to a sound foundation for the second century of work on this important topic.

Notes

1. As noted in chapter 1, we originally viewed the central contexts (history, culture, society) as influences on the content of the self and perhaps as moderators of the relationships between self and behavior. Thus, for example, self-definition might contain more references to other people and to social relationships in collectivist versus individualist cultures (Markus & Kitayama, 1991). The three context chapters in this volume do support this view of context. At the same time, however, the authors of these chapters have alerted us to broader and more basic issues raised by considering self and identity as historically and culturally bound constructs.

References

Baldwin, J. M. (1897). *Social and ethical interpretations in mental development.* New York: Macmillan. (Second edition reprinted 1973, New York: Arno Press).

Brigham, J. C. (1971). Ethnic stereotypes. *Psychological Bulletin, 76,* 15–38.

Bruner, J. S. (1957). Going beyond the information given. In H. E. Gruber,

K. R. Hammond, & R. Jessor (Eds.), *Contemporary approaches to cognition* (pp. 41–69). Cambridge, MA: Harvard University Press.

Cooley, C. H. (1902). *Human nature and the social order*. New York: Scribner's.

Fiske, S. T. (1993). Controlling other people: The impact of power on sterotyping. *American Psychologist, 48*, 621–628.

Fiske, S. T., & Taylor, S. E. (1991). *Social cognition* (2nd ed.). New York: McGraw-Hill.

Gergen, K. J. & Gergen, M. M. (1988). Narrative and the self relationship. In L. Berkowitz (Ed.), *Advances in experimental social psychology* (Vol. 21, pp. 17–56). New York: Academic Press.

Gilligan, C. (1982). *In a different voice: Psychological theory and women's development*. Cambridge, MA: Harvard University Press.

Hacker, A. (1995, November 19). Who they are. *New York Times Magazine*, pp. 70–71.

Hastorf, A. H., & Cantril, H. (1954). They saw a game: A case study. *Journal of Abnormal and Social Psychology, 47*, 129–143.

James, W. (1890). *Principles of psychology*. New York: Holt.

Lerner, M. (1980). *Belief in a just world: A fundamental illusion*. New York: Plenum.

Markus, H. & Kitayama, S. (1991). Culture and the self: Implications for cognition, emotion, and motivation. *Psychological Review, 98*, 224–253.

Marsh, H. W. (1993). Relations between global and specific domains of self: The importance of individual importance, certainty, and ideals. *Journal of Personality and Social Psychology, 65*, 975–992.

McCall, G. J., & Simmons, J. L. (1966). *Identities and interactions*. New York: Free Press.

Rand, A. (1964). *The virtue of selfishness, a new concept of egoism*. New York: Signet.

Stryker, S., & Statham, A. (1985). Symbolic interactionism and role theory. In G. Lindzey and E. Aronson (Ed.), *The handbook of social psychology*, Vol. 1 (3rd ed.,pp. 311–378). New York: Random House.

Thurow, L. (1995, November 19). Why their world might crumble. *New York Times Magazine*, pp. 78–79.

Author Index

Subject Index